HEYDAY AT FIFTY

H
HEYDAY
1974
2024
50

HEYDAY AT FIFTY

Selected Writings from Five Decades of Independent California Publishing

Edited by Emmerich Anklam

Introduction by Steve Wasserman and Gayle Wattawa

BERKELEY, CALIFORNIA

Some of the pieces in this book have been abridged from their original versions.

Heyday gratefully acknowledges Kyla Figueroa for her assistance in selecting material for this book.

Library of Congress Cataloging-in-Publication Data

Names: Anklam, Emmerich, editor. | Wasserman, Steve, 1952- writer of introduction. | Wattawa, Gayle, writer of introduction.
Title: Heyday at fifty: selected writings from five decades of independent California publishing / edited by Emmerich Anklam; introduction by Steve Wasserman and Gayle Wattawa.
Description: Berkeley, California: Heyday, [2024]
Identifiers: LCCN 2024012020 (print) | LCCN 2024012021 (ebook) | ISBN 9781597146531 (paperback) | ISBN 9781597146548 (epub)
Subjects: LCSH: California—Description and travel. | California—Social conditions. | Natural history—California.
Classification: LCC F861 .H49 2024 (print) | LCC F861 (ebook) | DDC 979.4—dc23/eng/20240528
LC record available at https://lccn.loc.gov/2024012020
LC ebook record available at https://lccn.loc.gov/2024012021

Cover Art: Anthony Sellari
Cover Design: Archie Ferguson
Interior Design/Typesetting: Archie Ferguson

Published by Heyday
P.O. Box 9145, Berkeley, California 94709
(510) 549-3564
heydaybooks.com

Printed in East Peoria, Illinois, by Versa Press, Inc.

10 9 8 7 6 5 4 3 2 1

CONTENTS

MAKING HISTORY

HEYDAY AT FIFTY

INTRODUCTION

Heyday was founded by Malcolm Margolin in Berkeley in 1974. A half century later—in an age of conglomeration, and as warp-speed technological change increasingly challenges literacy itself—it continues to thrive against the odds. Down the decades, Heyday has always understood that storytelling and indeed the physical book offer especially useful ways of apprehending the world. It is through the work of writers that we understand how we contend with the often-elusive forces that shape us as individuals and families, citizens and communities. And it is through our poets and historians and naturalists and scientists and journalists and essayists and novelists that we wrestle with how we have lived, how the present came to be, and what the future might bring.

From the beginning, Heyday was built around a big notion of California, a notion virtually synonymous with the very idea of the Golden State. Susan Sontag once remarked that California was America's America, a place of relentless reinvention, a magnet for people the world over who sought a new identity and an escape from history in a land of seemingly endless possibility. But that destination of desire came with a cost: the hunting down of its Native peoples, the plunder of its abundant natural resources, the hollow conceit that history's weight could be ignored.

Heyday has done much over the past five decades to recover that history, to celebrate and nurture California's bounty, and to explore our relationship to the land—a relationship that has given rise to both unrivaled prosperity and the stain of persistent inequity. Longtime home for some, refuge for others, California is both a place and a state of mind. Its literature reflects a range of affection and unease, or, in the words of Carey McWilliams more than half a century ago, a "curious amalgam of all America, of all states, of all peoples and cultures of America."

Since its inception, Heyday has been on a voyage of discovery. It seeks to stitch together an engaged community—an ambitious goal in a land so vast and sprawling that its very geography tends to separate one group from another. Malcolm Margolin taught us that what really counts in life (and in publishing) is imagination—the number of stars on your forehead. Sure, resources matter. But passion and vision and audacity matter more. Heyday was born out of Malcolm's deep commitment to "the way ideas are expressed, information is conveyed, and the public imagination is nourished." It began with a book he wrote called *The East Bay Out: An Unauthorized Guide to Hiking, Camping, Swimming, and Fishing in the East Bay Regional Parks*. As Malcolm described it, "More poetic than practical, the book was a song of praise for the beauty of the land and the abundance of life it supported. More, it was an expression of gratitude for the unexpected gift of freedom that allowed me to explore, to experience, and to enjoy a *Wanderjahr* in my own backyard with such joy and abandon." Heyday has always reflected the sensibilities and curiosities of its charismatic founder, who retired at the end of 2015.

In the San Francisco Bay Area, the early and mid-1970s saw an explosion of independent publishing houses across the aesthetic and cultural spectrum. There was, in Malcolm's words, "an interest in ideas and a zeal for social change," and the conditions were ripe for "a flourishing literary scene." As Malcolm has written: "Rent was relatively low and zoning lax, which allowed upstart publishers to run publishing enterprises out of their homes. There was a diversity of independent bookstores to support locally produced books [and] a major university that supplied readers as well as the basic fuel of all publishing enterprises—English majors eager to work in an industry noted for low wages and few material benefits. Berkeley also had a diverse population hungry to explore rapidly evolving concepts of race, ethnicity, and gender, and a mind-expanding offering of plays, concerts, art shows, films, and other forms of cultural wealth."

Heyday, like other independent presses of the time (North Point Press, Ten Speed Press, and Nolo, to name only a few), quickly achieved an unforeseen prominence. Based in Berkeley, Heyday's reach soon encompassed the entire state and the West Coast, and slowly but surely, book after book, its backlist grew. Many years were lean; some were flush. The whole enterprise was kept alive with Scotch tape and Malcolm's own special pixie dust. Somehow, Heyday survived. Its record of achievement was exemplary, as was the commitment and ability of its multitalented staff to inspire diverse communities across the state to collaborate. There was a deep understanding that, at bottom, Heyday's mission was to be a chief literary cartographer of California. It continues to map the state's still-to-be-discovered riches.

Heyday sought to expand the very idea of California, to help realize the California dream of equity and enfranchisement. Measuring the success of that ambition would always be ambiguous, not something that could be found in the passage of laws affecting policy, or in polls gauging shifting public opinion on this or that issue, or even, alas, in the number of copies sold that a particular title might enjoy or suffer. The metric of success lay elsewhere: in the belief that, as Shelley so memorably put it, "poets are the unacknowledged legislators of the world." Or, to say it another way, Heyday knows that books fall through time and circumstance, and success isn't always to be measured by immediate sales. A single book can change a single reader, who can in turn change the world. This, for the book conjurers at Heyday, has been—and remains—a principle of near-theological faith.

Heyday recognizes that here in the Golden State the local went global many years ago, as California has been an incubator of ideas influencing the culture at large. There is a certain sensibility, often as hard to define as it is palpable, that Heyday wishes to reflect and to explore. It is devoted to both historical and cultural reclamation as well as to works that reveal the state's astonishingly rich and interconnected natural habitat and that encourage us to become responsible stewards of a natural world now under siege. And it celebrates the many cultures—ethnic, social, aesthetic, and political—whose traditions, insights, and histories of resilience are even more precious in an era when relentless forces of avarice seek to thwart a more prosperous and just future for all.

For fifty years, Heyday has sought to inspire a beloved community of authors, readers, booksellers, and activists to help us cut through the noise of the culture and draw attention to the beautiful and deserving books we labor to bring into the world. We help birth the ideas of our invaluable authors, whom we nurture with love and devotion and respect. And we do so while ensuring that our staff works together in ways both fiscally sustainable and professionally satisfying. These core values were eloquently described in our strategic plan, articulated ten years ago: "We will continue to publish well-edited and well-designed books primarily about California. The acquisition and treatment of books will be informed by a love of the environment, a wide embrace of marginal and diverse viewpoints, a respect for authors and artists, creative courage, and a workplace marked by joy and collegiality. Laughter, kindness, wonderment, and genuine public service, along with stable finances, will be the measure of our good health and success."

Today, as we mark our fiftieth anniversary, we can, without hesitation or reservation, declare the same; our fealty to these ideals is stalwart and unshakeable. Our more than five hundred books published over the past five decades—books that explore the state's history and contested legacy, celebrate and defend its natural bounty, amplify the voices of Native peoples and others often marginalized and neglected, and examine issues of social justice—have garnered widespread acclaim. We take pride in having given readers books of enduring beauty and joy. We've sponsored hundreds of public events. And we continue to braid together the threads of community throughout the state, forging alliances with cultural and literary institutions, deepening public awareness, and encouraging civic engagement on a range of issues that press in upon the state's polity.

The volume you hold in your hands gathers three dozen highlights from across fifty years of distinguished publishing, featuring writers such as Deborah A. Miranda, Gary Snyder, Jane Smiley, Linda Ronstadt, John Muir Laws, Obi Kaufmann, Dorothy Lazard, Rosanna Xia, Leanne Hinton, Ursula Pike, Greg Sarris, Susan Straight, and our founder, Malcolm Margolin. Taken together, these pieces personify Heyday's work, past and present. (The Heyday canon contains an embarrassment of riches. Many worthy works were necessarily omitted, and so we urge you to peruse the extraordinary books listed at the end of this volume.) In the sensibility they reflect, they also provide a strong foundation for a robust future.

Heyday has never published a book cynically, never condescended to the reader, and we never will. We intend to continue building a sustainable publishing enterprise whose endeavors—books and events—will be as illuminating and enriching as they have been during our previous half century. Our pledge to you, dear Reader, is to bring to the public more works that astonish and delight, surprising folks with stories they didn't know they needed to know. We intend to be not merely a custodian of the past but a curator of the future. We believe that ideas matter, stories count, diversity of voices is crucial, and the book is still our best repository of knowledge and beauty. Heyday revels in its role as midwife to the birth of compelling, important, and often quirky books that embody the best of the human spirit and its longing for meaning and joy.

STEVE WASSERMAN, Publisher
GAYLE WATTAWA, General Manager
Berkeley, California
July 2024

HONORING NATURE

BRIONES

from *The East Bay Out*

Malcolm Margolin

Briones Regional Park is a 3,000 acre semi-wilderness area that lies between Lafayette and Martinez. It is an area of high bucking hills, broad valleys, creeks, meadows, ponds, waterfalls, and forests. You cannot drive your car past the two entrance gates, so this is a park primarily for hikers. And the hiking is splendid. The hills have a glorious, windy, high-country feeling to them—the sort of wild feeling that makes you want to break loose and run like a joyous crazy down the rippling meadows. The valleys (Abrigo, Homestead, Willow Flat, and Bear Creek) are wide, motherly valleys that gurgle with springs and song birds. People stop to picnic, often in the shade of a massive valley oak, and even those who have never so much as planted a radish seed begin to daydream about owning a farm in a place "just like this." Cattle graze on the meadows, deer browse at the edges of the woods, hawks play with the breezes overhead, and an occasional hiker wanders through this huge park, lost in wonderment at it all.

Briones is a park where—especially on overcast days—you are likely to see more deer than hikers. Deer are everywhere. They push their long, gentle faces into the cool grass of the meadows. They munch acorns thoughtfully at the edges of the forests. They cluster together in small clearings as if posing for a family portrait. Keep a sharp eye out, and sticking out of the brush you will probably see those erect ears, tensed bodies, frozen faces, and big unblinking eyes that watch your every move. Maintain a polite distance, and they continue to stare at you. Edge closer and they trot gracefully away. But move toward them suddenly and they boing-boing-boing away into the nearest thicket as if on pogo sticks.

While deer are always shy and demure, the cattle here seem at first to be almost malevolent—especially when a big herd of them is blocking your path. This puts the urban hiker into a dilemma. Should he act the role of a coward and give the cattle wide berth? Or should he plunge right through them, preparing to execute a half-veronica in the style of Juan Belmonte?

If you find yourself with this problem, be assured there is nothing to worry about. The brown cattle with the white faces are Herefords, and they are very docile. The black cattle are Angus. While Angus bulls are supposed to be testy, the young steers and heifers at Briones are far from dangerous. So walk resolutely toward them, and the herd of baleful looking beasts will obligingly scatter before you.

But what are cattle doing in this semi-wilderness park in the first place? Don't they trample the wildflowers, compete with the deer, and totally upset the balance of nature? Wouldn't Briones be much better off without them?

The truth is that rather than being intruders, cattle are actually the creators of the East Bay grassland environment. When the Spanish first settled here 150 years ago, the meadowlands of this area were covered with perennial grasses—the so-called "bunch grasses," with their long, tough roots and their ability to survive the summer's heat. The Spanish lost no time in introducing cattle. Tangled in the hair of the cattle were the seeds of the European grasses—grasses that die back each summer and grow again from seed in the fall, grasses that eventually were to take over the East Bay meadow lands almost completely.

By changing the grasslands of the East Bay, cattle may have

created a permanent niche for themselves here, especially in the drier, inland areas like Briones. Without their grazing, the annual grasses would grow waist-high, die back in the summer, and become a major fire hazard. Also, cattle are valuable for browsing on brush which might otherwise invade the fields of comparatively weak-rooted annual grasses.

Except for the change of grasses, though, Briones seems to be quite unspoiled. I doubt if the mosaic of dense forests and open meadows has changed much since 1829 when Felipe Briones, a retired Spanish soldier, fell in love with a waterfall here and decided to settle upon the land. For the next decade he lived peacefully, supporting his family of eighteen. But in 1839 a band of Indians stole horses from his neighbor, Ygnacio Martinez. Felipe Briones, the ex-soldier, was called upon to help recover the horses. In the battle which followed he was struck by an arrow and killed. After his death his widow, Dona Maria Manuela Valencia de Briones, received title to 13,353 acres (nearly 25 square miles), of which Briones Regional Park covers only a small part. Most of the rest of this once vast rancho has been acquired by the East Bay Municipal Utility District as part of the San Pablo Reservoir watershed.

Those of us who know Briones well feel that this is one of the most exciting places in the East Bay. It is a wild park with lots of space. Hikers along Briones Crest enjoy splendid views of the Bay, Mount Diablo, and (on clear days) the Sierras in the distance. But they are probably totally unaware of other hikers who are exploring the shady forested canyons, the creeks, ponds, and waterfalls.

I visit Briones often, but my own favorite time of year is fall when this big park first shakes off its summer sleep. As the days get cooler and shorter, certain trees (most notably the big-leaf maples) turn fall colors. The thick forests of Briones become dappled with yellows, browns, and russets. Leaves of the climbing grape vines shoot bold touches of red throughout the trees. Hark ye, hark ye, all you displaced New Englanders: there is a rich and colorful autumn to be found in the woodlands of Briones.

The second great autumn change in Briones comes with the first rains. All summer the meadows lay dry and golden, a slumbering giant. With the first rains the giant awakens. A million, billion grass seeds burst open, and waves of green wash over the golden hills.

Newts are among the first to celebrate. After the first heavy rains thousands and thousands of newts (or salamanders, as they're sometimes called) appear throughout Briones as if by spontaneous generation. On cool, rainy fall days it's hard to find a square yard of grassland or forest that doesn't have its own resident newt. They have the same shape as lizards, but totally different personalities. Lizards are sunshine creatures, light and fast. Newts, on the other hand, are creatures of moist dank places. They are stiff and sluggish, with cold rubbery skin. They act as if they had just crawled out of the refrigerator and haven't quite warmed up yet. You can easily pick one up, handle it, and put it down. Rub its back lightly and it will go into a "defensive position." It is a minor miracle that such a sluggish creature ever catches anything to eat.

By late autumn the ponds and lagoons in the hills fill once again with water. Freshwater ponds are rare in the Bay Area, so be sure to enjoy them while you're here. Peer into one of these ponds and you will see schools of tiny fish shimmering this way and that. Frogs croak at each other with unabashed machismo. Freshwater snails meticulously explore the newly submerged grasses.

The creeks of Briones also begin to flow again. In early fall there are only tenuous splatterings and murmurings, but by late winter the creeks become boisterous and high spirited. Waterfalls splash and dash happily along Cascade Creek, ferns spill over the banks, and in the dark canyons drops of water glisten like jewels in the green micro-worlds of moss.

By Christmas time the water has won its battle against the summer drought. Elsewhere snow may be falling and icicles forming, but in the East Bay we have every reason to be celebrating the annual miracle of a green Christmas.

By early spring the grasses become tall and loose, waving and rippling sensuously in the meadows. Thousands of sluggish newts now make their way to the ponds for their springtime mating orgy. In the water they take on a new, romantic identity. They tuck their legs in against their bodies, and with a few strong undulations of the tail they propel themselves through the water as quickly and effortlessly as fish. By late March the newts disappear entirely, the meadows are dotted with wildflowers and with cows, the grass bolts to seed, and the land prepares itself once again for the hot dry summer.

To me Briones has always been charming, but I remember one day in particular when the land seemed to reach out to me and become almost excruciatingly alive. I was hiking along, rucksack on my back, thoughtless and casual, when I heard a very distant, mournful, whistling sound. It was an eerie, monotonous song, and every so often the pitch would change. It seemed to be coming from everywhere at once.

For a long time this hollow, haunting song followed me along the trail. Were there Sirens here such as sang to Ulysses and his men? Was it the keening of the widow Briones for her dead husband? Was it the singing of a Costanoan Indian for his lost land, his lost language, his utter extinguishment? Was it the song of the land itself?

I found this distant whistling to be infinitely sad and infinitely beautiful. It was the song of the trees, the grasses, the soil, and all the strange, beautiful, and tragic people who once lived here. It was a simple song that flowed through the branches of the oaks, around the high peaks, between the blades of grass, back through the past and out into the future, through my mind and beyond—a lonesome, lovely song that was wrapping everything together in a thin strong blanket of sound.

I feel almost foolish telling you how the song ended. I reached into my rucksack for my canteen. When I turned the cap of the canteen the song popped and abruptly ceased. It had been air seeping in through a narrow opening of the canteen cap. I felt slightly chagrined, but still elated. The singer may have been a faulty canteen cap. But what remains with me is the feeling of enchantment that the song had drawn out of the land and laid before me like a precious gift—an enchantment that is a real and rightful part of Briones Park.

[1974]

BLUEBELLY LIZARD, OR WESTERN FENCE LIZARD

from *A California Bestiary*

Rebecca Solnit

The bestiaries, or books of beasts, of almost a thousand years ago contained much we no longer believe. There is no stone in the heads of toads that neutralizes poison and there are no unicorns at all, so the ability of their horns to likewise undo poison is not particularly helpful either. Those old books were compendiums of known and imagined animals, of eagles and dragons and elephants, with lore about their powers, lives, and meanings, often moral and religious meanings. They were also compendiums of sheer wonder, but the sense of wonder that emerges from scientific knowledge is at least as great, whether it's about the Belding's ground squirrel of the Sierra Nevada that hibernates about eight months a year or the elephant seal that not only can hold its breath underwater for an hour but often does so for twenty minutes or more at a time while sleeping on the shore. Or the blue whale, whose heart is bigger than an American bison and beats about six times a minute, a tenth the speed of ours, or the hummingbird in flight, whose tiny heart beats a thousand times a minute.

Toads can't counteract poison, but bluebelly lizards, it is now known, have a mysterious property in their blood that eliminates Lyme disease from the infected ticks, in their nymph stages, that bite them. They may be why the West Coast is so much less infested with this pernicious disease than the East. The bluebelly's blood now is as marvelous as the toadstone then. But it's important to celebrate the bluebelly for its own sake, for its twenty long toes as delicate as eyelashes, for its ball-bearing eyes, for its grainy camouflaging stripes in tones of dust and shadow, for the secret blue bands of its white underside—two long vertical lines and more blue on its chin, ranging from a soft sky blue in the young and female lizards to a fierce azure that saturates the males in rut.

The official name of this creature is the Western fence lizard, but they were all over the West millennia before fences were, and the California kids I knew called them bluebellies. Bluebellies were everywhere in the California hills when I was growing up, darting away from us, sometimes—like many other lizard species—shedding their tails when one of my brothers tried to catch them, so that the tail stayed behind flapping frantically, a tactic thought to have evolved to distract predators. I have seen thousands of bluebellies, held dozens, perhaps hundreds, but only twice have I seen the intensely blue males in rut fight each other, scrabbling and separating and gripping, doing pushups on the rocks betweentimes. (The pushups display their blue undersides and are thought to impress females.) Once they were under live oaks on Mount Tamalpais near the Golden Gate, once they were on the warm granite of the trail up Little Yosemite Canyon; both times I watched until all sense of scale fell away and I might as well have been watching sapphire dragons. But it is not the exceptional moments or exceptional beasts that are grounds for wonder. The everyday bluebelly found everywhere in California but the deep deserts and highest mountains is, with its purifying blood, its underside of sky, its speed and its talent for survival, already a small astonishment.

[2010]

HEART OF THE SIERRA SESSHIN: PIUTE PASS TO BISHOP PASS

from *The High Sierra of California*
Gary Snyder

AUGUST 24–26, 1969

Loading up: Nanao Sakaki, Nancy Tucker, Chuck Dockham and Marian Lincoln, and Rick the ardent disciple of Tarthang Tulku, into the new beige VW bus & heading east from Bay Area . . .

Next day walked over Piute Pass—Humphreys Basin slanting vast above us. Study the Mt. Darwin Col—crossed that once—from the east.

Camp below Golden Trout Lake. Mt. Emerson, Mt. Humphreys, Mt. Muriel, Mt. Goethe. Overflowing creeks, French Canyon.

Next day on down Piute Canyon, sharing the trail with Boy Scouts and a family with burros. Burros' dainty little steps. The hind legs stiffly and quickly.

Walking the excess out of body and mind. The flute player's chant. Piute Canyon lunch at the Muir trail—and sniffing Jeffrey pine bark, "Yes! that's it!" Nobody will ever agree: vanilla, caramel, or pineapple.

AUGUST 27, 1969

Today, up out of the Valley to the lower edge of Evolution Basin: right at timberline, the lake, the slopes of rock and talus, sitting on an orange two-man tent laid out as a ground-sheet, in the shade of a whitebark pine—for the shade it's cold—in the sun it's too hot.

> Morning sutra service,
> Making the altar up with lodgepole pine for "flowers"
> rising sun for the "candle"
> dawn breeze for the "incense,"
> a teaspoon of granola for the "food offering"
> —all the elements present
> a sitting and chanting session,
> the "Buddha-rupa" is the peak across the valley.

Today a free day, lake on one side, also under the wall of Mt. Darwin leaning over it. Rock, snow, moonlight, flowers. Last night a flaming meteorite that rose in the north—passed down the length of the sky with a sweeping tail and set in the south. (Much later heard it was a spent rocket stage.)

Wash clothes, take a bath. Treading the laundry on a shallow rock. Singing *kitanapo*
kitanapo! Humpbacked flute player mantra?

with Nanao and Chuck.

> O waters
> wash us, me,
> under the wrinkled granite
> straight-up slab.

And sitting by camp in the pine shade, about time for lunch now,

Nanao sleeping.
The mountains humming and crumbling
snowfields melting
soil building on tiny ledges for wild onion and flowers—
                    bare feet feel good.

AUGUST 28, 1969

to Sapphire Lake:

And climbing Mt. Haeckel, east from the trail and Sapphire Lake. A chock-stone in the final chimney that you have to go out over and around, much exposed, which made descending scary and shaky. Nanao for once got serious. Chuck on the summit, rolls his eyes, sticks out his tongue—we all laugh, the space, the exposure.

Blue polemonium
Great
Earth
        Sangha
                    —coming down the mountain.

AUGUST 29, 1969

to the Ionian Basin:

("Was it broken crust? Was it slush?"—the slidy snow).
Chopped swamp-onion, served on top the bulghur wheat.
Fresh-picked pennyroyal tea.
Walk up the length of Evolution Basin, no trees, all Tibetan
alpine zone, check out Muir Hut. Beehive stone shelter—
                    Belding's ground squirrels—"picket pin"

Mountain ground-for-a-mattress, rock-for-a-pillow dream: of a kitten bullying some big dogs and older cats until they all turned on it and beat it up. It seemed dead at first, but then wobbled unsteadily off—

Negotiated snowfields and slidy scree over the saddle from Muir Pass, now settling in at the first lake in the Ionian Basin, between Scylla and Charybdis peaks. This landscape is pure. Pure minerals, water, air.

AUGUST 30, 1969
Ionian Basin:

Dawn. Waiting for the sunrise to reach camp. The others are still sleeping but for Rick who is sitting in the icy shade. All our sleeping bags are white with frost, and there is a skin of ice on the blue tarn. This is high and cold.

> Water flowing under the cobble pavement, sun coming on, brilliant definitions of light.

—and a waning moon in the dawn sky.
Big rocks crack. Did I hear a howl in the night and dream it was a noon whistle?

> Black spider; small red spider; bumblebee; dead dragonfly; swallows. In the Ionian Basin. "Iona" a name for a girl.

> Dragonfly
> Dead on the snow
> How did you come   so high
> Did you leave your seed child

In a mountain pool
Before you died

Chasm Lake; still one-third ice, the guardian of the Enchanted Gorge. A second chilly night.

AUGUST 31, 1969

Sun hits first Nanao's, then mine, then Rick's bags, and we do the *Shingyo*, Heart Sutra, chanting together. Zazen sitting up wrapped in sleeping bags, below freezing.

The sun
is on
the
mountain peak

awake
          awake
                    awake—

The sun is on the peak.

Ah   high winter winds
Ah   the snows
Ah   the summer sun
which melts
            snow till it flows

blue flower
yellow flower blossoming together—
mountain peaks in greeting

morning wind—
each light-side-face awake and meeting
morning light
flowers and pines
The chanting streams.
Hundreds of peaks
greeting.
Hundreds of lakes. Gathering and passing on;
knowing each other
by the net of water; lying still.

Down LeConte Canyon and up to Dusy Basin:
Cross back over the saddle, set out cross-country down the long alpine talus, lichen, flowers, moss, snow, scree, water, slope.

SEPTEMBER 1, 1969

Last night what a moon. All the mountain ranges glowed blue. Night-long, Nanao was waking and sitting by our little fire, and in the pre-dawn dark singing along with the streams and hills.
How do I know?
I was awake too—

This morning went on over Bishop Pass and descended to South Lake—the trail noticeably dustier and dirtier where it's been used by horses. The cars and jumbled camps at South Lake a sorry sight. We get out on the level and into the shallow creekbed, standing on little rocks, our circle of hikers do a trip-end chant, *Shingyo*, to say good-bye to the mountain spirits.

[2002]

SPRING PLOWING

from *Letters to the Valley*

David Mas Masumoto

Dear Mr. Muira,

Spring awakens in our valley with the sun's warmth on our cheeks and a stirring of life within. We forget that other places still have snow, with threats of late spring frosts that hunt like a stalking wolf, howling reminders to both farmers and gardeners that winter isn't quite through.

But in our valley we are fortunate: life starts early.

You're an old farmer who can't retire from growing things and now have moved your itch to a city home and backyard. Farmers and gardeners share a spring calling: a longing to get outside, breathe in the air and touch the earth with our hands. We want to feel the damp soil under our fingernails, long to break winter's crust and turn the soil as if we free a spirit in the land. With the first signs of spring, we plow the earth and it plows something into us.

Growing things seems natural, a distinctly human act, part of our desire to reflect, build and create. But nurturing seems out of place in our fast-paced, high-tech information age. Gardens foster connections based on slow timelines, much like learning.

I've often thought all students and teachers should be required to grow something, to understand the patience required and the long learning curves of development. We all could benefit from planting seeds with patience to see the flowers bloom.

I sometimes fantasize: What if all professions required that you know how to garden? Could we be better off if businesspeople, lawyers, doctors and politicians had to pass a gardening test? Humility might be fostered alongside some humbling harvests.

Your gardens, Mr. Muira, help connect you to a real presence. I can tell as you prune a bonsai pine, skillfully guiding the clipper by feeling the needles with your hands and fingers and quickly snipping off unwanted growth. You could prune blindfolded, allowing a touch world to guide you. That's the secret calling of spring: we allow the senses back into our lives.

After the cold of winter and our thick blankets protecting us, we take off gloves and shed our clothes, wanting to feel weather with our skin: a tactile relationship. We seek to touch something and be touched in return—like a good hug.

The world of touch has become alien in our modern society. I find the seasons sometimes blurring together as I seek to insulate myself from the cold or heat as if to say, "Damn the weather, life should unfold someplace between 68 and 72 degrees!"

I too often ignore opportunities for touch to have meaning, as if I've been programmed not to pay attention. The great eating revolution of my generation has been fast food and the doing away of silverware. Yet I can't recall the sensation of a sesame bun or the feel of a French fry on my fingertips. We eat with our hands and have no memory of it.

Spring offers a reprieve, a chance to redeem myself and sharpen my senses. I connect with old friends: shovels, rakes and pruning shears that sat quietly in the corner of the shed all winter, ignored and forgotten. I imagine their feelings are hurt, but rationalize my neglect by believing that old garden and farm tools must hibernate and rest, waiting out the cold, trusting that following harsh winters will come spring. Then I run my hand along wood handles, cool and sleek to touch. I add my own body oils, leaving my mark as we warm up for spring work. A season of renewal for us all.

First contact with the spring earth, we stimulate all our senses. I like to think of this as an annual ritual. My eyes initially tell me the seasons have changed with more sunlight, less fog, longer days. Then I touch the damp earth and feel spring. Close up I can smell something rich, almost fattening, like an aroma of chocolate. This must be dessert.

Pause and stop. At first I hear nothing, then my breathing. I become lost in thoughts of a garden growing, a farm flush with green: the vegetables, fruits, grapes and harvest. My mouth waters in anticipation. Spring has sprung.

Later, I spy the first green shoots and realize they are weeds. They won't let me forget the work and the sweat. But I also continue to enjoy the moment, for these are not yet weeds, just misplaced plants. All green, the color of spring marking the end of winter.

Too quickly my moment of rhapsody passes with a reality check and the growing list of chores: beds to prepare, fields to plow, things to plant. This is about real work.

So then how do I begin the spring? I rub my hands together and chant: "This is a season to get dirty."

Good growing,
Mas

[2004]

I CAN HEAR WHEN THEY CALL

from *The Private Lives of Public Birds*

Jack Gedney

I have a simple formula for doubling the birds in your life: listen to the crows.

More Californians probably cross paths with them each day than with any other bird, although many fail to notice the meeting. Crows are the most ignored birds in America.

In some ways, they are a strange bird to overlook. The corvid family contains the most intelligent and socially complex birds of North America, which one might think would make them objects of interest and admiration. American crows are the great generalists of the family, with a continent-spanning range even wider than that of ravens, who, while not rare in California, are less enamored of human proximity—crows are the default corvid in urban and suburban settings. Where the two cousins in blackness overlap, recognize crows by their smaller size, more frequent occurrence in large flocks, and more flapping flight compared to the wide-winged soaring of the larger birds.

I see ravens some days. Every day I see crows. I see them from my window at home, and out in the parking lot at work. I see them at the corner playground and on the downtown streets. They perch in the trees, flap to the rooftops, walk on the pavement, and hop out of the way of approaching cars with one foot held in front of the other, imperturbably wrapped up in an insouciant lack of panic, as if they were performing some playful trotting that I've been too serious for since third-grade gym class.

Why look at crows? I am accompanied by black feathers, watched by black eyes, and discussed by black beaks everywhere

I go. To ignore their constant conversation would be to enclose myself within a bubble every time I step outside, to be an always-indoor person, whether inside of doors or not.

I have only a mild interest in encouraging people to go out looking for birds. The more valuable revelation is that birds already surround you.

CROW PARADISE IS HERE AND NOW

> The world was made by Prairie Falcon, Crow, and Coyote. . . . These three are in the east now, watching the dam that they made, to see that it does not break and the impounded waters destroy the world.
>
> —Creation story of the Western Mono

Crows have been here since before the beginning, according to the oldest stories of central California. When we now think of the changes the past centuries have brought to the natural world, we often focus on the idea that we live in fallen times: "the highway dust is over all," as Robert Frost's ovenbird laments. That's true for many birds, but not for this one. Modern human settlement displaced innumerable animals, but the transformation of North America also created "an Eden for crows." I see more of these birds today than the Mono did five hundred years ago.

At that time, California's crows were less abundant and more thinly distributed, without modern urban concentrations. Indigenous stories view them ecologically as scavengers, while centuries of European colonization considered them primarily as agricultural pests: crows were accused of stealing eggs, blinding newborn livestock, and above all feeding in great flocks on fields of corn and grains.

But where we go, they go. In the twentieth century, crows' concentration in agricultural areas was replaced by migration to urban areas, where human-provisioned food is even more reliable for the gleaners. Our broader changes to the landscape fit the preferences of crows: we create clearings in continuous forests, found irrigated oases in deserts, and plant lawns for foraging and trees for nesting in drained wetlands. These are the changes that create what John Marzluff and Tony Angell call an Eden for crows, adding up to "a nearly perfect arrangement of nesting and feeding habitat" and leading to an overall booming population. In the 1930s, a winter survey estimated a California-wide population of eighty-two thousand crows, spread among a number of rural roost sites. By the 1980s, all reported roosts were in urban locations, with a single roost in Yuba City estimated at one million crows. One million crows!

Now fewer crows shadow the poultry yards and cornfields than march among the parks and parking lots. Their movement to this new paradise has been encouraged by the increasing drawbacks of what at first seemed the unparalleled abundance of the farmlands, most notably shooting and disease. In the United States' more agricultural past, anticrow vitriol was more widely lethal. Governments and gun manufacturers sponsored crow hunts. Winter roosts were dynamited until the 1940s, killing tens of thousands of birds at a time. The result was not so much crow eradication as crow relocation: they moved to town, where both antipathy and trigger-readiness are much lower. People might complain about suburban crows—their noise or messiness or threat to smaller birds (which is easily overstated)—but this rarely reaches a point of deadly aggression.

The great threat to crows of late has been the advent of mosquito-transmitted West Nile virus, for which they are more at risk than any other bird in California. After the disease arrived here in the mid-2000s, one survey on mostly agricultural routes in the Sacramento Valley saw declines of 63 percent in crow counts from the 1990s, with the largest decreases in areas of mosquito-rich rice cultivation and lowest in areas of human habitation and associated vector control. The cities are safer.

As the world changed, so did they: crows persisted and thrived. From 1970 to 2019, California's winter crow population increased by over 400 percent. Sometimes we still fall into the error of thinking ourselves alone and separate, the unique possessors of these streets. But we've also built this place for crows, who prosper here among us. Today, a day without crows is a strange and empty silence and an aberration in my life.

Now I live within a double city, a town of people and a town of crows. To go out to the wild is to leave this bird behind, but here walkers chatter from the sidewalk, and the winged call from above. Running through all their varied conversation is a message I can hear:

Crow paradise is not a place unmarred by human hands. The age of crows was not the time before the plows and cars.

THEY WILL NOT FACE THE NIGHT ALONE

The sun settles behind the hill like a silent sinking stone. I see four crows in a line, steadily flapping toward the edge of town in the fading light. Orange glows from the horizon as it does from any dying fire, and the birds seem even blacker than they did during the day. At this distance, flesh and feathers dissolve into abstract forms, become holes cut through the planet's haze to show the night outside.

These receding black shapes are not the private plotting individuals that grab my attention in the day; now the crows show me only what they share in common. Another line follows, and another on a different tack, flying to converge somewhere out beyond my sight. Now I see the symbol clearer: these black-dashed lines across the sky are not mere lines but arrows, pointing to a single target. What they point toward is safety, and what they fly from is isolation, an enemy we share.

This is how crows live: they mate for life, and like many birds, the pair maintains a private territory in spring. Crow pairs are often joined by nonbreeding helpers, frequently offspring from the previous year, but also including older children or even unrelated adoptees. There may be a few of these helpers or there may be a dozen, and they help feed and protect the young, growing their own skills and experience before attempting to breed themselves.

In fall, when nesting is complete, most crows gather into larger roosting groups at night, which can contain hundreds or thousands of birds. Unlike most winter-flocking birds, they don't forget their partners and families: nonmigratory crows—as many are in California—continue to fly out to their territory as a group each day, foraging together until they return to the evening roost in those twilight arrows. The first benefit of the large group is safety: if you are ensconced within a thousand crows, you are unlikely to be seized by an owl in the night. Roosts also provide a chance to share information and meet others; adolescent or migratory birds can connect with local territory holders and join their foraging families.

This system allows crows the benefits of a Nation of Two—an established partner and a familiar territory—as well as the benefits of a larger flock: group safety, information about food sources, and opportunities to meet potential mates and allies. The essential requirement for such complexity is individual recognition, the a bility to distinguish over long periods of time among a mate, a family member, a tolerated stranger, and a territorial rival. Such enduring fine-scale distinctions are muted in most flocking birds: the participants in a swirling mass of blackbirds or sandpipers treat all their peers roughly alike, with perhaps some in-the-moment deference to age or size.

With crows it's different. I see half a dozen crows walking around the soccer field looking for grubs when a family member returns from an errand. She drops from the sky and descends, gives a little series of short caws, and a few birds return her greeting without interruption to their foraging. But a few minutes later, an unwelcome neighbor attempts to simply fly by in silence and is greeted by a host of raucous voices, who rise into the air to escort him from the family territory. Crows have enemies and allies.

Another day: I see a bulky nest high in a pine, with one black head barely protruding. I assume it's the incubating or brooding female, and that the approaching bird carrying something in his beak is her mate. Then something subtle, and less common, occurs: another bird approaches and lands with a burden of his own—now there are *three* birds at the nest. Baby crows are the only birds in this book likely to have a big brother bring them food.

What does it mean to be part of a crow family? Members cooperate in defense and in feeding children—and in play. Crows compete at aerial acrobatics with their siblings, play tug-of-war with sticks, and like to belly-sled down snow-covered roofs. Carolee Caffrey tells a story from Southern California in which a sister plucked flower petals for the clear and express purpose of dropping them on her brother's head to observe his startled confusion.

Above all, there is one social behavior that is vital and unmissable: crows' irrepressible conversation. "Vocalizes while perched, on the ground, and in flight, while alone or interacting with others," summarizes the *Birds of the World* account. They could have just written: "talks at all times." What do I hear when I hear a calling crow? A bird who speaks to those she knows, her neighbors, parents, sisters, and adopted siblings. In those conversations, I hear a system more familiar than solitude or the flocks of shifting hundreds, and find meanings I can follow.

One afternoon in spring, I step out back among the dumpsters and see a crow perching on a streetlamp: *CAAAW . . . CAAAW . . . CAAAW.* Three long, evenly spaced caws, each given with a theatrically exaggerated lean forward and pump of the tail. A brief look around, and a repeat performance. And in the gaps between bouts I watch and wait, and hear an answering series of three more rough caws from somewhere out of sight. These are territorial declarations, the corvid equivalent of song.

Usually, crows of neighboring families are urged to keep their distance, but such disputes are put on hold when a larger threat appears. One of the clearest and most common calls for clamor is when a predator is discovered: I look up to see three crows cawing in the air above the neighborhood nest, making little dips and dives over a nearby tree. But then more crows flood in and converge on that point, until there are twenty black shapes screaming at the hawk in the canopy's top tier.

On another morning, I'm watching from my window when a crow flies in carrying an enormous piece of bread. It's early and the streets are quiet. She settles on the edge of the pavement and places her burden on the ground. *Caw, caw . . . caw . . . caw . . . caw, caw.* A longer train of notes, quicker and less intense, not with the slow-spaced ceremony of the territorial calls, nor the rough screams of maximum volume to summon all the full county militia. She lowers her head again to her haul and starts to tear and hammer. Two more crows fly in and land beside her, and they all begin to share. These are calls of neither "Neighbor stay away" nor "All crows assemble now," but of "Brother, sister, I've found something!"

How do the crows survive and thrive, here where so many others falter? They are not the biggest or the smallest, not the fastest or most cunningly disguised. But the thing that crows do best is talk, to build the bonds that mean that their beaks are more than one and their eyes are more than two. A great roost of crows mutters in the night like the ocean on the shore or the wind sweeping through a forest. And like the ocean, it can't be silenced, and like the wind, it can't be caught.

A VOICE THAT SPEAKS TO ME

> What a delicious sound! It is not merely crow calling to crow, for it speaks to me too. I am part of one great creature with him; if he has voice, I have ears. I can hear when he calls.
>
> —Henry David Thoreau, *The Journal*, January 12, 1855

Like us, crows work together, play together, form long-term bonds, isolate in family groups while making efforts to meet others, and join together when facing outside threats. People often dismiss crows as just another bird, winged and beaked and thoughtless. Correct this false conclusion: count the crows among the thinkers. I love to hear the singing birds, but like us, crows live their lives in prose. They are the second speakers of my town, and everything they do is accompanied by speech. They are our closest social cousins, more like us than other birds. This is not merely an interesting abstraction, but the grounds for our connection. More than any other bird, crows and people interact.

A foundational crow skill, I argued earlier, is their ability to recognize other individuals. Many birds can recognize their mate, but crows might have significant personal memories of twenty birds and passing acquaintance with many more. There is another allied and dramatic difference that sets crows apart: there are no birds more likely to recognize individual humans. (Other corvids are capable of human recognition, but often don't particularly care who we are, whereas crows routinely find us relevant.) The most scientifically well-known example of this was a study at the University of Washington, in which masked researchers visited crow nests to take measurements and band young birds. In the future, they were routinely abused around the college campus if seen wearing the masks.

Conversely, people who regularly feed crows at a particular place will come to be recognized and trusted, and sometimes followed or greeted. There are many anecdotes of regular crow feeders even receiving gifts from their corvid friends. One girl in Seattle was particularly generous with her local crows and received dozens of objects, including buttons, balls, beads, Legos, a broken light bulb, and jewelry. Much as I love the chippies, there is no chance of them bringing me treasures.

Bonds between humans and crows used to be commonplace, rather than newsworthy stories. In the less cautious past, crows were popular pets (now illegal, for reasons I find at least somewhat worthy of reconsideration). Old books are full of stories of pet crows' personality and mischief: caching berries in one owner's shirt pocket (while he was wearing the shirt), perching on a shoulder for companionable preening of their owner's hair, and imitating human phrases and laughter are just a partial anthology. When you've lived with a crow, you don't need studies to tell you that crows can recognize, remember, play, and speak with meaning.

Encounters with wild birds can reveal this too. Crows are always watching, and in each human face look out for potential friends and dangers. Crows are the birds whom we ignore most often, but they are the birds who ignore us least.

I step out into sight, and a junco bursts away to change her sphere of action. Brown birds disregard me from the bushes' edge, and a woodpecker flies to a higher branch to continue feeding without further concern. But the crows keep watching. Some humans are a threat; others may bring gifts or tools. They watch what objects hold my interest, for they use the things we use.

If I leave a garbage bin unclosed or a grocery bag unguarded, then they will be there to investigate in the wake of my departure. In the morning, I fill a birdbath with water, and in the afternoon find submerged in it a piece of no-longer-crusty bread, softening for the crows' consumption. They've long known that our wide, hard roads are good for cracking snail shells, but some items offer more resistance, and more human labor must be harnessed: I ride my bike to work and look up ahead at the sound of a sharp tap on the pavement—a crow has just dropped a walnut taken from a tree we planted and now awaits the sequel. *I'm not going to crack a walnut on my bike, bird. Not as clever as you think!* Then a car comes up behind me, and I hear a crackle under tires.

Falcon watches from the wild, and Coyote from the shadows, but Crow watches from among us to see that the dam he made won't break, to see the work he did to make California safe for people. I know the story has some truth: Crow was here before I came. But I also know how crows live now and that we have returned the favor. Now we are cocreators of the world we share.

To look across a room and find our thoughts reflected in another's glance is an inexhaustible surprise. But look further out and further up. Look across the room, and out the window, and up into the trees and on the rooftops. My eyes move through our human scaffolding, and black eyes return my gaze. A sea of crows is gathering to murmur in the night, and when black arrows streak across the sunset, I understand their call.

[2022]

POISON OAK

from *Secrets of the Oak Woodlands*

Kate Marianchild

Over the past several years, against the advice of friends and relatives, I have fallen for someone new. At first I was barely aware of his existence, much less his steady presence in my life. But whenever I sat down at my outdoor writing table, there he was, eight feet away, always available and interesting. Eventually I became aware of his radiant good looks, his enticing fragrance, and his gentle way with birds, who fearlessly land on his upstretched arms. I noticed his height, which is greater than my own, and his breadth, which is almost twice his height. I admired the supple grace with which he moves in a breeze, and the way light radiates from his many soft surfaces. I began envying the birds who sleep in his arms at night, knowing that I will never so much as hold his hand.

The object of my affections is a luminously healthy male poison oak bush who has been quietly growing on the edge of my yard for many years. I have been present at the birth of his little flowers each spring and the spectacular demise of his spent leaves every summer and fall.[1] I have witnessed his easy relationships with birds, mammals, and insects, admiring the stable and generous role he plays in their lives. I don't know how he feels about me, but I am grateful for his faithful presence and the entertainment he often provides. More than any plant I have ever known, I have come to count Poison Oak as a friend and an important member of my community.

1 Poison oak bushes generally have either male or female flowers. This one has male flowers, which is why I refer to it as "he."

VERSATILITY

To the dismay of most humans residing in western North America, poison oak has a legendary ability to adapt to a wide variety of soil, climate, and light conditions. It also resprouts easily from damaged stems and root fragments. It is so adaptable, in fact, that it may have a wider geographic range than any other California native. This plant can grow as a bush, a vine, a groundcover, and occasionally even a single-stemmed tree. It is most likely to become a vine in shady areas, where it climbs toward the light using the trunks of nearby trees or shrubs, wisely saving energy by not investing in a thick trunk.

In the fall, poison oak drops its leaves, leaving nothing but thin reddish stems. You wouldn't expect these bare whips to be attractive to anyone, but during the winter I often see as many as sixteen golden-crowned sparrows and several spotted towhees perched silently on the stems of my shrub at one time—always low, and always on the same side of the plant. They may be intentionally keeping the broom of stems between them and a sharp-shinned hawk who sometimes swoops in from the other side, hoping for an easy meal at my bird feeder.

When spring arrives, glossy poison oak leaves begin to unfurl like wrinkled little embryos, adding dark red accents to an otherwise gray-green landscape. The red quickly turns to green, and by the time the bushes are attired for summer, the golden-crowned sparrows have departed for Canada and Alaska and the spotted towhees are hidden from view by new leaves.

TINKER BELLS, HONEY

The wildlife show picks up again when loose clusters of small yellow-white flowers emerge in late April or early May, sending plumes of clove-like fragrance into the air around them. In the heat of the day, you may see hundreds of glowing forms hovering about a bush like a halo of tiny Tinker Bells. If you tiptoe close to one of these fairy galaxies, you will see native bees, honeybees, crane flies, butterflies, and/or lizard beetles crawling on flowers or hovering in the air above them, presumably for the purpose of sipping nectar or gathering pollen.[2] Close-focusing binoculars magnify the insects and flowers in a marvelous way, turning each tiny wing, antenna, and petal into a magnificent work of art. The nectar gathered by honeybees makes its way harmlessly into commercially sold honey.

In mid-spring, small green berries appear on female plants. As they mature and turn into seeds, tan-colored papery skins called exocarps form on the outside. These husks cover white seeds scored with dark longitudinal grooves that mark resin canals.

FALL FINERY

As early as June, or as late as October, when poison oak plants begin to go dormant, warm tints start creeping into their leaves, intensifying until they set woodlands and streamsides aglow. Bushes and vines growing next to each other often "go off" at different rates, as do individual leaves on plants, creating spectacular palettes of yellow, peach, orange, magenta, red, and green foliage. The colors often linger for months, treating Californians to more

2 Lizard beetles are short narrow beetles (.1 to .4 inches long) in the *Languriidae* family. The ones I've seen on poison oak are dark with reddish heads. Beetles are thought to be important pollinators of plants in the *Toxicodendron* genus.

varied, vivid, and widespread art shows than those produced by any other native plants.

When the last leaf has drifted to the ground, nothing remains but bare stems hung with forlorn-looking clusters of seeds. These little jawbreakers, which are the size of small peas, are surprisingly attractive to birds and mammals, whom you might see eagerly harvesting them.

CALLING ALL WILDLIFE; WRENTITS, DEER

Few humans realize that we and a few other primates are the only animals to suffer ill effects from poison oak. Everyone else seems to love it! At least fifty California bird species eat its berries and seeds, while others forage on the leaves for insects, and yet others nest and hide in it. I wonder, in fact, if poison oak provides food and habitat for a wider variety of birds than any other California native plant. Wrentits, secretive little birds that spend their lives in dense shrubs, are heavily dependent on poison oak, relying on its berries and seeds for seven months of the year and hiding inside its foliage for safety. Ruby-crowned kinglets and yellow-rumped warblers also rely heavily on its berries and seeds, and endangered least Bell's vireos prefer poison oak to other plants for nesting sites.

Many of California's seed-eating birds have evolved a symbiotic relationship with poison oak. They eat the seeds, scarifying them (abrading or softening their surfaces) with their digestive acids before excreting them away from the shade and competition of the parent bush. Scarification allows water and gases to penetrate the seeds' gummy coats, reducing germination time after the birds "plant" them.[3]

3 Unlike the seeds of many chaparral plants, poison oak seeds do not benefit from scarification by fire.

Black-tailed deer browse heavily on poison oak leaves, which are rich in phosphorus, calcium, and sulfur. In some areas, deer eat poison oak more than any other plant. Elk, horses, and other ungulates also consume the leaves, as do rodents, such as Merriam's chipmunks and western gray squirrels. Squirrels, woodrats, and pocket mice eat the seeds as well.

NURSE PLANT

In addition to providing important food and cover for birds, mammals, and insects, poison oak plays a key role in the regeneration of plants in areas that have been burned or cleared. Sprouting quickly from root crowns, new poison oak bushes serve as nurse plants, providing shade and protection from herbivores for species that sprout underneath them. If poison oak disappeared, California's landscapes would change radically, and many animal populations would undoubtedly decline or disappear.

CONTACT DERMATITIS

All parts of poison oak plants are covered with urushiol, an oily resin that causes contact dermatitis in 85 to 90 percent of modern humans when it binds with specialized white blood cells in the skin.[4] Only the nectar, pollen, and fallen dead leaves are free of urushiol. To avoid oozy, itchy misery, or even anaphylactic shock (rare), susceptible people must avoid touching poison oak plants, no matter what state the plant parts are in: living, dormant, or dead; red, yellow, or green. Even hundred-year-old herbarium specimens have caused rashes. You must be careful not to build a campfire with dead branches, as the smoke is toxic, and you must

4 Other familiar urushiol-producing plants in the same family include the cashew, mango, pistachio, sumac, and Chinese lacquer tree.

avoid touching tools, gloves, shoes, pets, or other things that have contacted poison oak. Contrary to popular opinion, it is not possible for a person to contract a case of poison oak by simply standing near the plant or inhaling its pollen.

TWO LEAVES KISSING

To identify poison oak in spring and summer, look for "leaves of three," with "two leaves kissing and one leaf running away": the leaflets usually occur in groups of three, with the two side leaflets meeting at the base while the middle one "runs away" on a short petiole (stalk). Watch out, however, for the rare plants with five or seven leaves per leaflet. In winter, novices have a hard time recognizing the bare stems and the woody vines of poison oak, but with expert guidance you can quickly learn to identify them. In the meantime, avoid touching any upright leafless stalks or climbing vines.

Unless you have pets, please leave this shrub for wildlife to use except where it infringes closely on areas of human activity. If we could hear the bewildered reaction of a bird who has just experienced the death of a poison oak bush, it would resemble the shocked reactions of humans in the aftermath of fires, hurricanes, and earthquakes: "What happened¿ Where is my home¿ Where is the food that was supposed to last me through the winter¿ Where am I going to sleep tonight¿"

If you do need to remove poison oak, it is best to do so by mechanical or low-impact chemical means rather than by spraying it with RoundUp® or other toxic herbicides. POEA, the so-called inert surfactant in RoundUp®, has been implicated in the massive worldwide decline of amphibian populations. Far from inert, it also damages and destroys human embryonic, placental, and umbilical cells. It is difficult to kill poison oak roots, which are actually rhizomes that creep horizontally under the soil and send up sprouts from their nodes, but there are various ways of keeping the plant at bay.[5]

USES BY NATIVE CALIFORNIANS

Ohlone basket makers and weavers of several other tribes reportedly used poison oak shoots to make baskets. Pomo women mixed the sap, which turns black when exposed to air, with other substances and used the resulting slurry to dye bulrush (tule) fibers. Each weaver had her own secret recipe. Kashaya Pomo, Coast Miwok, Maidu, and Karuk peoples made tattoo ink from poison oak ashes. Chumash peoples broke the stems and used the black juice to treat warts, cankers, and skin cancers. They also put powdered poison oak on wounds to staunch the flow of blood. Some Native Californians also reputedly cooked with poison oak, for instance wrapping the leaves around the bulbs of wavy-leafed soap plant before baking the bulbs underground. The Karuk people used the stems as skewers for cooking salmon. Most contemporary health practitioners discourage all of these practices, as the consequences could be severe.

Native American herbal lore is full of remedies for poison oak dermatitis, suggesting that many individuals had allergic reactions to it; others seem to have been partially or totally immune. As all tribes were not of the same genetic stock, their levels of immunity probably varied, undoubtedly more so after European genes

5 St. Gabriel's Poison Ivy Defoliant, a clove oil and citric acid product available on the Internet, will remove the leaves of poison oak, making it easier to cut off the stems and dig up a section of rhizomes. The plant will probably resprout, but if you starve it of food by repeated defoliations, you might eventually cause localized rhizome die-off. You can also let goats loose on small plants or get help with mechanical removal from one of the lucky 15 percent of people who are immune to poison oak.

entered the gene pool. Frequent exposure and the widespread practice of eating small amounts of poison oak may have enhanced immunity for some peoples.

[2014]

FIFTY DREAMS FOR FORTY MONKEYS

from *A Salad Only the Devil Would Eat*

Charles Hood

1. Shrink Los Angeles so it fits inside a snow globe, then shake it. The dots won't be white. Not snowflakes—when does it ever snow in Los Angeles?—but swirling specks of red and green, hundreds of them, hundreds and hundreds of vivid green dots.

2. Each dot is a parrot. Shake it and watch them fill the sky. Parrots also fill the domes of Bakersfield, San Francisco, La Jolla, and even the well-tended, richly treed grounds of the Getty Villa in Malibu. Temple City. Altadena. Most of Southern California, one way or another, and plenty of other places. Phoenix? Yes, even Phoenix.

3. "Parrots" means parrots, but also everybody else: lorries, conures, budgies, red-crowned Amazons, yellow-chevroned parakeets, and even the occasional and very expensive blue-and-gold macaw. Parrots means the collective tribe of psittacines who generally live in jungles, and generally have green bodies and red heads (lots of variation there, of course), and generally make a screechy racket streaking around overhead, and generally like big, tall, exotic trees like the silk-floss tree, but which pretty much never met a tree they didn't like, from native sycamores to feral pomegranates.

4. Call them exotics, they don't mind. Call them anything you want, really.

5. People love pets; people love parrots as pets; people are stupid; from llamas to pit bulls, pets get loose; among the things that get loose, it makes sense that parrots got loose/get loose (past tense and continuing present tense); years ago all those loose parrots started to find each other and form chattering parrot gangs; and on Saturday night when the daddy parrot loves the mommy parrot very, very much then they make baby parrots, and then as teenagers, those once-baby parrots get drunk at prom and have babies of their own, and now some of the free-flying, baby-making, sky-screeching feral parrot species number in aggregates of hundreds, even thousands of individuals.

6. And not just parrots.

7. In the long list of introduced birds, watch for bishops, bulbuls, mannikins, waxbills, whydahs, and white-eyes.

8. And not just birds.

9. All hail the flowerpot snake, small and blind, and beware the dreaded coquí frog, coming to ruin a night's sleep somewhere near you. And listen for a modest, cricket-like chirp from the Mediterranean house gecko. Where did they come from? Oh, a pet store probably, or a houseplant somebody shouldn't have imported, or they got trapped in a crate of macadamia nuts. All of the above, none of the above. Who knows. How did *you* get here?

10. Besides parrots, besides geckos, what other things have I seen

sold in pet stores? If I think back as far as I can remember it becomes a sad and infinite list, because I can remember seeing for sale—seeing with my own eyes, here in America—chipmunks, skunks, ocelots, squirrel monkeys, gibbons, chimpanzees.

11. Admittedly, this is all back in the day, but while I am old, I am not *that* old.

12. And the pet trade still carries on today, albeit more clandestinely and with a higher profit margin for the really rare stuff.

13. The escapees create complicated feelings in many of us. Birders often hate on starlings and exotics, won't count them on their lists and speak as harshly of them as Trump does of immigrants. Yet I must say, when it comes to starlings, they are snappy looking birds, aren't they? Just considered objectively, they *are* worth appreciating for their plumage and their willingness to make a living even in the middle of our very busy cities.

14. Because the thing is, I live when I live, and while I can yearn for the passenger pigeon or the truly stupendous and entirely extinct Carolina parakeet, that won't help me get through the day. I have to love what the day allows me to love, and my days include—for better or worse but they do—plumped-up little balls of starling-ness in the morning sunshine on the tops of my neighbor's Italian (I think?) cypress, and when the light catches them, oh how they shine.

15. Margaret Millar: "Occasionally I am asked what difference bird watching has made in my life. I can only repeat, the days

don't begin quickly enough, and never last long enough, and the years go by too soon."

16. Memory of childhood, happy and indelible: I was on vacation with my family, we were at a zoo (maybe Portland, Oregon?), a gang of squirrel monkeys had gotten loose somehow and were free-roaming on the zoo grounds. The thrill, in those innocent and presexual days, my thrill in coming across these seemingly wild monkeys, oh my gosh, it was like being filled with five hundred volts of electricity. I can taste it still, feel it, remember it. Just about the best thing ever.

17. Am I a bad birder to admit that on my expeditions to the Amazon, I like seeing monkeys even more than I like seeing wild parrots? *Like* as a word may be too brief, too shallow. LOVE in block caps, that's closer. I *love* seeing wild monkeys, as does my wife; it is one of her favorite nature things, and as she says, "Monkeys—*they have people fingers*."

18. Henri Rousseau called them his "Mexican paintings," the exotic jungle landscapes he conjured up, like the one that has a chain of monkeys linked up hand to foot to shake oranges out of a swan-winged tree. Flowers, foliage, and monkeys fill the canvas; there is hardly room for the sky, which sits on the top of the forest like a forgotten hanky. Rousseau implied he based these scenes on what he had seen in military service abroad, but in actuality he made them all in Paris, and they were just versions of the zoo and botanical gardens and illustrated magazines, garden plants taken in by his generous heart and scaled up ten-fold. It works, though: The paintings read like jungles and monkeys, and you know that if he had found a spider monkey sitting at his table one morning, he

would not have been surprised at all. He would have halved a grapefruit and shared it over, and he and the monkey would have eaten toast and read *Le Figaro* in companionable silence.

19. Ages ago when I was a docent at San Joaquin Marsh in Orange County, there was talk about the Alligator of Back Bay. For three years it evaded capture. Not truly an alligator: in the end, it turned out to be a spectacled caiman, native to South America. Locals called it Wally. But it was five feet long and terrorizing the mullet. (It also supposedly ate coots and opossums.) Discussions circulated among the staff about what to do if we saw it, how it could be captured. It usually lived in Upper Newport Bay, but also ranged upstream in the creek that ran past the marsh and UC Irvine. It all sounded rather jolly to me; I hoped to see it myself, and doubted it was having all that much impact. It was just doing what its nature told it to do: live in an estuary and eat whatever it could catch. It probably took out fewer raccoons per week than were killed by cars speeding on University Drive. Before that, there was a capybara (largest rodent in the world) loose in Orange County, and even a contingent of Marines from Camp Pendleton couldn't track it down. I found that amusing as well. Wildlife: 1, humans: nil, and if I am betting on the long-term results, my money is on the wildlife.

20. Of course, it is bad (*very bad*) to release pets into nature. Do not ever do it.

21. That said, I do wish—secretly but fervently—I wish that the same careless dolts who let their parrots escape had accidentally let their pet squirrel monkeys escape too. Not hundreds, but enough so that they could have met up,

formed a self-sustaining colony. Can you imagine the thrill of it? How utterly supercalifragilisticexpialidocious it would be if you were by Golden Gate Park or the LA River, if you were out birding or walking the dog or doing a slow, struggling, five-mile run, and suddenly you came across a frisky, scampering troupe of thirty or forty squirrel monkeys, feral and happy and chittering excitedly as they raided an abandoned orange tree.

22. Because that's why parrots do so well: fruit. Not just citrus, but exotic fruit more generally. All the off-the-charts tropical landscaping makes for a year-round, lavish abundance of fruit. If we can support thousands of wild parrots and not feel a burden (and we can), why then not feral monkeys too? Not big kinds, they might bite or fling poo; but some species of marmosets are small as hamsters—their ecological footprint wouldn't be much bigger than that of LA's introduced fox squirrels.

23. To repeat, it is bad, very bad, to release pets into nature. *Do not do it.*

24. But if you were going to do it . . .

25. No, *bad*. It is bad to introduce nonnative species into any ecology, even an urban one.

26. Some species introduction stories have surprise endings. Los Angeles had a bird from Asia that is mostly but not entirely gone, the spotted dove, which looks like a regular mourning dove but with an added back-of-nape black bandana speckled with white stars. Common as all get-out, once upon a time.

Here one day, seemingly permanently so, and then, suddenly —*whoosh*, they all disappeared.

27. Happens all the time. Some introductions fail. Most do, in fact, and that is a good thing. (They don't fail often enough.) One bird that seemed to be established in the New World was the crested myna, native to Asia. Wayne Weber, from a thread on the bird forums: "The history of crested mynas in North America is interesting. They were first reported around Vancouver in 1897, and the last ones were seen in 2003. In other words, they were present for at least 106 years. The population was estimated to be about 20,000 at one time, and they spread as far as the outer limits of the Vancouver metropolitan area." Yet now they are gone. Vancouver is a myna-free zone. Other myna sites have replaced it, and since 1997, the birds have been present in Lisbon, Portugal, so far doing fine. What makes one population able to linger while other populations die out? No clear pattern reveals itself.

28. At the end of Werner Herzog's hallucinatory movie about the Spanish Conquest, *Aguirre, the Wrath of God*, the titular character gives a final soliloquy to a crazed horde of squirrel monkeys. He does this in rusty armor, floating down the Amazon, while his daughter and final companions sprawl around him, dying on their moss-covered, barely intact bamboo raft. How did a movie made with a stolen camera and barely enough money for rice and beans ever afford an animal wrangler and four hundred trained monkeys? Answer: well, they didn't afford it because they couldn't. They were filming in the jungle, so Herzog hired a local trapper to round up some wild monkeys, all of which they would release after the day's shooting. Fine, except the trapper double-crossed him and

tried to export the monkeys to the great and grand US of A, a country where we have a bottomless appetite for mahogany, tequila, cocaine, looted Mayan artifacts, and all manner of exotic pets. Remember that the exotic pet trade was legal up until the 1990s. Herzog found out about it and raced to the airport. He pretended to be the regional medical officer, and began screaming in outrage. These monkeys! They had not been vaccinated! Everybody who tried to handle them was at tremendous risk! He must confiscate them all, RIGHT NOW. After he retrieved the monkeys, filming continued. The monkeys survived. You can see for yourself: released on the raft, they all promptly swam back to the flooded forest, aside from a few inadvertent movie stars who for sixty seconds were on the receiving end of the mad ravings of the famously mad Klaus Kinski.

29. Squirrel monkeys are adorably small and nimble, with long tails and a scampering gait, hence the name. They pee on their hands to mark territory.

30. If I were a monkey, I might very well prefer Los Angeles to my native jungle. In the Philippines there is a bird called the monkey-eating eagle. What does it eat? Ah, hmm, yes. It does not occur in California though. And in the South American jungle, there is the harpy eagle, and it takes things as large as a sloth, so a baby monkey, that is no problem at all. Meanwhile, California's native peregrine falcons mostly eat birds—pigeons, ducks, seagulls—so no threat there, while the golden eagle is an open-country bird, so is not going to be hanging around Brentwood waiting to snack on a golden lion tamarin. Cooper's hawks zip among the urban trees nailing robins and juncos, and they hope to pick off the random

squirrel or two as well, but trying to snatch dinner by stooping a gang of monkeys? I don't think they would take that risk. Bobcats hunt on the ground and specialize in rabbits, so they don't factor. In the end, urban monkeys might thrive, and I can imagine a scenario where in the same urban tree one could see feeding parrots, feeding warblers, and feeding squirrel monkeys. (Be still my beating heart.)

31. Some introductions are not benign. An escaped tiger lived outside Los Angeles once, giving even the mountain lions reason to flinch. Vaqueros reported tracks the size of dinner plates. It had been an illegal pet and it lived wild until it was seen by somebody in their backyard and was tracked down and shot near an elementary school.

32. If tigers are too much of a good thing, mountain lions seem about the right size, and everybody loves the fact that P-22 made Griffith Park its home. The famous puma crossed multiple freeways to end up in an island of habitat between Hollywood and the Los Angeles River. In Mumbai, official population thirteen million, wild leopards live inside the city limits, and they eat dogs mostly, and manage to carry on year after year. Nobody knows how many live there—one Indian biologist told me he guessed about three hundred—and when I asked him, "How did they get there?" He just shrugged. "They were always there."

33. All the things in the dark we never notice or think about. What a list that would be.

34. And just as long, a list of the things we wait until dark to do.

35. "Draw me your map of utopia and I'll tell you your tragic flaw," says Laurie Penny.

36. That's okay, as I have many tragic flaws, and at the head of the list is an unreasonable hunger for interesting aesthetic experiences. Animals in trees provide that.

37. Historically, California had zero native parrots, or at least none that we know about, but adjacent New Mexico and Arizona did: the thick-billed parrot, generally considered a Mexican species but one that ranged north to Flagstaff. It was nomadic and/or irruptive, following pinecone crops. Mostly gone now. Circumstantial evidence suggests it was kept as a pet by the Pueblo Indians in the Southwest, who also raised captive macaws, received via trade from Mexico, whose feathers had ceremonial value. This lasted more than a thousand years; macaws were kept from 300 to 1450 CE, and it makes sense that at least once in a while some got away, living out their lives in New Mexican forests.

38. Recent attempts to reestablish the thick-billed parrot in Arizona didn't work out (too few birds, too many hungry hawks) but a stray—perhaps genuinely wild—thick-billed parrot showed up in New Mexico in 2004. Let the lists swell with joy.

39. To think about the urban jungle is to admit that humans destroy habitat but humans also create habitat, and to discount what I call blended ecologies (part-indigenous, part-cloud cuckoo land) would be like refusing to eat Tex-Mex because it lacks haute cuisine pedigree. Thomas Keller never served fajitas for Christmas dinner, but in my house we're big

fans. Out with the old, in with the new, and somebody pass the Cholula.

40. Which brings us to a central problem in wildlife management. On paper, restoration ecology sounds like a noble profession. The hidden gotcha is, restored back to what state? What year do we use as baseline—1950? 1850? 1500?

41. Meanwhile, it may seem impossible, but the birdiest place in all of North America, at least during spring migration, is Los Angeles County. Not Florida, not Alaska, not Monterey. In a single weekend, in a nation-wide competition, Los Angeles County ends up with the most bird species tallied—often surpassing 270 species. As a site, it can cheat in the sense that it has a mountain range *and* a desert, but it also has something on the order of twenty million people driving sixty million cars or whatever, and so to achieve multiple hundreds of bird species in one weekend, finger snaps for the collective productivity of urban jungles, vacant lots, stony ridges, and muddy culverts.

42. So instead of trying to resurrect an imagined state of lost purity, we might do better to take blended nature at face value. If we say to ourselves, "Okay, this is where we're at: we have x percent native, y percent exotics; what do we have to work with?" we not only might do some good for a certain percentage of species, but I think we could also find some optimism in these days that seem suspiciously like end times for much of life on earth.

43. Aren't these the end times?

44. Not according to all the parrots I saw yesterday.

45. Not according to the coyote pack celebrating the poodle they just brought down.

46. Not according to the leopards of Mumbai and not according to the raccoons who now live in golf courses around Palm Springs and not according to P-22, the ghost king of Griffith Park. Does anybody remember that he used to go into the LA Zoo at night, have a look around? One night he snatched a koala from the Australia exhibit, bounded out of the pen, and ate it. (Does koala meat taste like cough drops?)

47. There are four hundred species of monkey in the world, and another four hundred species of parrot. Some of the parrot species we have already wiped out, permanently and inexorably. Some we have saved. Some live in our cities. Maybe in each lifetime we get no more nature than we deserve, and in that case, shame on us, shame on our fathers before us. But it is not too late: We can make better choices now, a minute from now, in ten minutes. We can always make better choices. *It is not too late.*

48. Camille Dungy: "Ask me if I speak for the snail and I will tell you / I speak for the snail."

49. If the insidious message of capitalism is You're alone; you're not good enough; be worried, be fearful, then the default message from a parrot flock is, Dress loud, make noise, and tell everybody to meet at the silk-floss tree—Mom's not home and ain't nobody gonna call the cops.

50. At night my dreams flare red and green, and each day when I wake up, I look out the window and there it is again, brighter, more saturated: a tree, a flower, a squirrel, a cloud, the shadows of leaves applauding against the driveway, the one dandelion I forgot to weed, the subtle jostle that could be a passing box truck or a train or a very minor earthquake or maybe just the dome of the globe inhaling to fill itself with light, ready for another day of crescendo and shine.

[2021]

INTENTIONAL CURIOSITY

from *The Laws Guide to Nature Drawing and Journaling*

John Muir Laws

You can train yourself to be more curious. Be active, bold, intentional, and playful in your questioning. Seek out mysteries and the world opens itself to you.

THE JOY OF CURIOSITY

There is a marsh near my house that I visit frequently to watch wildlife. On one visit, I was making observations and became interested in the directions that shorebirds face while resting. Over the course of an afternoon I watched the birds move, noting their positions relative to wind and sun. As I watched and recorded my observations, patterns began to emerge. I decided that these birds were pointing their breasts into the wind. On a subsequent afternoon I spent quality time with a group of ducks resting along the shore. I was already primed to think about sun, wind, and body direction from my previous exploration but there was something different happening here. The ducks tended to orient their breasts toward the water and their backs to the land, often with their heads turned over their backs. This pattern makes sense when I think of predator alarm response. The shorebirds take to the air at the first sign of danger, but the ducks slip into the water.

Throughout this process I felt heightened focus and awareness. The experience was one of delight and wonder. It also made me want to know more. How do ducks orient when they are away from the water's edge or when the wind really picks up? I will be heading out again with these questions in my mind. It was the process of intentionally, actively questioning that opened all of this to me. I would have missed it if I had not been playfully engaging the world with my questions.

Curious investigation stimulates the reward center in your brain. It triggers the release of dopamine and activates the hippocampus, a brain region involved in forming new memories. As a result, in a state of heightened curiosity you will learn more easily—and not only about what caught your attention in the first place. Surprisingly, people in intense states of curiosity are also primed to absorb unrelated information that they were not innately curious about. Essentially, interest in one thing creates a curiosity vortex that sucks up unrelated material, making it easier to assimilate and remember.

Develop your curiosity and find that the mysteries that have drifted just outside of your attention come into focus, enrich your world, and stimulate a cascade of delight and inquiry.

EMBRACING MYSTERY

We are born into curiosity, a quality that can either be developed or degraded by experience and can always be enhanced by practice. Think of curiosity as a skill that you can improve over time. You can train yourself to find rich questions hiding everywhere.

Spending time with children can be a delightful reminder of just how many questions are possible. On a walk in Muir Woods National Monument I overhead part of a conversation between a boy and an adult:

Child: "How come the redwood trees are so big?"
Adult: "They grow taller than other trees so they can get more sunlight."
Child: "Why do they need to get sunlight?"

Adult: "All plants need sunlight. They get their energy from the sun. Sun is like food for trees."
Child: "Why don't the other trees just grow taller too?"
Adult: "Because they can't."
Child: "Why?"
Adult: "Enough with the questions already."

The admonishment to stop asking questions usually happens when adults reach the boundary of their understanding. Yet we don't only do this to children: silently and unconsciously, we suppress our own internal curiosity when we run out of answers to our own questions.

Rather than step into the realm of the unknown, embrace our ignorance, genuinely wonder, and look for an answer, we ignore the questions. Perhaps it is psychologically safer to stand on known ground; in schools, students and teachers are often expected to know the answers to all questions. If a pupil doesn't have an answer, it is assumed he or she wasn't paying attention or didn't study hard enough. Now, as adults, fighting for status in social and professional situations, the vulnerability of not knowing is still a threat. In any profession, answering "I don't know" can be viewed as a weakness. Some naturalists can name every species they see. Some doctors have a prescription for every ailment. Some consultants can produce an answer for every question. There is a special word for these sorts of experts: liars. No one knows it all. This pressure to look smart and competent keeps us from publicly wondering and admitting when we do not know the answer. It can also prevent us from trying new things, being open to new ideas, or learning new skills. Being aware of the pressures that stifle our curiosity helps us to push back against them. Not knowing the answer is okay. In fact, it is where the fun begins.

ASKING QUESTIONS

Embrace your curiosity. When mysteries are given the dignity they deserve, coming up with and "dancing with" a rich and interesting question can be as pleasurable as answering one. If you can come back from a stroll in the woods with a new and provocative question in your head, you have tapped into a rich part of being alive.

"What species is that?" is one of the first questions many people ask of nature. Identifying plants or animals is challenging and fun. Species names are useful for communicating with other people, but they can also be a trap. Many birders will stop looking once they have identified a bird. The name is not the thing. Identifying a species is only the tip of the iceberg of inquiry. It is not necessary to know something's name to ask an interesting question or make a discovery about it. Ask as many questions as you can, and don't worry if an answer seems beyond your reach at first. The process of asking questions in and of itself is important.

By asking a rich question, you engage your brain to explore more deeply and to focus on a chosen topic. A question provides structure within which to organize observations and related thoughts, and it prompts you to look for other details that are germane. Suppose that you notice that the iridescent sheen of a mallard's head shifts between purple, green, and blue. To help focus your exploration, you transform the observation into a question: "How do the colors on a mallard's head change with different light angles?" With this question in mind, you find yourself walking around a pond, observing backlit, sidelit, and frontlit ducks and watching individuals swim back and forth across your field of view. You form a giant protractor with your arms, capturing the angle between the sun and the bird from each observation spot. Time disappears as the pattern emerges in front of you. This discovery unlocks deeper questions. Do males orient themselves relative to the sun and a female in order to display a specific color? If so, do males compete for this spot? How are hummingbird display flights oriented relative to females and the sun? The next time you see a group of mallards displaying, your brain will be ready for the next step in the investigation. In this way, a question pulls you into a more sustained and focused exploration.

Many of the most fascinating questions in science have never been studied, and there are perhaps even more questions that have never even been asked. Challenge yourself to ask as many questions as possible. If you are struggling to come up with questions, try a couple of the following strategies to help heighten your curiosity.

MOVE FROM OBSERVATIONS TO QUESTIONS

As you make observations, see if there are any questions that pop up in relation to them. Try to focus on questions you might be able to explore in the field rather than questions like "How much does it weigh?" or "How long does it live?"

LOOK FOR PATTERNS

Practice searching for patterns as you scan the environment. Patterns are clues to mechanisms or processes at work in nature, and asking questions can be a useful way of identifying them. Imagine you encounter a flock of ducks floating in a pond. Start asking questions that would identify patterns at work: "How are they oriented?" "Are they all facing the same way?" "How does this change as the wind direction shifts?" "How close are they to each other?" "Are there any differences between the ducks at the center of the group versus those on the edges?" Looking for trends, similarities, and differences will lead you to many different questions.

USE THE SIX INTERROGATIVES

Who, what, where, when, how, and why questions are just as useful for a scientist as they are for a journalist. Use them to focus on different types of information:

1. "Who" focuses on identity and identification: "Who made this nest?" "What kind of bird is that?"

2. "What" focuses on describing events, broad trends, phenomena, behaviors: "What foraging strategies is this bird using?" "What is happening here?" "What happens when the sun comes out?"

3. "Where" focuses on location, whether local or large-scale geography: "Do I spot this species at the forest edge or deep in the woods?" "Is this bird a resident or is it migrating?" "Where is it going next?" "Where will it spend the night?" "Is this nest hole oriented for protection from the wind or water?"

4. "When" focuses on timing: "What part of the nesting cycle are we in?" "How does the approaching winter play into what the bird is doing right now?" "How long can this cormorant hold its breath?" "How long does it take for the newt to crawl over a log?" "How long do elephant seals move on land before pausing to rest?" "Does that change if they are traveling up a slope versus down a slope?"

5. "How" focuses on mechanism or process: "How do those pelicans fly so close to the water without hitting the surface?" "How do bushtits weave such delicate nests?"

6. "Why" focuses on reason or meaning: "Why are the wings tilted up like that?" "Why is that bird on such an exposed perch?" "Why is this bird singing in the middle of winter?" "Why" questions can be asked of any observation and are a good follow-up to other questions, to push inquiry deeper.

SEEKING ANSWERS

It is not necessary to answer every question you stumble upon, but if you do choose to investigate, your approach must match the type of question you have asked.

Science is a tool for studying observable experiences and phenomena—the stuff you can see, hear, taste, feel, or measure. "What causes the sea to change color near the horizon?" "How many holes are in this tree?" "What time do moths begin to fly in the evening?" "How long is this earthworm?" These questions can be explored and in some cases answered through observation and experimentation.

Some things cannot be observed, measured, or tested. "What is God?" "What is kindness?" "How do trees feel about the wind?" "Does the Gray Wolf have a soul?" These questions are outside of the realm of science. It is an important part of the human experience to consider them, and you can use disciplines like poetry, theology, and philosophy to explore them.

Some of the questions you come up with may not be answerable in the field, but they may have been asked before and studied by other people. Write these in your journal so you can look them up later. Use field guides, natural history books, and published research to identify organisms and learn basic natural history information. While I was working on *The Laws Guide to Drawing Birds* (Heyday, 2012), I was baffled by the variation of how wing feathers overlap. I discovered that another naturalist had extensively explored this topic—and had published the results in the *Proceedings of the Zoological Society of London* in 1886. What a delight. Not only was my question answered but I felt a kinship of curiosity with someone from over a century ago.

If your question can be addressed through observation, engage in a focused study. For example, while watching a grebe dive below the water, you might wonder how long it stays underwater and how long it stays up between dives. You can answer these questions through direct observation. Imagine another example: if you find a branch and notice that there are lots of aphids on its green leaves, you might ask, "Are there generally more aphids on green leaves or on brown leaves?" Within a few minutes of poking around you will have an answer.

If you are able to answer one of your questions, do not stop there. Use that answer as a springboard to formulate a deeper follow-up question and keep observing, or return to the same place in the future in different conditions to see if your answer to that question has changed. Keep asking deeper questions: "On the green leaves, are there more aphids on the top of the leaf or on the underside?" If that too can be answered, go even deeper. Things get really interesting when you get a few questions into an idea.

"Who," "what," "where," "when," and "how" questions may be answered by direct observation (though not always). If you cannot directly observe your subject, you may still be able to infer a possible answer by making related observations. "Why" often comes out after a few cycles of questioning. While it is easy to wonder "why" a phenomenon occurs, it is not possible to observe the answer definitively. You can, however, move toward an answer through a different approach: making explanations and investigating alternative hypotheses.

[2016]

JUSTICE AND NATURE

from *The Coasts of California*

Obi Kaufmann

Why does there need to be a discussion of justice in a book about nature?

When we talk about conserving, restoring, and preserving ecological services in terms of applied justice, we can make ethical arguments for the defense of nature. In an age of so much divisiveness in our popular discourse, the core desire for justice can be either a unifying or a divisive force. When we present the defense of nature as a human issue, as a way to assert the necessity of equitable access to a healthy and happy life, the denial of that access becomes commonly identifiable as an injustice. As climate breakdown, spurred by global warming, accelerates in the coming decades, the tenuous balance between societal, environmental, and economic pursuits must be in the forefront of our considerations. [. . .] Justice is a force that transcends personal or political agendas. It encompasses not only the relationship between people but also the relationship between humanity and the biosphere.

There is a postideology era coming. It is hard to see now, through the smoke of divisiveness that belabors every breath we take when talking about the future. Soon we will be ensconced in a new and bigger round of climate fires, a new and bigger round of drought events, and a new and bigger round of civil unrest. But we are forewarned and thus forearmed. Regardless of any individual events, the trajectory holds. We've got plans to make California carbon neutral in the next twenty-five years; we've got plans to restore 30 percent of California's natural habitat in the next two decades. We are transforming now inside a complex system, a terrain of dancing variables where catastrophic success is at least as probable as any other outcome.

For our purposes, let's double down on the word *justice*. There are other words that ecologically minded people use to discuss such things; most notably, the word *sustainability* is used to describe some practice or business-related aspect of adaptive capacity, and that is a good start, but it does not include the unifying, cosmopolitan yearning we have for harmony, for witness, for grace, and for love. The word *justice* does that. In the context of biodiversity, the word reveals a world where we let go of the scarcity myth—a myth that unregulated capitalism relies on in order to dismantle the working biosphere—and where we begin to see equity in diversity. In this world of inclusion and abundance, we are no longer being chased down the consumerist tunnel of the linear economy. Instead, we are held in a round basket, and we make ourselves within a world of replenishable resources—ones whose intrinsic value overrides their rote, utilitarian, disposable worth.

Racial justice. So often when we talk about restoration of California's natural world, we fail to realize that California's natural world is a landscape that for at least ten thousand years was intimately managed by indigenous Californians. Restoring California habitat space means engaging the active native Californian community and restoring those cultural traditions that the natural systems of California coevolved with. All of the other kinds of justice I am naming must get behind racial justice. There can be no environmental justice without racial justice, and in so many regards, the inverse is true as well: racial justice is environmental justice.

Climate justice. With the advent of a warming globe, California has been shocked by a number of environmental calamities that threaten so much of our daily life. The big one has got to be fire. Fire policy over the past one hundred years has been dictated by incomplete and overturned science, the timber industry, and colonial violence toward indigenous cultural practice. As fire transforms and resets the forest, we too are realizing our own capacity to transform and reset. Within the next five to ten years, we will have at least another year of terrible fire; there will be (more) towns lost across the west slope of the Sierra Nevada. But it is not too late to begin to redress every one of our policies toward forest and land management, based on what we already know: pyrodiversity equals biodiversity, and saving the old trees means reintroducing healthy fire to make way for new trees.

Water justice. When you are talking about water in California, you are not talking about water—you are talking about worldview. You are talking about what is worth what. As we test our values against the eighty-year-old water infrastructure system, we find misalignments, we find injustice. Freedom, it turns out, is not being able to do whatever you want; freedom is having the agency to attend to your social responsibilities without a government entity dictating exactly what those responsibilities are. Our responsibility as Californians involves respect for water—water as a living relation, as a resource that transcends property—and if we were to honor it as such, if we were to restructure the story we tell ourselves about our relationship to it, we can align ourselves with a grander, more equitable vision of the future than the trajectory our current paradigm suggests.

Economic justice. Healthy coasts, strong with a good complement of their ancient biodiversity, provide a litany of invaluable services for the citizenry. Our coastal wetlands are polluted, desiccated, drained, diverted, and invaded. Our coastal forests are simplified, overcrowded, fragmented, stressed, and diseased. But the ambition to transform our habitat that made this mess in our forests is the same force that can clean it up. We should continue the economic transformation already begun by building restoration as a legitimate trade skill. To this end, we should enlist an army of young Californians and arm them with scientific knowledge and ancient wisdom to steward tomorrow's world.

Ecological justice. All the solutions to all the problems are on the table. The missing pieces on one level are expressed by actual geographic gaps, connectivity gaps between habitat spaces where private interest overruns public need, but on another level, the more important gaps are between members of our own species. As we recognize the disaster that a broken ecology demonstrates, as we feel the squeeze from missing species that play key roles in the health of functioning systems, as we begin to see climate breakdown for what it is—a disastrous act of self-robbery—we will reach for bold solutions. Some of these may be simple—for instance, with the dismantling of the four dams on the Klamath River, we are giving California salmon populations their best possible chance for continued survivability. Our course then is to couple that kind of initiative with a full campaign to reintroduce the beaver across the California Floristic Province. Increased biodiversity follows these industrious ecosystem engineers, once incredibly numerous but largely expelled from California before American settlement.

So often, our daily diet of popular media asks us to absorb fatalistic, dystopian visions of the future and also technological panaceas that tease the perpetual, unfettered growth of the status quo. So often, we are asked to individually internalize an unfair share of the burden for what we sense are the necessary, systemic changes that our society needs to make in order to tackle the problems at hand. In a movement that has swelled over the past fifty years, concerned citizens who were told to reduce, reuse, and recycle were never given the economic tools to do any of those things to any consequential effect. Believing you are part of that movement, how do you reconcile that betrayal, that lie of personal agency over the well-being of the biosphere with the media's message from the hourly news that by consuming more and more, always more, you assist a nationalistic entity called the Economy, which is the measure of your worth as a citizen?

The genius of industrial society is its hyperefficient methods of creating disposability. Our extraction-based economy is built from the exploitation of capital resources, including human capital, and turning those resources into goods of temporary utility that then are labeled as garbage. Our ability to reconfigure the nature of our economy from a linear basis to a circle is metaphorically akin to learning how to curve the shot of the arrow from our proverbial bow; and in order to do that, you shoot the arrow far enough, with a big enough bow, to follow the curve of the earth.

[2022]

FIGHTING INJUSTICE

PREFACE

from *Only What We Could Carry*

Patricia Wakida

During World War II, the United States government suspended due process, rounded up more than 110,000 Japanese resident aliens and American citizens of Japanese descent, and banished them to prison camps in desert wastelands. They were not charged with any crime, except, of course, being Japanese.

Although rooted in decades of anti-Japanese and anti-Asian prejudice, the internment of Japanese Americans was triggered by Pearl Harbor. At dawn on December 7, 1941, Japan launched a surprise attack on the U.S. fleet at Pearl Harbor, Hawaii, killing or wounding nearly 3,500 Americans. One hundred forty-nine airplanes and two battleships were destroyed, four other battleships sunk or run aground.

The devastation at Pearl Harbor inflamed an already pronounced resentment toward Japanese immigrant communities. Initiatives and legislation throughout the first four decades of the twentieth century had restricted or prohibited Japanese immigration, land ownership, and U.S. naturalization. Despite such initiatives, sizable communities of Japanese and their American offspring were scattered throughout the United States. In 1941, 127,000 Japanese Americans were living in the United States, of which 50 percent were engaged in agricultural businesses with notable success; 93,000 of them lived in California, mostly in rural farming communities, and an additional 19,000 lived in Washington and Oregon.

Within hours of the attack on Pearl Harbor, FBI agents swept through Japanese communities in California, Oregon, Washington, and Hawaii, arresting community leaders: teachers of the Japanese language, its culture, or its martial arts; Buddhist reverends and Christian ministers; businessmen; those with prominent political beliefs—indeed anyone who might be suspected of having sympathetic ties to Japan. Hundreds were rounded up, questioned, and shipped off under Justice Department orders to detention camps in Santa Fe, New Mexico; Bismarck, North Dakota; Crystal City, Texas; and Missoula, Montana. Some disappeared for months or years. Meanwhile, with United States entry into World War II, anti-Japanese reactions intensified, fueled by a storm of propaganda, hysterical stories of sabotage, and reports of American battlefield casualties. All Japanese branch banks were closed, and the U.S. Treasury froze all bank accounts belonging to anyone born in Japan. Ostensibly to protect people of Japanese descent from suspicion and arrest, a mandatory curfew was imposed, first on Japanese aliens and then on Japanese American citizens as well, while all were required to carry identification. Under Army pressure, the FBI and the Department of Justice conducted unannounced searches and seizure of "contraband" items in "enemy alien" homes, with special attention to cameras, weapons, and radio transmitters that might be used to signal Japanese ships offshore.

On February 19, 1942, nearly ten weeks after the outbreak of war, President Franklin Roosevelt signed Executive Order 9066. This order authorized the exclusion of all persons of Japanese descent—citizens and aliens alike—from designated areas of Washington, Oregon, California, and Arizona, with an emphasis on zones around airports, dams, power plants, railroads, shipyards, and military installations, in order to prevent any possible acts of sabotage and espionage. Although E.O. 9066 applied to German and

Italian nationals and eventually to Aleutians in Alaska as well, it was clearly aimed at those of Japanese ancestry.

Within weeks of the signing of E.O. 9066, all Japanese Americans within the hastily defined exclusion zone were instructed to secure or sell their houses and possessions and report to designated civil control stations. Here they were first registered and labeled, then herded into buses and trains and taken to "assembly centers" until more permanent camps could be built. These assembly centers were, in fact, just off-season racetracks, unused fairgrounds, and abandoned stockyards. After an average of about three months, internees were moved into isolated prison camps surrounded by barbed wire, where they were kept under armed guard for most of the duration of the war. In all, there were sixteen assembly centers, all but three of them in California, and ten internment camps, scattered throughout the more remote areas of the United States: Utah, Arizona, Colorado, Wyoming, California, Idaho, and Arkansas. The last internment camp did not close until March, 1946.

These, at least, are the bare facts. But bare facts tell only part of the story. We created this wide-ranging anthology to further explore the complex thoughts, emotions, and personal histories of those affected by the internment—largely Japanese and Japanese Americans, but also the American population at large. All of us who worked on this book have realized that the tragedy of the internment should be part of every American's knowledge as part of our collective history, and we have strived to create a book capacious and varied enough to reflect that understanding.

Putting this book together involved an arduous process of gathering material up and down the valleys and coastal communities of California. Stories sometimes came from unlikely places. We began research starting with an extended community of friends, acquaintances, and advisors. As we asked people about their experiences in the camps, they gladly gave us their stories. They pulled typed diaries from dark closets and dusty boxes tucked under beds; they slipped carefully preserved letters and memoirs into the mail; they let their stories unfold during long telephone conversations.

We also dug deeply into material that had already been gathered by libraries and historical societies. Institutions that had preserved vital pieces of history opened their files to us. One astonishing voice after another emerged, some in typed and bound volumes of collected oral histories, some written longhand in spiral-bound notebooks, their pages bent from wear. In contrast, other selections in this anthology had already had a distinguished history as literature. We selected from published novels, short stories, poems, and memoirs that had long served as powerful testimony to wartime experience.

While we became aware of the wealth of material available to us, we also became aware that much was already beyond our reach. Much writing from the internment period has been lost over the decades. Some writers hastily fed their poems to fire in the rising panic following Pearl Harbor. Others lost their personal records because with each relocation, only the most necessary belongings could be taken, and at such times, who would have given priority to short stories and private journals? Another dimension of literature—work written by the Issei in Japanese—has remained untranslated and thus is all but lost to younger generations. In making our selections, therefore, we tried to include the spirit of these voices, if not their actual words.

For many Californians—including most of us who worked on this project—the attitudes and events of World War II and the internment are distant history. Words and emotions that prevailed in the daily culture of 1940s America are lost on us today: Fifth column? The coming Gestapo? How many Americans under the age of fifty know the real meaning of these words, let alone feel their fear and threat? It's hard to picture receiving letters cut so full of holes that they resemble nets—and accepting the censor's damage as military necessity. The very thought of picking up a morning newspaper covered front to back with maps of the European theater, complete with military strategies in bold arrows and star patterns, strikes those of us from younger generations as in the realm of fantasy.

Despite the yawning gap between pre-war generations and those born after the war, there is nevertheless an unnerving familiarity to many of the dark themes running through this book. The neighbor who watches from a safe distance, the church employee who tries to make the best of a horrible situation, the racist politician whose vitriol fires others up with hatred, the anguished apologist who accepts egregious injustice as "necessity," the victim who blames himself—such voices are all still heard today. The story of the internment, while in most ways unique to its time, is disturbingly relevant. The targets have changed, but the themes have remained constant. Recent immigrant groups, gays and lesbians, those belonging to minority racial, ethnic, or religious groups still experience prejudice, hatred, and contempt. A larger purpose of this anthology, then, is not just to explore history, but to use that exploration to understand more deeply the consequences of racial prejudice, to confront more fully the harm that it does and the strengths that it calls forth, and by increasing intellectual and emotional awareness, to help ensure that such events cannot occur again.

As we worked on this book, we also came to realize how important it is to listen to the stories of those who came before us. As we move further and further away from the war years, the opportunity to gather firsthand accounts from a generation of people who experienced or witnessed the internment is rapidly diminishing. Fifty years has, of course, altered people's remembrance of the past and rubbed the edge off many memories. But as memories fade, so fades an entire period of culture and history. The writers of these pieces must have known, whether they wrote their thoughts down at the time, or with a different determination years later, that their words were a part of history in the making. With this in mind, we have compiled a collection of stories and pictures created by those who were there. They saw and they wrote down what they saw, so that one day their words could carry their burdens for them.

[2000]

UNCOVERING LIES, 1982

from *Fred Korematsu Speaks Up*

Laura Atkins and **Stan Yogi**

One January morning
Fred receives a phone call.
A man named Peter Irons
wants to meet with him.
He has new information
about Fred's case.

It has been nearly forty years since
the United States Supreme Court
ruled against Fred.

Though several people have
asked him to talk
about what happened,
Fred has almost always said no.

Now
Fred says
yes.

Peter arrives with a tape recorder in hand
and gives Fred documents to read.
Peter found them in the
National Archives—

the place where government papers
are kept.

Fred reads page after page
silently
for thirty minutes.

He finds out that people in the military
and lawyers for the government
lied.

They had no evidence
that Japanese Americans
were spies or a risk to the country.

The whole case was built on lies.
Lies that locked up Fred,
his family, and
120,000 Japanese Americans.

Lies that stole toys from children
and pets from families.

Lies that ripped people from their lives
and then threw them back in
without homes or jobs.

Fred puts down the papers.

They did me a great wrong,
he says.

Peter tells him that it is possible
to reopen Fred's case
based on these documents.

Are you a lawyer?
Fred asks.

Yes, I am.

Would you like to be my lawyer?
Fred asks.

A team of lawyers gather
and get to work.
Most of them are young Japanese Americans,
children of people who were imprisoned.

When they first crowd into
Fred and Kathryn's living room
Fred leans over and whispers to Peter,
Hey, these look like high school kids.

Oh no, they're the best,
Peter replies.

When Fred sees them in action
he agrees
and the team becomes
part of the Korematsu family.

The lawyers
work for no money,

but from a firm belief
that it is time for the truth to be told.

Almost two years pass
as they gather evidence
and figure out the best way
to challenge Fred's conviction.

At first Fred stays in the background
letting the lawyers do the talking.
Then he decides it is important
to step forward.

When he speaks
out loud again
about what happened to him
and other Japanese Americans,
his courage glows through
his no-nonsense words
and quiet voice.

[2017]

BUILDING COMMUNITY

from *Biddy Mason Speaks Up*

Arisa White and **Laura Atkins**

On Sunday afternoons, guests drink Biddy's
homemade elderberry wine as they discuss
community news and politics—the presidential election
and Reconstruction, the recent Fourteenth Amendment,
and nationwide fights against discrimination. Biddy's home
is the gathering place for Los Angeles's Black community.

Over the years, a bustling downtown has grown
around Biddy's homestead.
Spring Street now has banks, hotels,
gas street lamps, a fire-engine company,
stage coaches dashing up and down paved roads.

More and more Black migrants are coming
to the city from the North and South.
Families with school-aged children
and pregnant mothers
are growing the community.

One afternoon, Ann Pepper,
Hannah's eldest daughter,
tells about twelve-year-old
Mary Frances Ward in San Francisco,
who's not allowed to attend
an all-White school. A lawyer

was hired to fight for Mary in court.

Biddy says, "It's a shame.
I had to send my grandbabies
five hundred miles away to Oakland.
There they have good schools
that will educate our children."

Winnie Owens suggests
that they hire a lawyer themselves,
and get schools integrated in Los Angeles.

Heads nod, there are "Amens,"
and then a collective "Yes!"
from these women and men born
in states like Biddy's Georgia homeplace.
Now property owners, boardinghouse keepers,
barbers, maids, and teachers—this is Biddy's
pulled-together family. Their passion
and strength spreads like a network
of roots reaching to uplift.

There are times when the line of people
seeking Biddy's care and medicines
wraps around the corner. And Biddy
turns no one away. Granny Ellen's
words continue to ring truth
in her ears: *Nothing good comes*
when we close our hands to others.

Biddy looks around her living room,
sees her guests together in the service

of Black people's physical, political,
and spiritual well-being. She feels
the weight of Granny Ellen's hand
like a feather in her palm, and says,
"We need a church."

The guests begin to discuss
what kind of church, where it will be,
who will be the minister, and time
quickly passes, day turns to dusk.
By meeting's end, the evening air
is sweet with jasmine, and the first
African Methodist Episcopal church
in Los Angeles is officially organized.

Feeling accomplished, everyone raises
their glasses to cheers. Biddy's guests
give a special thanks to her for offering
to pay the church's property taxes and
minister's salary. With an open heart,
Biddy acknowledges everyone
for their contributions and ideas,
because she knows we all grow together
when our hands and hearts are open.

[2019]

SHADOW AND LIGHT: MIFFLIN WISTAR GIBBS AND DEFIANCE OF DISCRIMINATION

from *Gold Rush Stories*

Gary Noy

In early 1850, Mifflin Wistar Gibbs was in Rochester, New York. He was dejected and depressed. The twenty-seven-year-old free black man from Philadelphia had just completed a whirlwind tour throughout the eastern United States as an assistant to abolitionist Frederick Douglass. With Douglass's speaking tour finished and the excitement fading, Gibbs felt that his prospects were severely limited. As he later wrote, "The outlook for my future, to me, was not promising." Mifflin confided his gloom to Julia Griffiths, a British antislavery leader and a colleague of Douglass's. Griffiths responded with seven words that changed Gibbs's life: "What! Discouraged? Go do some great thing."

Armed with this powerful directive from Griffiths and a ticket provided by a sympathetic friend, Gibbs booked passage on the steamship *Golden Gate* and headed toward the distant realm of the dreamers. He had all his possessions in a trunk and sixty cents in his pocket. As Gibbs later noted in his autobiography, *Shadow and Light*, "Fortune . . . may sometime smile on the inert, but she seldom fails to surrender to pluck, tenacity and perseverance."

Mifflin Wistar Gibbs arrived in San Francisco in September 1850. After paying fifty cents to have his trunk delivered to his lodgings, he immediately spent his remaining few pennies on a cigar to celebrate his arrival in the land of golden opportunity. Over the next decade, his California experience would involve the full range of success and disappointment, exhilaration and exasperation, shadow and light.

Gibbs never seriously considered making a foray to the goldfields, preferring instead to remain in San Francisco. In the beginning of his time in the city, he was desperate for work and offered his services in the building trades. He was hired as a carpenter for $10 a day—nearly ten times the going rate for carpenters elsewhere in the United States— but that opportunity was short-lived. As he recalled in *Shadow and Light*, "I was not allowed to long pursue carpentering. White employees finding me at work on the same building would 'strike.'" He worked briefly as a bootblack and then entered into a partnership operating a haberdashery with another African American man, Peter Lester. Gibbs and Lester made a fortune selling boots and men's clothing in boomtown San Francisco, and Gibbs rose from bootblack to prominent merchant and, later, to newspaper publisher. Despite his success, however, he could not escape the sharp sting of prejudice. A vicious incident involving his partner would place Mifflin Wistar Gibbs on the cutting edge of the effort to secure rights and respect for the African American community during the Gold Rush, and although Gibbs did not fully succeed, he never lost hope that his people would ultimately triumph over discrimination.

There were few African Americans in California during the Gold Rush. The notoriously inaccurate census of 1850 showed that the entire state was home to about one hundred black people that year, although the number rose significantly—to around twenty-five hundred, including ninety women, in 1852—as word spread that no other place in the United States offered greater opportunities for free blacks than California. But still their numbers remained low compared to other ethnic groups. By 1860 the census showed fifty-four hundred African Americans in California.

Although the state constitution had an antislavery proviso,

that did not mean Gold Rush California was a sanctuary for African Americans. Especially galling to the black community, and particularly to Mifflin Wistar Gibbs, was the denial of the right to testify against white people in court. Gibbs saw his business partner, Peter Lester, robbed and beaten by a white thief, and as Gibbs was the only eyewitness but not allowed to testify, the assailant was not prosecuted.

Seeking equality before the law, petitions calling for the immediate removal of the testimony ban were circulated in African American enclaves, most notably in San Francisco. Newspaper editorials were published in support of the movement, hundreds of signatures were gathered, and the petitions were submitted, several times, to the State Assembly for consideration. The documents were repeatedly rejected. By 1855, advocates in the black community were considering another, hopefully more fruitful tactic. They called for a state convention to formulate an activist response to the testimony ban.

In November 1855, the first in a series of "California Colored Conventions" assembled in Sacramento. The three-day convention was comprised of leading black citizens primarily from Northern California, and especially from San Francisco and Sacramento. Mifflin Wistar Gibbs was a prominent member and an official of the Committee on Credentials. The press cast a mocking eye on the proceedings, and when a grass fire broke out near Sacramento on the first day of the convention, dropping ash on the city, the *Sacramento Daily Union* connected the fire with the opening of the Colored Convention: "A shower of ashes, proceeding from the burning tules of Yolo, fell upon the city and vicinity yesterday. It was in reality a colored snowstorm, gotten up for the benefit of the Convention."

The delegates considered many pressing concerns but focused almost exclusively on the testimony question. As delegate David

Lewis of Sacramento passionately explained:

> The law is to us a dead letter, a broken staff to lean upon. The oath that should protect life, liberty, and property, all that should throw the shield of law around ourselves and families, is denied us. Now we have no protection, and stand as nothing. "The oath" would make people careful how they act before us. We should have a voice. As it is, we are scarcely recognized as human beings.

The convention resolved to circulate more petitions and pledged to obtain numerous endorsements from white men—that is, people who had the right to vote. The outreach was a success, and petitions teeming with hundreds of signatures from empathetic white citizens were delivered to the California State Senate. Unlike the earlier documents, these were received by the legislature, but after that the matter was quickly buried in committee. But inertia was overcome and additional optimism began bubbling when a San Francisco grand jury report recommended that the testimony of non-white people be allowed.

A second Colored Convention was called for December 1856 in Sacramento. It was the largest gathering of its kind that California had ever seen. Gibbs was a member of the Executive Committee but remained in San Francisco to circulate petitions. Over four days, convention delegates once more concentrated on the testimony question. Building on earlier efforts, they authorized the circulation of additional petitions, and within weeks, signed petitions flooded the state capitol. The documents were accepted, yet again, by the state legislature, and, yet again, the question disappeared in the legislative labyrinth.

Many were discouraged as 1857 dawned, and a third convention gathered to rally supporters. That year also saw the dispiriting

Dred Scott decision, in which the United States Supreme Court declared that African Americans had no status as legal citizens of the nation and, in the words of Chief Justice Roger B. Taney, were "beings of an inferior order, and altogether unfit to associate with the white race, either in social or political relations, and so inferior that they had no rights which the white man was bound to respect." Things would get worse for black Californians before they got better.

In 1857, as later court transcripts detailed, a white man named Charles Stovall brought a slave named Archy Lee to California and sold him to Robert Blakely. Lee fled from Blakely, who then had Lee arrested, and Blakely asked that his slave be returned to him under provisions of the federal Fugitive Slave Act of 1850. But United States Commissioner for California George Johnson determined that Archy Lee was not a fugitive under the meaning of the law and refused to order Lee back into Blakely's custody, instead ordering that he be released. The commissioner's reasoning was that Stovall had become a permanent resident of California and therefore could not own or sell a slave in a free state. In 1858 the Sacramento County Court upheld Johnson's decision, which was widely regarded by the black community and its supporters as a victory, as well as a much-needed, much-desired clarification of the status of African Americans in California.

Alas, the moment was short-lived.

The county decision was appealed to the California Supreme Court, where two justices, both Southerners with unmistakable pro-slavery sympathies, took it under advisement. One of them, Justice Peter Burnett, had been the first governor of the State of California and had previously tendered numerous anti-black pronouncements. For this case, he remained true to form and declared that Archy Lee was not free and should be reunited with his master Stovall without delay. Burnett argued that Stovall warranted an exception to the permanent-California-resident clause due to his inexperience and poor health and should be allowed to retain his slave despite the law clearly indicating otherwise. For black Californians, this judgment doused a long-awaited sunbeam of justice. Burnett's reasoning was a flimsy subversion and misinterpretation of well-defined California law, and his finding was roundly criticized not only in antislavery circles but in the legal community as well. Even Justice Burnett's colleagues on the supreme court condemned the finding. The *San Francisco Daily Alta California* called Burnett's opinion a "crowning absurdity and the greatest mass of legal contradiction that has ever come under our notice." The ruling was a disgrace, the newspaper added, and had rendered the California Supreme Court "a laughing stock in the eyes of the world." Within a month, the California Supreme Court's decision on Archy Lee was overturned by a federal district court in San Francisco, and although there were additional legal maneuverings, this federal court ruling stuck and Archy Lee was declared free, once and for all.

On March 19, 1858, emboldened by the Dred Scott decision, Nevada County assemblyman J. B. Warfield introduced Assembly Bill 339, titled "An Act to Restrict and Prevent the Immigration to and Residence in This State of Negroes and Mulattoes." It seemed likely to pass. Gibbs and editorial writers for black newspapers expressed outrage. Even though relatively few numbers of black people were immigrating to California, the act would have imposed severe restrictions on those who tried, and there were no protections for black individuals simply visiting the state for business, pleasure, or family or personal matters. Under the proposed law, black citizens would have to register to prove their residency and would be required to carry their registration certificates at all times or risk fines and imprisonment. This type of regulation was not compulsory for any other group in the state. Surprisingly, due to technicalities the measure did not pass, but its near approval proved to be the final straw for hundreds of black Californians. They had endured enough and decided it was time to leave the Golden State.

Several hundred African Americans sought a new home where they would find tolerance, opportunity, and acceptance. This "promised land" appeared to be sparsely populated British Columbia, which was in the early days of a gold rush of its own. In April 1858, a vanguard of two hundred embarked on an exodus to Victoria, British Columbia, aboard the sailing ship *Commodore*. Among its members was Archy Lee. Mifflin Wistar Gibbs offered a farewell address and was seriously considering joining the migration himself, as were hundreds of others.

As positive word filtered back from the Victoria migrants, plans were accelerated for additional settlers to head north. Ultimately, more than five hundred would join the early arrivals in Victoria and Vancouver. Nearly 15 percent of all black people in California migrated to British Columbia during this period, and the *San Francisco Daily Evening Bulletin* predicted that "the day when colored people fled persecution in California . . . may yet be celebrated in story." A conference of ministers for the African Methodist Episcopal (A.M.E.) Church issued a resolution that referred to the Victoria mission as "God's rescue."

In June 1858, Mifflin Wistar Gibbs left San Francisco for British Columbia. He carried with him stores of supplies needed by the settlement and, upon arrival in Victoria, immediately flourished there as a merchant. The community was succeeding, too. Letters home described that nearly all the jobs in Victoria were held by black people; that the migrants had purchased considerable tracts of land; and that the police force—the only police force—was the black unit known as the Victoria Pioneer Rifle Corps. It was a step up from conditions in California, but it was not idyllic. Many white Americans had rushed to British Columbia for its gold, and they harbored the same familiar prejudices; tension between these old adversaries was inevitable. There were a few efforts to segregate churches, theaters, and saloons, but, in general, these new black Canadians found support and protection from both the British government and local clergy.

Mifflin Wistar Gibbs sunk roots in the new colony and became one of the wealthiest men in Victoria. His five children were born in British Columbia, and he was elected to the Victoria City Council. But even then he could not escape intolerance and social indignities. In 1861, while attending the theater, a white bigot objected to sitting in the same section with Gibbs and threw a container of flour at him and his wife.

When the Civil War ended, prospects for African Americans in the United States initially appeared brighter. While the members of the exodus to B.C. had pledged allegiance to the British crown, many retained unbroken loyalties to American family and friends, as well as to the United States, and in the postwar years there was a reverse migration. Hundreds of black Americans remained in Canada, but a significant portion of the migrant community ended their exile and returned to the United States, where they resumed their former lives. Among those starting anew in his former homeland was Mifflin Wistar Gibbs.

After more than ten years in Victoria, Gibbs migrated to Ohio, where he obtained a law degree at the age of fifty. After hearing of promising potential in Arkansas, he moved to Little Rock in 1871 and hung up his legal shingle. Within two years, Gibbs was appointed County Attorney in Pulaski County, and, in 1873, he was elected Municipal Judge in Little Rock. His election generated national interest, as the majority of the voters were white and he was the first elected African American judge in United States history. In 1877, Gibbs was appointed the Registrar of United

States Lands in the Little Rock District by President Rutherford B. Hayes. Gibbs received another federal appointment from President Benjamin Harrison in 1889, and in 1897 Judge Gibbs was selected by President William McKinley as United States Consul for Madagascar.

Mifflin Wistar Gibbs died in 1915 at the age of ninety-two. His passing came sixty-five years after abolitionist Julia Griffiths had urged the nearly penniless young man to "Go do some great thing." It is likely that Griffiths would have felt that Mifflin Wistar Gibbs—California Gold Rush civil rights champion, defiant migrant, successful merchant, respected lawyer, city council member, county attorney, judge, federal official, and ambassador—had succeeded.

[2017]

THREE YEARS BEFORE STONEWALL

from *Wherever There's a Fight*

Elaine Elinson and **Stan Yogi**

California has been the site of transgender activity since at least the nineteenth century. (The term "transgender" encompasses people who do not conform to gender stereotypes, refuse to identify with a gender, or manifest a gender different from their birth-assigned sex. While some transgender people identify as lesbian or gay, not all do.) At the turn of the century, the Los Angeles Merchants Association even encouraged cross-dressing on All Fool's Night, the culmination of a weeklong commercial Carnivalesque celebration called La Fiesta. Bowing to religious leaders offended by the gender confusion of the event, the Los Angeles city council in 1898 not only banned All Fool's Night, but also passed an ordinance making it a crime for "a man to masquerade as a woman, or a woman as a man."

In 1922 the council revised the law, imposing a six-month jail sentence and five-hundred-dollar fine on anyone caught on the street dressed in clothes of the opposite sex. This gave police the legal basis to stop and harass women and men who did not conform to officers' notions of gender-appropriate clothing. The harassment continued even after Los Angeles municipal courts ruled, in two separate 1950 cases, that a woman could not be convicted for wearing men's slacks and coats and short hair unless there was further evidence of intent to conceal her identity.

Transgender people in California had been quietly organizing since the 1940s for recognition of their rights. Louise Lawrence, a male-to-female transgender person, began in the 1940s to live full-time as a woman in San Francisco. She learned of other transgender people in the U.S. and elsewhere and built a wide correspondence network. She worked with pioneering sex researcher Alfred Kinsey to educate social scientists about the needs of transgender people. Lawrence also mentored another transgender pioneer, Virginia Prince. Born in 1912 into an upper-middle-class Los Angeles family as Arnold Loman, Prince, who as an adult adopted the pseudonym Virginia Prince, began cross-dressing as a teenager. After earning a PhD in biochemistry, Prince moved to Oakland and worked at the UC San Francisco medical school. There she encountered transvestite patients. Feeling isolated about her cross-dressing, Prince contacted one of them, and they began meeting with other transvestites. Prince's wife filed for divorce, incorrectly believing her husband to be gay. The local press learned of the story and publicly identified Prince as a cross-dresser. Although the publicity was unwelcome, it spurred other cross-dressers to contact Prince, and they formed a small group in her home city of Los Angeles, to which she had returned.

In 1952 Prince and a group of transvestites that met in Long Beach published the newsletter *Transvestia: The Journal of the American Society for Equality in Dress*. Historian Susan Stryker considers the short-lived publication "arguably the first overtly political transgender publication in the U.S."

In 1960 Prince began publishing another iteration of *Transvestia*. The following year she formed the Hose and Heels Club, which soon changed its name to Phi Pi Epsilon, not only to mimic sororities but to reference the initials "FPE," an acronym for "Full Personality Expression."

These pioneering organizing efforts were a prelude to the more radical transgender political protests that erupted in 1966 in San Francisco's Tenderloin neighborhood. The mid-1960s were a time of transition for the Tenderloin. Urban renewal projects on the neighborhood's edge had brought tourism and convention-related hotel construction. City leaders wanted to polish the tarnished area, one of the most run-down in San Francisco.

At the same time, America's escalating involvement in the Vietnam War was bringing more military personnel to San Francisco. As they had during World War II and the Korean War, civic leaders and police cracked down on bars and prostitutes catering to soldiers and sailors.

Transgender people in the Tenderloin faced rampant discrimination and could not find jobs or decent places to live. Though nightclub managers hired male-to-female transgender people with talent and glamorous looks as drag performers, those jobs were few and far between. Lacking marketable skills and confronting discrimination, many male-to-female transgender people turned to street prostitution for economic survival. Police officers routinely harassed and arrested them. Many transgender people who lived in the neighborhood's seedy hotels were jailed for no reason, or on such flimsy charges as impersonating a female or obstructing the sidewalk.

In addition to adult transgender prostitutes, teenage hustlers of all genders worked the tough Tenderloin streets. To address their needs, Reverend Ed Havens of Glide Church formed Vanguard, a night ministry for young street prostitutes. Motivated by the then radical idea that, like racial minorities, sexual minorities were the targets of discrimination, Havens secured funding from the federal government's War on Poverty program to address the problems of the Tenderloin's transgender and youth prostitutes.

The spring and summer of 1966 were active in the city's lesbian, gay, and transgender communities. In April, the Society for Individual Rights, an early San Francisco gay rights organization, opened a community center in the Tenderloin as a locus for gay community activism and to organize residents to lobby for federal anti-poverty funds. In May, lesbian and gay activists gathered at the San Francisco federal building, at the edge of the Tenderloin, to protest the military's exclusion of gay people. In August, the Daughters of Bilitis convened its fourth biennial conference in San Francisco.

In the mid-1960s, police were known to allow prostitution, drug dealing, gambling, and other vice in the Tenderloin, if they were paid off. But in 1966, pressured by politicians, they targeted the Tenderloin for a prostitution crackdown.

That summer, the flashpoint for the Tenderloin's poor, disenfranchised, and dispossessed transgender people and young gay street prostitutes was a twenty-four-hour restaurant on the corner of Taylor and Turk streets. At Compton's Cafeteria, a diner where waitresses with paper doilies pinned onto their starched uniforms poured coffee for them, regulars gathered in the vinyl booths to gossip and talk. The police department's Elliot Blackstone recalled: "Compton's was a drag queen hangout. They'd buy coffee, then sit there for four or five hours. Compton's was losing money because of it." When Compton's management imposed a twenty-five-cent service charge on all orders, teens in the Vanguard program saw it as a thinly veiled attempt to keep customers like them out. They began picketing outside the restaurant.

Late on a hot August night, the collective rage of the Tenderloin's transgender women and street youth erupted. A boisterous group at one table upset the manager, who called in the police. An officer accustomed to harassing the restaurant's disempowered patrons grabbed the arm of a drag queen and tried to arrest her. Fed up with disrespect and police abuse, she threw coffee in his face.

Her action released the pent-up anger of the other patrons. They threw cups, saucers, silverware, and plates at the retreating officer, who called for reinforcements. The ensuing melee, which involved fifty to sixty people, spread into the street, with

Founder Malcolm Margolin with his boxes of books.
From *The Heyday of Malcolm Margolin* by Kim Bancroft, 2014

"Horse Creek Trail" (left) and "Half Dome from Glacier Point" (right) by Tom Killion, from *The High Sierra of California* by Gary Snyder and Tom Killion, 2002

"McWay Rocks, Big Sur, 2013" (left) and "Golden Gate Sunset, 1997" (right) by Tom Killion, from *California's Wild Coast* by Tom Killion with Gary Snyder, 2020

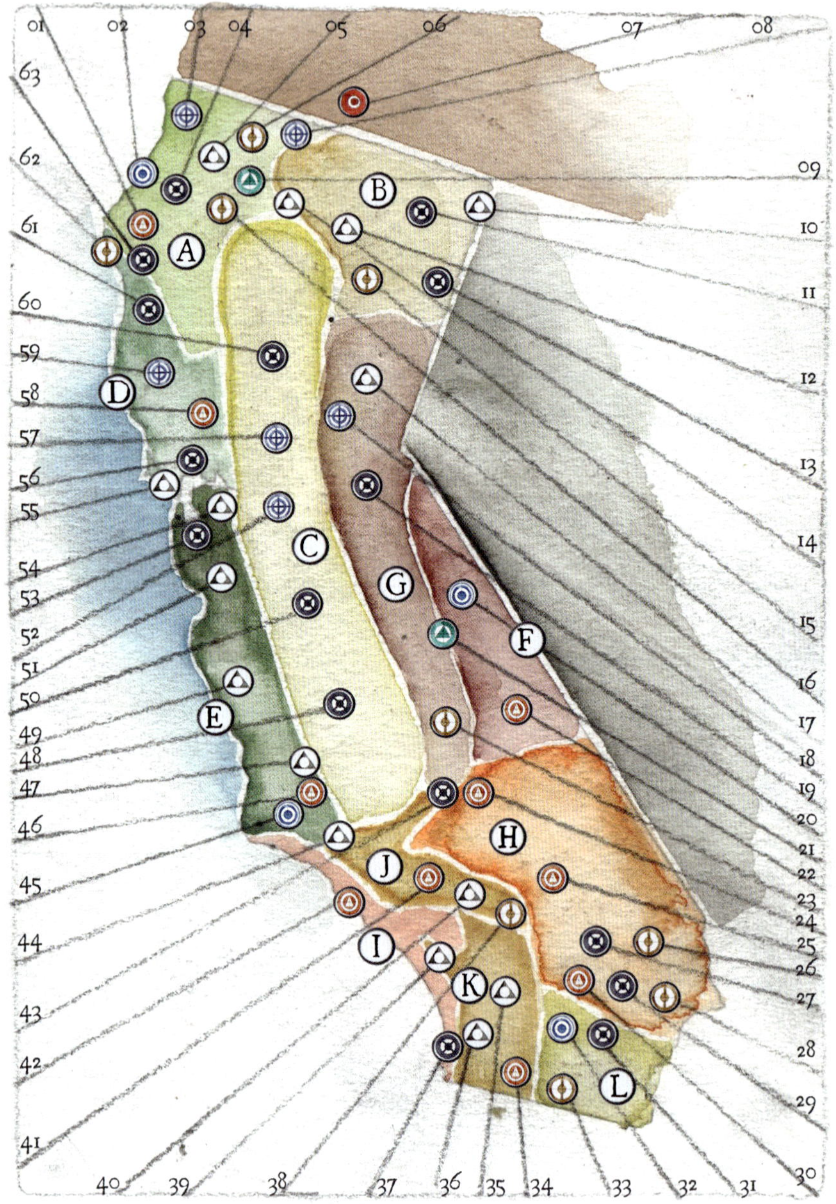

Illustration from *The California Field Atlas* by Obi Kaufmann, 2017

Illustration from *The Forests of California* by Obi Kaufmann, 2020

Illustrations from *The Coasts of California* by Obi Kaufmann, 2022

Mojave yucca
Yucca schidigera

Joshua tree
Yucca brevifolia

Font's Point and the Badlands

Anza-Borrego Desert State Park

Illustrations from *The Deserts of California* by Obi Kaufmann, 2023

Illustrations from *The Laws Guide to Nature Drawing and Journaling* by John Muir Laws, 2016

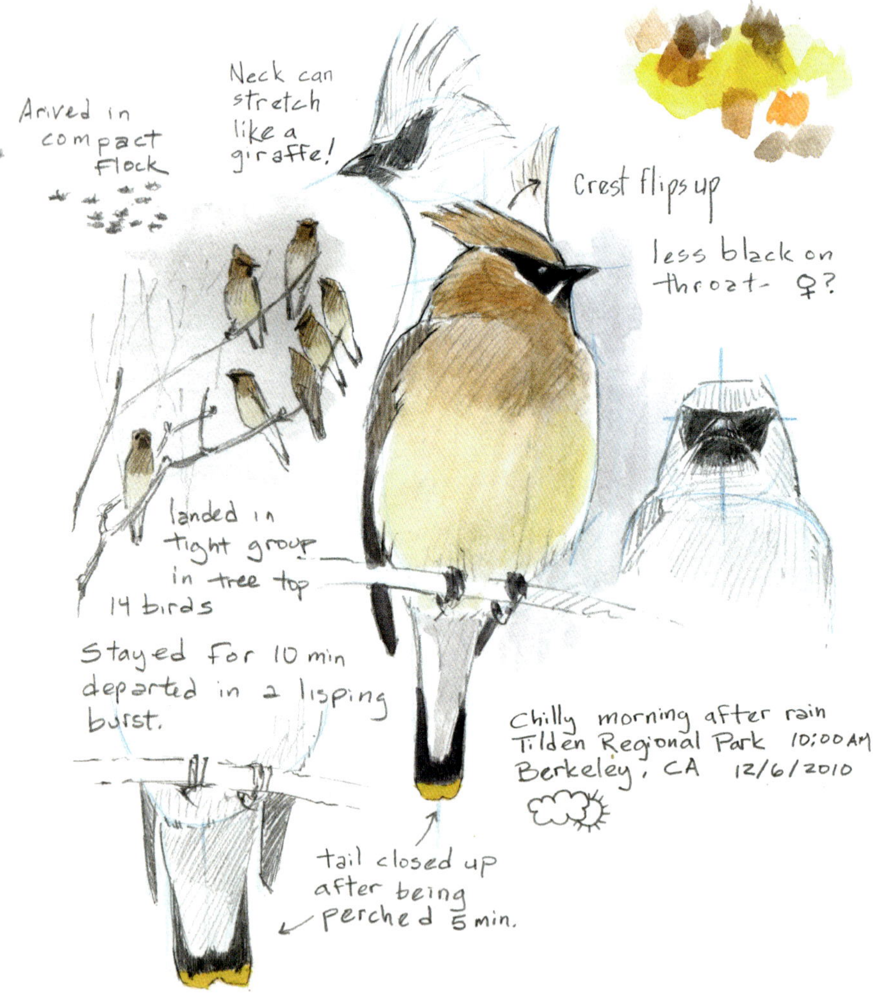

Illlustration from *The Laws Guide to Drawing Birds* by John Muir Laws, 2012

Illustration from *Birds of Point Reyes* by Keith Hansen, 2023

Illustration by Yutaka Houlette, from *Fred Korematsu Speaks Up*
by Laura Atkins and Stan Yogi, 2017

Illustration by Laura Freeman, from *Biddy Mason Speaks Up* by Arisa White and Laura Atkins, 2019

Photo by Charles Hood, from *Nocturnalia*
by Charles Hood and José Gabriel Martínez-Fonseca, 2023

drag queens hitting police with their purses and kicking them with their high heels. Rioters broke restaurant windows and set fire to a nearby newsstand.

Susan Stryker explains that the riot at Compton's was "the first known instance of collective, militant queer resistance to police harassment in United States history." It took place three years before similar resistance by gay people and drag queens at New York's Stonewall Inn, the event many consider the birth of the movement for lesbian, gay, bisexual, and transgender equality.

"There was a lot of joy after it happened," explained Amanda St. Jaymes, who participated in the riot. "A lot of them went to jail, but there was a lot of 'I don't really give a damn. This is what had to happen.'"

In late 1966, Elliot Blackstone, by then the police department's liaison with the federally funded Central City Anti-Poverty Program, received a visit from a woman he later described as a "tall, football player–type female." The visitor was Louise Ergestrasse, a male-to-female Tenderloin prostitute, who explained to the burly officer that she and other transgender women traded sex for money because of employment discrimination. Ergestrasse demanded that Blackstone do something to reduce police abuse and help prostitutes out of sex work.

Together, they organized Conversion Our Goal (later changed to Transsexual Counseling Service). The group succeeded in reducing arrests under gender "impersonation" laws. With funding from the Erickson Educational Foundation, a philanthropy formed by a transgender man who was heir to a lead-smelting business, they connected clients to supportive social services and medical programs, including city-funded clinics that provided hormones to facilitate gender reassignment.

[2009]

MOMENT OF TRUTH

from *Grave Matters*

Tony Platt

California was the first state in which a grassroots organization was created to specifically halt the desecration and looting of cemeteries. The Northwest Indian Cemetery Protection Association (NICPA), an intertribal nonprofit organization with strong Yurok participation, was officially established in 1970. Its first chairman, Milton Marks, and its second chairman, Walt Lara Sr., were well-known Yurok leaders. In 1988 NICPA gained national prominence for its role as the respondent in the "G-O Road" US Supreme Court case involving Native American religious access to public lands. But long before that case was decided, the association's militancy in California generated widespread recognition and a flurry of results.

The official founding of NICPA in 1970 was the result of a perfect convergence: an accumulation of grievances stretching back at least a hundred years, combined with a receptive political climate, the rise of a new generation of native leaders and strategic activists committed to building organizations for the long run, and the emergence of a cadre of ethically responsible anthropologists willing to play a supporting role in defense of Native American rights. And a triggering incident.

In October 1969, a young assistant professor of anthropology who was working on his doctorate and had just started his first teaching job, at San Francisco State University, received word from Tom Hannah at the Clarke Historical Museum in Eureka that the site of the Yurok settlement of Tsahpekw in the state park at Stone Lagoon (north of Big Lagoon) was being torn apart by collectors. When Michael Moratto checked out the area, it "resembled a battlefield with contiguous potholes and shattered bones from desecrated graves covering about two acres." Moratto sought and received permission from Francis Riddell, chief archaeologist of the California Department of Parks and Recreation, to initiate a salvage operation. In January and February of 1970, he and two colleagues carried out a reconnaissance of Tsahpekw, refilled potholes, and "made surface collections." With "all the standard permits" in hand, he planned to return in June with twenty students to carry out an excavation of the Yurok site. He felt confident that he had received a go-ahead from "two influential Yurok Indians" who "were fully informed of the proposed excavations and seemed in complete sympathy with our efforts to stabilize the site and to salvage whatever of archaeological value remained, while avoiding cemetery areas."

Moratto must have known—as did archaeologist John Mills during the 1949 excavation of Tsurai—that it would be impossible to carry out an excavation of an important native site without disturbing graves. When an attorney for California Indian Legal Services wrote to him in April 1970 expressing "a strong feeling among the Indians of the North Coast against this constant digging up of Indian burial grounds" and asking, point blank, "whether in fact San Francisco State plans to send a project up there to desecrate this burial ground," Moratto hedged and covered himself on this eventuality: "If we do encounter any burials, it is our intention to re-inter them with proper respect in a part of the site that will not be disturbed by subsequent Stone Lagoon Park developments." The concerns of the attorney for the Yurok were not assuaged by this promise. "It is felt," replied Robert Donovan, "that one of the reasons why there is so much exploration in the North Coast area is that archaeology professors desire to give practical experience to their classes and to do so they must go on a dig. The Indian communities' dignity is constantly infringed upon by these efforts and Indians wish that such efforts would be directed at white cemeteries."

Despite these warning signs, Moratto returned to Stone Lagoon with a crew of eager students who were ready to learn by doing. But by June, NICPA was on the move and the political mood had changed. Now he was facing an organization of "dedicated, self-determined Indians," not just a couple of sympathetic Yurok.

Sometime in 1969, a small group of influential Yurok, Hupa, Karuk, and Wiyot at the core of what would become NICPA began to discuss "the wanton desecration of Indian family cemeteries by archaeologists, art collectors, hobbyists, necromancers, and commercial and amateur curio seekers." This was a group of visionaries who understood that grassroots organizing requires patience and stamina; and who had a knack for building political relationships with other organizations and generating publicity for their campaign. Its leaders also had a toughness and resiliency hewn from their experiences in working-class jobs and the labor movement. These qualities served them well in confrontations with authority, whether in the form of professional archaeologists or government functionaries or academics.

The founding organizer of NICPA, Milton Marks (1915–1980), was from a Yurok family whose activism spans four generations. His father, Jimmy Marks, grew up in Morek—according to Thomas Waterman, a "very important" Yurok town on the Klamath and site of "impressive ceremonies." He was known as Morek Jimmy until school authorities further Anglicized his name. "He belonged to an era to be remembered," noted his obituary. The teachers "couldn't spell Morek, couldn't even sound it out," recalled Jimmy's daughter in 1990. "Morek, that's our main name." Her father played a leading role in the community as a dam builder and was "held in high esteem." Later in his life, when he lived on the coast, he supported the state's taking over the area around the native site of Espaw from a gold mining company. He thought the state parks would do a better job of protecting the settlement and allowing Yurok to gather berries, roots, ferns, and other traditional materials.

Jimmy's wife, Josephine Brown McDonald Marks (1877–1965)—known as Josie or Sin-gi-wa—was one of Waterman's informants about Yurok culture, the "very intelligent woman" who wouldn't tell the anthropologist her native name. Margaret and Milton, founding members of NICPA, were two of their children. Milton's daughter Diane worked with NICPA until her untimely death at the age of thirty, and his first daughter, Sandy, was a member of NICPA and went on to develop an innovative Indian education program for Eureka's public schools. Milton's nephew Walt was his right-hand man in the early days of NICPA. Three of Margaret Marks's children—Frank, Jeanette, and Walt—became leaders within the Yurok Tribe and are currently members of its prestigious Culture Committee. Walt Lara Sr. is married to Callie Lara, who served for several years as the director of the Hupa Language, Culture and Education Center, and their children are emerging as leaders-to-be in their tribal communities.

While the driving force behind the formation of NICPA was Milton Marks, his older sister Margaret Marks Lara (1912–1996) was at his side and more than held her own. Born and died in Ooh-sa-mech, south of Orick, she worked in the sawmills to support her children, was active in her union as well as NICPA, spoke Spanish, and was part of the first cohort of postwar Yurok to emphasize the importance of reclaiming native languages before they died with the elders. As a child she was suspended from school for fighting back when a teacher hit her. And as an adult, she inherited her mother's resiliency and unsentimental views about anthropologists: "They just talk to us like we're the most intelligent people in the wide old world, and when we give them all this information and everything, then they slough us aside." Margaret, who as a young woman had stayed with the influential native rights advocate Ruth Roberts in Oakland, had no trouble operating confidently in the milieu of white, middle-class professionals. A university-based expert on community organizing remembers her as a formidable foe in the 1970s: "She cried, stomped the floor, shook her fist at archaeologists. She gave archaeologists a hard time."

But within her own community, she was a patient and tireless organizer, serving as chairperson of the Yurok Organization before it became officially incorporated. Despite "always working," recalls her niece Sandy Burton, "Auntie Margaret pounded into our heads 'You come from a long line of well-bred Indians and you must live up to that expectation. Be respectful at all times.' A lot was expected of our family. She would come over to my home on Friday nights and teach me the Yurok language. 'This is your inheritance,' she said. This kind of leadership was also instilled in Milton."

By the time that Milton Marks became the organizational leader and public face of NICPA, he was fifty-four years old and a person of considerable experience, charm, and self-earned knowledge. In the mid-1930s he had received a Bureau of Indian Affairs loan to attend the Sherman Institute in Riverside—a boarding school that no doubt raised his pan-Indian consciousness. After graduation he stayed on in the Los Angeles area, attending junior and business colleges and working various jobs, including a walk-on role as a generic African soldier in a turban in the 1941 Hollywood movie *Sundown*, starring Gene Tierney. After serving in the army from 1944 to 1946, he returned to Humboldt County, where he was employed as a timber faller for the rest of his working life. One of his jobs was with Hammond Lumber, the company that clear-cut the area around Big Lagoon.

By all accounts, Milton Marks was an extraordinarily effective organizer who combined a steely resolve to keep his eyes on the prize with a capacious patience for diplomacy and education. He was "persistent and amicable," recalls Jim Benson, the first Native American archaeologist to work with NICPA. "I've never met a person who knows more about traditional Yurok culture than Milton. He could go up to anybody and get them to talk. He listened, was very inquisitive. . . . He had his own body of knowledge, told story after story." Dave Fredrickson, one of the first white archaeologists to develop a working relationship with NICPA, remembers Milton Marks as a "charismatic presence. . . And he always let me know what was going on." He also had a profound impact on Polly Quick, fresh from her doctoral dissertation in anthropology at Harvard. "It was a pivotal moment in my career," she recalled recently. "He took me on as a protégé. He's the one who taught me how to reach out to native communities, how to listen. My relationships with Native Americans have all been patterned on what he taught me: it takes time to build relationships." Other people who worked with NICPA describe Milton Marks as an activist who didn't tread lightly when there was a need to take principled stands, but who understood the importance of tactical alliances with people and organizations that had access to power.

The proposed excavation at Tsahpekw had special meaning for the Marks family: they had relatives buried there. The confrontation with Moratto, recalled Milton, "inspired" the formation of NICPA. "Being raised by my grandparents and a working mother," says Walt Lara Sr., "I can understand the hurt when a site is destroyed. I was there and I saw what it did to my grandparents when these excavations occurred." His experience at Tsahpekw gave him a lifelong suspicion of the motives of academics and a fierce determination to protect Yurok sites. "He didn't like archaeologists," recalls Dave Fredrickson. 'Too much science,' he'd say." And Lara, who to this day exudes a palpable energy, had a reputation for keeping even white supporters of NICPA anxiously on their toes. "He was a very physical person," recalls Tom Parsons, who allowed the association to use his office on the campus of Humboldt State as a mailing address during its formative years. "He was about 80 percent supportive of what I was doing." But Lara's garrulous roughness was as much tactical as it was a reflection of his personality. "You had to be tough," recalls another NICPA activist, "because people were always speaking down to you." As a tag-team, Milton and Walt were a match for any opponents: "I would strong-arm them, then Milton would smooth-talk them," says Lara.

Like his Uncle Miltie and mother, Margaret, Walt Lara worked in the timber industry and was active in its union. By the mid-1960s, some 70 percent of native workers in rural areas and on reservations in California earned less than three thousand dollars annually; and in the Hoopa area, one out of three people was unemployed. The average age of death for Native Americans in the region was forty-two, twenty years younger than the general population; and the Indian infant mortality rate was 70 percent higher. So a job in logging, with an annual income of as much as six thousand dollars, was highly desirable, despite its rigorous physical toll.

When the Lumber and Sawmill Workers union mobilized its membership to oppose the Carter administration's proposed expansion of the Redwood National Park in 1977, Milton Marks and Walt Lara joined a truck convoy and hundreds of angry loggers who traveled to Washington, D.C., and paraded a peanut-shaped redwood log in front of Congress. An Arcata newspaper captured the two of them in hard hats, suspenders, and work shirts on the Capitol steps, with Lara giving an interview to a television crew. And back home in Orick, Margaret Lara buttonholed a sympathetic Senator Sam Hayakawa during a visit to Redwood National Park, telling him that most of her relatives, who worked directly or indirectly in logging, would lose jobs if Phil Burton's legislation passed.

Another early participant in NICPA was Joy Sundberg, a Yurok descendant of Big Lagoon who later chaired the Trinidad Rancheria for twenty-five years. Like Margaret Lara and Milton Marks, she accumulated a great deal of worldly experience early in life— her grandparents visited [Alfred] Kroeber in Berkeley—and whatever her private fears, she thrust herself into "the white man's world." She was, and is, fiercely independent. "I went to school at the college of hard knocks. Look at all these chop marks on my neck," she says, pointing to the back of her head. "Always sticking it out. We fought for things that were right. We didn't do it for ourselves. None of us got rich doing it."

Sundberg admired women like Jane Fonda, who opposed the war in Vietnam, because "she stood up for what she believed." In Washington, D.C., Sundberg lobbied sympathetic senators, such as Daniel Evans and Daniel Inouye, for native land rights, while locally she supported the campaigns of a white activist, Sara Parsons, the first woman elected to Humboldt's Board of Supervisors, in 1977; and of African American Tom Bradley in his unsuccessful 1982 run for governor of California. In 1974 she led a delegation of California Indians, including a troupe of Tolowa and Yurok dancers, to the Festival of American Folklife in Washington, D.C. She also transported a redwood log provided by Walt Lara for a canoe-building demonstration.

Sundberg brought to NICPA her experience as a member of the Trinidad School Board and many local political and cultural organizations, and as an appointee to the State Historical Resources Commission and United Indian Health Services Board. "There was just a few of us when NICPA started," she recalled recently. "We had to pound on doors, talk to organizations, get up and speak in front of politicians. I didn't give up. It was hard, but we had to do it." She learned that "a ragtag group of folks can defeat the big guys."

By the time that twenty-six-year-old Michael Moratto arrived in Humboldt with his students in June 1970, ready to excavate Tsahpekw, native insistence on the need to protect cemeteries had already caught the attention of local officials and the press. In March 1970, the *Times-Standard* in a moment of rare candor reported that "Indians opposed people digging into the graves of their immediate ancestors." A few weeks later, the Humboldt County Sheriff, Gene Cox, issued a public warning that "every person who mutilates, disinters or removes from the place of interment any human remains without authority of law is guilty of a felony. We sincerely hope that the guilty persons who are committing these acts not only realize the magnitude of the crime they are committing, but also that many bodies they are disturbing have close living relatives in the area."About the same time, the director of the state's Parks and Recreation department added his voice to the growing if belated outcry of indignation by recognizing that "vandals and souvenir hunters" were destroying Tsahpekw. "Evidently, many people aren't aware of the laws protecting these historic sites and, if they are aware of them, they don't understand the serious consequences of their actions."

Meanwhile, Milton Marks was building the foundations of NICPA and looking for political alliances. "He came to me and we talked about a plan to do something to stop grave robbing," recalls Tom Parsons, who came to the Arcata campus in 1965 as de facto director of the university's newly formed Center for Community

Development. Parsons arrived with degrees in education from the University of Michigan and experience as a seasoned community organizer in the mold of Saul Alinsky. He was a good match for Marks, his equal in charisma, energy, and determination. Parsons's politics were influenced by the New Left and civil rights movements, with their emphasis on grassroots, cross-racial organizing. Recently married, he and his wife, Sara Mitchell Parsons, were a formidable team. She was a white, upper-middle-class reformer from Georgia who, as a member of the Atlanta Board of Education, had worked with Martin Luther King and civil rights organizations to integrate the public schools. She had divorced her first husband after thirty years of marriage to marry Parsons. "I felt sorry for my first husband," she said, "because he married a sweet southern girl. And I turned out to be this civil rights activist and a flaming feminist."

Under Parsons's leadership, the Center for Community Development received federal and state funds to work with a variety of grassroots groups and to develop field placements for students committed to public service and social justice. "We are community developers, not planners nor technical advisors," explained the center's manifesto. "Our clients, in all cases, do their own program planning in interaction with us. And they must, because the motivation that propels their projects' vigor comes directly and only from their active involvement in planning on their own behalf." Parsons sought out local native leaders and provided resources to support the resurrection of Yurok languages by teaching the basics of vocabulary and grammar through a system of phonetics. "I went to them, won their trust," says Parsons. "Other than a blood transfusion, you couldn't get closer than language." The center is credited with helping to revitalize the Yurok language.

While Moratto's twenty students set up camp at Patrick's Point State Park, he and two colleagues (including the chair of his department at San Francisco State) attended a meeting at Humboldt State, at the Center for Community Development. Moratto naively thought that the meeting would be the beginning of a mutually respectful collaboration. Instead, he recalls, "I listened to a great deal of animosity. I can understand why they felt that way. I caught the brunt of their anger. I paid for the sins of our fathers."

The meeting, which was chaired by Milton Marks and attended by Walt Lara, Margaret Lara, nine other members of NICPA, and their lawyer (with Tom Parsons on hand as an observer), quickly turned tense and argumentative. After Moratto nervously explained that the sheriff's ban on excavations did not apply to state land, and that he hoped to salvage what remained of Tsahpekw and "to avoid cemetery areas," he sat and listened to a lecture of complaints: "Archaeologists have not contributed much beyond what is already known of Yurok history and traditions. . . . Archaeologists and anthropologists take artifacts and information away from the Indians and their territory without returning anything of value to the Indians. . . . It is sacrilegious to store the artifacts and bones of deceased Indians in museums. They should all be respectfully reinterred."

"I was totally intimidated," recalls Moratto. "A big guy there—about six feet across his shoulders—spoke up: 'I don't know about you archaeologists, but you ain't going to dig at Tsahpekw." Moratto recalls "one particularly irascible Yurok logger"—Walt Lara—who "spiced the dialogue with periodic threats of actual violence. Not wishing to jeopardize lives or future Indian-anthropologist relationships, I conceded to leave Tsahpekw and undertake research elsewhere." Moratto was too stunned to turn the incident into a learning experience for his students. "I was shellshocked for several days." Even now, forty years later, he finds it painful to recall.

The showdown over Tsahpekw quickly became a widely recounted tale, a cause célèbre in native circles and a topic of debate and gossip in archaeology. The "unprecedented accord"—in reality, a victory for NICPA and defeat for the San Francisco State team—was reported in the press and retold as legend. I've heard versions of the story that turn what happened into a subversion of the cowboys-and-Indians narrative by locating the confrontation in the rugged wilds of Stone Lagoon rather than a sedate university office, with the Yurok running off the archaeological team at gunpoint, rather than by the ferocity of their words. One outcome, however, was clear to everybody who was directly involved or heard about the incident. The rules of engagement had changed: anybody planning to collect or dig at native sites in Humboldt County better have the cooperation and authorization of NICPA.

[2011]

LA FRONTERA

from *Feels Like Home*

Linda Ronstadt and **Lawrence Downes**

When I was a girl you could get across the line easily. The border station in Nogales was a small building with a turnstile. It took a few minutes and across you went. We'd go down from Tucson for shopping in Nogales or for road-trip vacations or for social functions like pachangas. And people came up from Sonora to shop and do business on our side. We all crossed the line.

Mexican ranchers and farmers were a big part of my dad's business. They came up to Ronstadt Hardware for pumps, windmills, and other heavy equipment, and for tools and rifles and kitchenware and whatever other supplies they needed. And my dad would go to them. He drove all over Sonora to meet his Mexican customers, and sometimes he'd take me along.

I learned about the desert driving back and forth with Daddy pointing stuff out. He knew that area like the back of his hand. We'd be in the middle of the desert, driving for hours with nothing in sight, and he'd say, "Well, around this next little corner, you're going to see Don So-and-so. He's going to ask me if I want a little whiskey, and I'm going to stop and have a little drink with him."

And there the man would be, sitting on his chair by the road. He'd see my dad and say, "Un whisquito¿" and my dad would go, "Sure, why not¿" I'd stay in the car and they would talk business for a while. Maybe he needed a new cultivator or a windmill or something like that. My dad knew all the ranchers. They knew what he could supply, what kind of price he would give them, and that he was going to treat them fairly.

Sometimes we'd all go to Sonora as a family, singing harmonies in the car. That was before there was air-conditioning in cars. Our vacation trips were super hot and dusty, but with great food. We would stop in Hermosillo and little towns like Caborca and Oquitoa and end up in Guaymas, a fishing town on the Sea of Cortés. We would marvel at the ocean. I had never seen so much water. My father would hire a boat, we'd all go fishing, get la turista—Montezuma's revenge—throw up, and go home all sunburned. It was wonderful.

We went down for special occasions, too. Hermosillo would have a black-and-white ball for the debutantes of ranchers' families, and many Tucson families would be invited as well. The connections between Tucson and Sonora went deep because, until relatively recently, Tucson *was* Sonora. With the Treaty of Guadalupe Hidalgo, in 1848, the United States took possession of more than half of Mexico's territory, including California, New Mexico, Texas, Colorado, Nevada, Utah, and a big chunk of Arizona. In 1853, the Gadsden Purchase moved the border again, fixing the line below Tucson. Even then, the line remained fuzzy, and more work was needed to pin down exactly where Mexico ended and the United States began. It's little wonder that southern Arizona kept close affinity with Sonora, and that all kinds of connections—economic, cultural, and familial—continued to bind both places together.

When I went back to Sonora from Tucson in the 1990s, I saw what the border fence had become. It wasn't a chain-link afterthought anymore. Now it was an ugly scar, a gash in the landscape that made you feel like you were doing something bad when you crossed in either direction, there was so much fear and tension.

The border in Ambos Nogales—what they call the two Nogaleses, American and Mexican—used to be a formality between neighbors who got along. It was rich on one side and poor on the other, but the rich side wasn't always so frightened. It saw no need to fortify itself against its poorer, weaker companion.

But that was long ago. The fence has gotten hulking and monumental. Under the forty-fifth president the wall was extended in both directions and draped, in Nogales and other places, with parallel coils of lethal concertina wire. A little desert border town suddenly looked like a cross between 1950s Berlin and a supermax federal prison.

The construction was a disaster for the Sonoran Desert. Wall-building crews scraped and bulldozed miles of pristine desert floor into bare dirt track on either side of the barrier. They drained springs and aquifers, stealing life-giving water from plants and animals, to mix concrete. Quitobaquito Springs, a sacred spot for Native peoples and a rich oasis for wildlife, was depleted. Enormous saguaros, which take decades to mature, were toppled and piled and left to rot. What the crews left behind—a thirty-foot wall—stops many migrating and grazing animals in their tracks, endangering their survival.

Because of the wall and the Border Patrol, with its trucks and drones and floodlights and sensors, many migrants end up stalled in Mexican Nogales. Migrants caught on the American side are dumped there without money or prospects. People seeking refuge, who were ordered by the United States to remain in Mexico while they wait for their asylum hearings, bide their time in grimy tent camps. Migrants who are determined to keep going wait in Nogales until they are ready to cross—to try their luck for the first time, the second, or the tenth. All the while, they are vulnerable to robbery and kidnapping by the narco gangs and human traffickers who control the northbound routes, and to the abuses of the Border Patrol waiting on the other side.

And yet, in the heart of Mexican Nogales, in the middle of all this ugliness, there is an outpost of love and human decency. It's known as the Comedor, Spanish for the dining room. It's run by the Kino Border Initiative, a partnership of Catholic sisters and priests and laypeople from both sides of the border. Migrants are welcomed there.

They arrive weary and stunned by exposure to the elements and raw from their encounters with immigration authorities, known as la migra. Their feet are blistered and bleeding; they have other injuries and traumas. Many of the women and girls have been sexually assaulted. And that is just the damage from the journey of the last few days and weeks, piled atop the terrors of the lives they fled.

The migrants get the basics. Volunteers keep the Comedor supplied with donated clothing and diapers, toothbrushes, soap, and, most important, clean, dry socks. But maybe the most restorative thing the migrants receive is a hot meal. Eggs and tortillas and beans and salsa for breakfast. For lunch, chicken in mole or menudo, the rich stew made of tripe and hominy, a fragrant, steamy bowl garnished with lime and cilantro.

The Comedor began humbly, as an improvised effort by several Catholic nuns who fed deported migrants outdoors, near a bridge by the Mariposa port of entry. The sisters then worked alongside the Jesuits to establish an indoor shelter that could give migrants food and other necessities and services. The Comedor has been doing its vital work since 2008.

I first visited there with my friend Shura Wallin, one of a group of volunteers from suburban Tucson who have supported the Comedor for many years, collecting donations of food and clothing, greeting migrants, helping them to adjust to the place, learning their stories, answering their questions, and easing their fear through simple kindness. I met Shura through my brother Mike, who had gone with Shura's group on one of their regular searches of the Arizona side of the desert to find and help migrants who were lost or abandoned and in danger of dying.

Shura, who is in her eighties, is tiny, almost elfin, with close-cropped gray hair, boundless energy, and an uncanny ability to spot people in trouble. She speaks little Spanish beyond the basics like "amigos," a word she would call out over and over when she walked the dusty trails beside the highway, looking for migrants who might be injured or sick.

Shura solves problems. She will meet somebody in the Comedor and learn he has a toothache, then find a guy with a car who can drive him to the dentist, and then work her magic to persuade the dentist to do the work at no charge. She'll coax a friend to help fill a migrant's blood-pressure prescription at a Walgreens on the American side. She'll let migrants use her phone to call their families so they know their loved ones are alive.

Many of the migrants who visit the Comedor are determined to keep pressing on, beyond Nogales, past the wall, to jobs and families in the United States. They are aiming at Tucson, seventy-two miles up Interstate 19. The drive takes about an hour. The walk takes about a week. It's dangerous, and not just because of the Border Patrol. No one knows how many thousands of migrants have died in the Arizona desert; many bodies are unidentified, and many are never found. Volunteer groups such as No More Deaths try to lower the death toll by leaving lifesaving caches of water and food in the desert. Border Patrol agents are known to empty and destroy the water jugs when they find them. Sometimes they arrest and charge humanitarian aid-givers for sheltering and transporting migrants. Advocacy groups who keep track of the reported deaths—the corpses who are turned over to medical examiners in Tucson—mark maps with red dots that cluster all along the Arizona border, and thickly in the Tohono O'odham lands, which are sparsely populated and all the more dangerous for their isolation.

Those dots sprayed out across southern Arizona look like a map of a disease outbreak, and in a sense they are. They show the results of the disease of exclusion and hostility. Each dot is a story of hope and reckless courage that ended terribly.

[2022]

MAO'S LITTLE RED BOOK

from *What Kind of Bird Can't Fly*

Dorsey Nunn with **Lee Romney**

I hadn't been at DVI [Deuel Vocational Institution] but two days when a friendly voice called out, "Hey, Dorsey!" It was the best sound someone in my circumstance could hope to hear. After Vacaville I was feeling the loss of my big brother. I was lonely and scared. But here was someone who could make out who I was, and even sounded happy to see me. I was walking the hallway that led from J Wing to the chow hall, trying to keep my head down, and when I heard my name, I turned around to see Nate Harrington's smiling face.

Nate, my childhood friend. Nate, who got harassed by the pigs with me for picking up a sprinkler on the wrong side of the freeway. Nate, who ran away from home with me and chickened out with me damn quick when we got cold and hungry. Running into Nate was sure as shit a better welcome surprise than watching a brother get stabbed in the back. Still, my first response was confusion. Because even when Nate was young, I knew he was brilliant. Seeing him here, locked up, gave me cognitive dissonance. I recognized that *I* might have been an asshole. And when I later reflected on my life up until that point, there were many instances that could confirm that opinion of myself. Nate, though? I had fully expected him to be someplace else in life. Nate had promise. It wouldn't be long before I'd learn that a lot of the other brothers locked up with me did too.

Nate's presence at DVI added a piece to the puzzle my mind had been working since I arrived. As soon as our escorts marched us to J Wing, I noticed all the Black faces in the yard that separated East Hall from West Hall. I saw them in the chow line, and on the tier. "Damn," I mumbled to myself, "it's more Black men here than everybody that went to high school with me." More Black men than I'd seen in church. More brothers than I'd stood shoulder to shoulder with at a packed concert infused with the sweet smell of weed. Nate's presence seemed to provide the answer: we were *all* destined for prison.

Racism was not surprising to me, given my childhood. But the composition of DVI shocked me. It's how I imagined Jews might have felt in Auschwitz or Dachau. They may have occasionally seen a Gypsy, or a gay person, but they knew *they* were target number one. Because they were *all* there. It'd be like, "Fuck, you the doctor!" "And *you* was the baker!" DVI established one fact for me fast: prison had a color scheme, and it didn't match the larger society.

A couple of weeks later, the prisoners organized a baseball game on the yard by hometown. Oakland gathered in one spot, San Francisco in another. When East Menlo Park/East Palo Alto grouped up in our corner of the yard to represent, we looked around and recognized our whole Little League team was there, reunited—everyone but the one white kid. And that was the tip of the iceberg. I'd soon run into kids I'd seen in continuation school, guys I'd hung out with in the pool hall, and just about everybody else from my youth. There was William Charles, a solid brother and a decent burglar too. And Tommy Moore, who'd learned to sing and play the piano at the Nairobi Cultural Center in East Palo Alto and boogied right next to me on dance nights. Tommy had a political consciousness before he arrived. DVI was a mix like that. There were those of us whose opportunities and ambitions had been limited by racism and the poverty it engendered, so we'd turned to taking other people's shit and getting high. Then there were brothers already affiliated with the Black Panthers who'd broken the law in the service of their ideals or had straight-up been framed by the FBI. Black Panther Party members Arthur "Tha" League; Jalil Abdul Muntaqim, who I knew at DVI as Anthony Bottom; and Geronimo Ji-Jaga Pratt were all politicized before they came to prison, and when they hit the yard, they brought that with them. They seeded the global prisoner rights movement and cultivated us newcomers to fight for justice.

When I arrived at DVI, my political consciousness was still nine parts rage to one part reason, and there were plenty of others like me still flipping through the pages of girly magazines. When we'd get lonely, we'd turn to each other and ask, "Hey, you think I could write your sister?" Still, I could *feel* revolution in the air, even if I couldn't articulate it. Nate would help with that. Even as the system stole my physical freedom and trampled my humanity with its impossible choices, he and some other brothers gave me the key to intellectual freedom, and that was a lasting gift. They helped me understand structural racism so I could strategize ways to blow that shit up and put something better in place.

Nate never spoke from a place of ego, and he never dished out bullshit. A lot of guys you run into in the pen are more than happy to have pretend conversations. "Man, when I was out there, I was moving pounds of dope. I don't know how in the fuck I got caught. Some snitching-ass motherfucker told on me, you know?" *That's* a bullshit conversation. But Nate and I weren't going there. That day we first reunited, we sat down with our trays of cold mac 'n' cheese at one of the steel four-person tables bolted to the floor. Nate was even taller than I remembered, thin as a green bean with long limbs that each seemed to march to their own tune. He was keeping his big warm smile in check—that's what men in prison do—but I could sense love for me in his liquid brown eyes. We were as tight as if no time had passed.

"What happened to you, homeboy?" I asked him. "Where did you go?"

Nate's family hadn't been healthy. As dysfunctional as my own household felt sometimes, his was worse. So much so that the county had dumped him in the foster care system. The last time I seen Nate, I rode one of my stolen bikes fifteen miles down El Camino Real to visit him in a group home in the city of San Mateo—and fifteen miles back. Sitting in the chow hall, Nate caught me up. He'd wound up in San Francisco and even attended the same high school as Alma for a while. Then dope came into the picture, just like it had for me. Nate got busted for selling smack and here we were, in the same grim space at the same fucking time, together again. Nate wasn't about regrets though. He was only nineteen years old, a year younger than me, but he was intellectually more grown, inquisitive, analytical, and generous with his mind. As we picked at our food, he changed the subject.

"Have you read Eldridge Cleaver's book, *Soul on Ice?*"

Nate consumed books like a chain smoker consumes cigarettes. He didn't have time for girly mags. He wouldn't just teach me *how* to read, he would teach me *what* to read. Thanks to Nate, big boobs got boring even for me. He would walk up to me in the yard and without so much as a "What's up?" start breaking down dialectical materialism for me. He'd read Karl Marx, and soon I would too. Nate also turned me on to Ralph Ellison, talking about the *Invisible Man* in such a way that I had to find out what was exciting him. The system had eyes though, and our revolutionary fervor landed both of us in trouble, for hanging around too close to the BGF [Black Guerrilla Family] and for raging at the pigs. There were weeks, even months, when I didn't see Nate because I was locked in K Wing. Back on the mainline, we'd seek each other out and pick up where we left off, sitting in the bleachers on the yard.

"Come on, man," Nate would coax, "read to me a bit."

My ghetto education had brought me into prison at a third-grade reading level, but Nate never judged me. He was a gentle teacher who helped me embrace knowledge without feeling shame about my lack of it. Nate could tell right away I was grasping stuff. It wasn't that I was just mimicking. I was having real opinions about the shit I was consuming. And he appreciated that. After giving me a book to read, he'd wait around like an expectant father for a couple of days, then jump at me with questions: What did I see in there? How did I arrive at my conclusions? Was I willing to pass the book on?

Nothing gave me a stronger appetite to learn how to read than being told certain books were prohibited. That made them sexier than all the *Hustlers*, *Playboys*, and girly calendars in the pen. Censorship came in waves for people caged in California prisons. Before 1968, people sentenced to life were considered "civilly dead," which meant you had no civil rights at all. If you wrote shit down, you didn't own your own words, because legally you more or less didn't exist. As for reading material, the prison chose all of it. Prisoners couldn't even write confidential letters to lawyers and lawmakers. What became known as the Prisoner Bill of Rights changed a lot of that. In 1968, long before I knew where I was headed, it deemed prisoners undead, limited prison censorship, and expanded what people locked inside could read. Governor Ronald Reagan signed that, believe it or not. In 1975, right after my transfer to San Quentin, the law changed again under Governor Jerry Brown, giving us prisoners a list of new and specifically enumerated rights, including the right to own property, make a will, marry, and have conjugal visits with spouses. If prison brass wanted to withhold those rights, it was on them to cite specific security reasons. They threaded a lot of bullshit through that loophole.

We had some intellectual freedoms when I was at DVI. But with more of us behind bars getting hip to notions of revolution, Marxist or otherwise, plenty of reading material was on the contraband list, broadly interpreted as anything that might incite violence. *War of the Flea: The Classic Study of Guerrilla Warfare*, for example, was definitely on the unofficial syllabus. I had two educational tracks at DVI. I managed to get my high school equivalency degree, studying for the exam through clouds of tear gas. I also learned how to put a timer on a bomb. At the *very* top of our contraband list, though, the book that was like water to a man on a desert island, the one the goon squad guards and prison bureaucrats least wanted us to have, was George Jackson's *Blood in My Eye*, the book he'd finished writing just a few days before San Quentin guards gunned him down. It was in equal or higher demand than *Soledad Brother*, Jackson's first book, which the *New York Times* had called "one of the most significant and important documents since the first black was pushed off the ship at Jamestown colony." It prompted a generation of white leftist radicals to take up our cause. If that's how large the brother's impact was on mainstream notions of prison oppression, imagine how important it was to us. Jackson was one highly relevant motherfucker.

One night when I was back in K Wing, I got my first chapter of *Blood in My Eye* by special delivery—folded up in legal paper attached to fishing line and banked through the open bars of my cell. Some brother I never did lay eyes on had copied Jackson's words in longhand in a blend of pencil and ink. (When I finally got free, I bought a used copy of *Blood in My Eye*, just to make sure the dude in that cell down the hall hadn't made shit up.) I stayed up for hours reading and rereading those pages, and by the looks of the smudged ink and graphite, a small army of us had done the same. This was how real men made love to each other in lockup, not through force or violence, but through the sharing of information and dreams about what we *could* be.

The next night, I leaned up against the cell bars like I was hawking rugs at a Turkish bazaar and made my pitch. "I've got chapter number one. Anybody got chapter number two?"

Eventually, it came to me, sailing across a floor that smelled like piss and shit and sweat and right into my cell—thanks to fishing line and prison ingenuity. Over the coming decades, I'd insist to anyone who would listen that you can't lock up millions of people without locking up genius. The person who taught me geometry may not have been able to read, but he had serious skills when it came to banking books off the wall to pass a note three cells down. He taught me the importance of a fucking triangle. By the time I got to San Quentin in late 1974, prisoners who could afford one were allowed to get their own televisions. I'd get a nice little mirror instead and rig it just right to catch Gladys Knight and the Pips on my neighbor's set.

[2024]

THE PEOPLE'S COAST

from *California Against the Sea*

Rosanna Xia

It's no coincidence that the coast today is mostly white. Racism laid the groundwork for excluding certain people from the shore, but California's sticky history with affordable housing is largely why this system of privilege continues to be reinforced.

Decades ago, the Coastal Act's original vision for public access had included the need for less-expensive housing that would enable people of all incomes to live near the ocean. Peter Douglas and his fellow authors of the law had recognized that access was not just about physically getting to the beach but also about having the opportunity to live by the sea. As originally enacted in 1976, the Coastal Act called on the Coastal Commission to protect and ensure that affordable housing continued to exist along the shore:

> Lower cost visitor and recreational facilities and housing opportunities for persons of low and moderate income shall be protected, encouraged, and, where feasible, provided.

The commission used this authority to require developers who were seeking construction permits to turn as much as 35 percent of their proposed units into affordable housing. The commission, through the permitting process, also built in resale controls to ensure that these units would continue to be affordable if they were sold. By 1981, within a span of just five years, officials had managed to lock in permits for approximately 5,000 units of affordable housing along the coast. (They also prevented the demolition of roughly 1,300 existing units.)

The backlash was immense, particularly from real estate developers and property rights groups, as well as politicians who ran into their own permitting issues with these new rules. After various attempts to weaken the Coastal Act, a senator from Monterey, Henry J. Mello, managed to introduce a measure that got signed in 1981 by a governor who was increasingly resentful of the commission's power. Senate Bill 626, known as the Mello Act, changed the course of modern California history by altering this key phrase in the law:

> Lower cost visitor and recreational facilities ~~and housing opportunities for persons of low and moderate income~~ shall be protected, encouraged, and, where feasible, provided.

Under these revisions, the Coastal Commission could no longer require developers to include affordable housing units, nor require cities to include housing policies in their coastal planning. As for the already-issued permits that required a certain percentage of a project to be affordable housing? Developers were allowed to go back and remove the conditions that the commission had demanded. To that end, most of those 5,000 affordable housing units on the coast never got built.

The amended law also allows existing affordable housing to be turned into luxury developments, as long as "replacement units" are constructed elsewhere in the city or within 3 miles of the coast. This, in effect, institutionalized the relocation of affordable housing into less desirable parts of California. The law also exempts this replacement requirement for any building with less than three units, so the trend of turning an old duplex or surf shack into a multimillion-dollar beach house has gone unchecked since 1981. Systematically excluded as a result of these changes are the families who did not have the opportunity to buy or hold on to coastal properties before they got too expensive—coastal properties that could've been passed on to their kids and grandkids.

To this day, the people of California have no way to ensure accountability when it comes to affordable housing along the coast. Within a generation of the Mello Act, what used to be more modest, more diverse, more working-class neighborhoods had become unobtainable even for those who consider themselves somewhat well-to-do. Without an inherited property, most working professionals today cannot afford to own a home on the coast. When Effie Turnbull Sanders went for a walk in Manhattan Beach that morning in the spring of 2021, four oceanfront homes were listed for sale along the Strand: The cheapest, a four-bedroom home, was priced at $6 million. The other three asked for $7.5 million, $13 million, and just under $20 million. Today, the properties once owned by the Bruce family [of Bruce's Beach] are also worth millions of dollars.

These injustices run deep. When Turnbull Sanders was first appointed to the Coastal Commission, she noticed California's Native communities were strikingly absent in many of these discussions on affordability and access to the coast. There are more than 180 tribal groups in California, but generations of Native people—first pushed out, and now priced out—have been disconnected from the shore. When she met with Indigenous advocates, they made the point that while the Coastal Act never precluded the commission from engaging with tribal members, someone in power needed to interpret this law in a way that broadened the definition of who is included when we say "access for all."

In recent years, the state has made notable strides in formalizing the need to consult with tribal leaders when making environmental decisions. "Tribal cultural resources"—sites, features, and objects with cultural value to a California Native American tribe—must also now be protected under the state's environmental laws. But building trust takes more than just a change in policy. Very few coastal city planners, environmental engineers, and state officials are Native American. No California Native has sat on the dais of the state's coastal decision-making board.

One way to diversify the people in charge of planning decisions is to create more career pathways for Indigenous people, Turnbull Sanders said. In today's world order, getting a job at the Coastal Commission or as a city engineer requires highly specialized degrees and a particular experience working in environmental science. There must be a way, she said, to provide more internships and science trainings to people who are grounded in the knowledge of their communities. She has also been reflecting on the people that society tends to value as experts: Lawyers. Researchers with PhDs. White historians. Are there also ways to broaden who we choose to listen to—and whose experiences we choose to validate as expertise?

For Angela Mooney D'Arcy, a member of the Juaneño Band of Mission Indians Acjachemen Nation, addressing these gaps requires a hard look at reality. The arrival of the Spanish—fraught with disease and invasive plants and livestock—upended the ecological balance of her people's homeland and forced hundreds of villages into the mission system. And when California's first legislature convened in 1850 and Peter H. Burnett became the state's first elected governor, he declared that the "war of extermination will continue to be waged between the races . . . until the Indian race becomes extinct." For years, the state authorized Indian-hunting expeditions and awarded scalp bounties for the killings. By 1873, California's Indigenous population had plummeted by an estimated 80 percent. Along with these state-sanctioned massacres and the diseases unleashed onto the Native people of the land, the land itself also suffered. "Settler colonialism isn't just a history of the racist violence that happened here—it's a history of ecological violence," Mooney D'Arcy said. Within a few decades, California managed to destroy, or forcibly alter, the many estuaries, meadows, and oak-covered foothills that coastal Native communities had once maintained for thousands of years. "Think about this from the perspective of California Indigenous people who were overtaken and forced into the mission system: We saw such a dramatic, ecological, violent change in our homelands over the course of a single lifetime."

And long after tribal nations were forced to abandon their coastal villages, long after the country and the state's extermination policies finally tempered, Native people were still forced to feel foreign on their own homeland. Their sacred places had become private property, others transformed into unrecognizable developments. Children were taken from their families and redistributed into boarding schools that taught them the Western way of seeing the world. Generations of Indigenous people have since lost their connection to the sea. Some today may grow up listening to the songs of their people that describe the sand softening their shores, but few have the opportunity to actually see the ocean. Mooney D'Arcy herself grew up in Kansas, landlocked and longing for the sea. She followed the water, guided over the years by tribal elders, and eventually made it to the coast as an adult. She lives today in Los Angeles, once a flood plain dotted with vibrant Tongva villages and the comings and goings of Acjachemen, Tataviam, and other neighboring people. It's hard to imagine the city today as a place where the rivers once flowed freely and the stars sparkled without a blanket of smog. "Think what it must be like to see a phenomenon like Los Angeles spreading over your meadows and valleys, diverting your rivers, building parking structures on your holy sites, transforming the land that nurtured your ancestors into something unrecognizable," she said, quoting one of her elders, L. Frank Manriquez.

By examining how these past wrongs continue to shape present-day injustices, more people could perhaps understand how to advocate for a different future that is healing for all. Mooney D'Arcy has spent years finding ways to bring more students to the beach, creating programs for them to experience this shoreline once celebrated by their ancestors. She hopes that by helping more Indigenous youth see themselves reflected in these spaces, a new generation of traditional-knowledge bearers could feel empowered to pursue environmental studies and other fields that may have otherwise felt inaccessible. They, too, can become scientists and experts of the sea. They, too, belong on this coast.

"It doesn't have to be your culture or science," she tells them. "It could be both."

Mooney D'Arcy, who went to Brown University and studied federal Indian rights at the UCLA School of Law, said it's important to value Indigenous history not just as stories from the past but as valid knowledge that informs both science and policy. As the founder of Sacred Places Institute for Indigenous Peoples, she spends her days speaking at public meetings, hearings, and workshops and figuring out ways to get nonprofits and government agencies to work with Indigenous leaders in deeper, more substantive collaborations. In her firm but patient way, she has spent more than 20 years navigating the bureaucracy of local, state, and federal environmental regulations, building partnerships, and reminding anyone who would listen that Indigenous people still exist today—as real people, not just some ghosts of the past. "I exist because my ancestors resisted multiple and sustained state- and church-sponsored efforts to eradicate us physically, culturally, and spiritually," she said. "They resisted and they continued—

continued to live, laugh, love, speak their language, sing their songs, . . . build and sustain their communities through all the violence. It is therefore my responsibility to do what I can to plant the seeds for a just and sustainable world for our descendants."

On a warm but overcast morning in May 2021, Mooney D'Arcy made her way down the coastal highway toward Balboa Pier, the center of another postcard-perfect, well-to-do beach town not far from Manhattan Beach. She lost a few minutes of time circling for parking, thinking as she hurried along the seawall that so much of this land of ice cream shops and art galleries had been engineered to stay above water. She reached the docks just before 9 a.m. and boarded the *Nautilus*, an old fishing vessel turned whale-watching boat. Her voice rang with purpose as she greeted a group of local Indigenous leaders, activists, and educators who had gathered that day for a field trip on the water. They were doing a ride-along of sorts with the education team at Crystal Cove Conservancy, an environmental nonprofit that has been working with Mooney D'Arcy to deepen the way coastal history is taught to the thousands of schoolchildren that visit each year. "We are committed to uplifting voices and perspectives that benefit the land," said Kate Wheeler, the conservancy's president, who acknowledged that "we grew up telling the story of Crystal Cove in a way that overlooked—and frankly sometimes erased—hundreds of years of history, whole cultures, and important events."

Most people today know Crystal Cove as a state beach lined with colorful, eclectic cottages that families can rent for a quiet weekend by the sea. (Saving Crystal Cove from becoming a luxury resort is an oft-cited success story of the Coastal Act.) But these 3.2 miles of coastline, one of Orange County's largest remaining stretches of open space, is also the site of a former village—land that was, and still is, sacred to Tongva and Acjachemen people. Today, to Mooney D'Arcy's knowledge, not a single Acjachemen or Tongva person lives in Newport or Laguna Beach. No one with her on the boat that day had been to Crystal Cove before. Few had spent time on the water in this manner, so as they made their way out of the harbor, the deck was quiet as her guests faced this coast that they had been alienated from. Deep in thought, they contemplated the rocky formations. The tucked-away coves. The patchwork of bluff-top mansions and private seawalls that they could not usually see from land.

Once the roar of the engine had puttered to a hum and the *Nautilus* started to bob more gently on the open water, Mooney D'Arcy gathered everyone in a wide circle and began making introductions. She encouraged her Indigenous experts to jump in as the conservancy's program educators walked through the lessons on ocean chemistry and marine protection that they usually taught students at each station on the boat. The goal was to share ideas and identify places in the curriculum where historical context or traditional knowledge could be woven into the way the students think about the present—and ultimately the future.

"I have one," said Jessa Calderon, a Chumash and Tongva singer, songwriter, and poet. She held out her hands and gestured to the water that had announced its presence with a splash. "I was thinking, as we were stepping onto the boat, that we should acknowledge the ocean and ask for permission."

"Yes, like knocking on your grandma's door before entering," said her mother, Tina, who made the distinction of seeing the land and water as relatives, rather than as resources to extract. "The ocean has a spirit."

It's a relationship, Jessa explained, one where humans are no better than the ocean or any other life on these shores. She motioned to each mansion along the water, fortified behind concrete walls and manicured hedges that helped determine where each parcel of land ended for one owner and began for another. "In today's society, we control, control, control," she said of the coast. "I think that's the biggest difference between our people and the modern-day colonized mentality: We knew not to stabilize in one place for longer than fifteen, twenty years, because we needed to let that place regenerate, grow, heal—that's part of the relationship. If I'm with you, and you and me are together, and I'm just depleting you and depleting you and depleting you . . . that's not a healthy relationship at all. I shouldn't use you until I kill you; I should love you, and help you heal, and help you grow."

"It's about respect, too," Tina said, as she considered the various places their ancestors had chosen to live for thousands of years. "If you look at where we placed our villages . . . You want to be near the water, but not *on* the water, because it could take you out. And that's what this teaching is about: asking for permission, blessing yourself with the water—because it keeps you alive, but it can also take your life."

Mooney D'Arcy nodded, encouraged to see this conversation happening among educators who wanted to share this worldview with future scientists, coastal planners, and environmentalists. It is uncomfortable for many people today to think about just how long this land had been inhabited before white settlers arrived. It is uncomfortable to reckon with just how much a few decades of history have altered our age-old relationship with the coast. But this is not necessarily an indictment, just the reality, Mooney D'Arcy said. She is encouraged by the many college students today asking her the tough questions that few before had been willing to confront. "The big thing for me is I don't see defensiveness from younger white people when they're called white or talking about white privilege, because they don't see it as a personal attack. In my work, I often encounter a lot of resistance and folks taking really personally something that is not personal but is in fact historical and institutional."

"But you can't heal," she said, "if you're still in a place of erasure or denial. So now that there seems to be less defensiveness in younger generations, we're finally at the point where we can begin to have the real conversations. We can finally reimagine what living in relation with each other, and with place, could look like."

She pointed to the work of Charles Sepulveda, a Tongva and Acjachemen professor in the University of Utah's Department of Ethnic Studies. In a 2018 essay titled "Our Sacred Waters: Theorizing *Kuuyam* as a Decolonial Possibility," Sepulveda introduces the concept of *kuuyam*, which means "guest" in Tongva. Could non-Native people today, on the land that is now known as California, acknowledge that they are actually guests of this land? It is not easy to think of yourself as a guest, Mooney D'Arcy acknowledged, when you and your family have lived somewhere for generations. Letting go of that personal attachment to a place takes courage. But by being better guests, by reframing our relationship with place and with the Native people of this land, could *kuuyam* ultimately lead to more people taking care of the environment, this coast, this planet we all share?

"*Kuuyam* allows for a re-centering of place," Sepulveda wrote. "Instead of dividing peoples into categories (and binaries) it allows all peoples to understand themselves as guests of the land—either they behave appropriately, or they do not. Either they act in ways that are respectful to the earth or they do not."

[2023]

CELEBRATING NATIVE CALIFORNIA CULTURAL RENEWAL

LEARNING HOW TO FISH: A LANGUAGE HOMECOMING JOURNAL

from *Bad Indians*

Deborah A. Miranda

"And he saith unto them, Follow me, and I will make you fishers of men. And they straightway left their nets, and followed him."
—Matthew 4:19–20

MONDAY

8 a.m.: coffee
9 a.m.: blessing

10 a.m.: welcome. "Give a person a fish, and she'll eat for the day," Leanne tells us, "but teach her to fish and she'll feed herself and her family forever." I sit in a classroom at UC Berkeley and take notes. I can't believe I'm here. Can't believe I've done this to myself again: an intensive summer language program. Didn't I go crazy enough the first time around, with Spanish? Teach me to fish. Yeah, right. The Franciscan missionaries assigned to Alta California loved their metaphors too. Father Serra wrote of California's Indigenous inhabitants that "before long, they will be caught in the apostolic and evangelical net," likening himself and his fellow priests to the Fishers of Men called upon by Christ to spread the Gospel. I've always been a bit bothered by this image, however; the comparison between catching fish and catching souls just never worked for me. After all—one *eats* what one catches; swallows, consumes, devours. One uses that flesh as fuel for one's own body. Catching

Indian bodies and souls like catching fish? It makes me wonder about alternative, darker definitions of the word "save."

I'm not sure I can survive an entire week here, submersed in California Indian languages. It all started with a phone call and my sister Louise gushing, "This is incredible," in a voice happier than I had ever heard her use before. "I'm learning new words every hour, I seem to understand them even before David explains what they mean, I wrote a prayer, we study all day and all night. . . I never thought this could happen, but our language is out there, *we can learn it!*"

It was as if someone had given her a brand new pole and a big box of tackle and said, "Come on in, which hook do you want to try first?" My sister had become a Fisher of Words.

So here we sit, two years later, at the Breath of Life conference, a biannual event sponsored by UC Berkeley's linguistics department, in partnership with the nonprofit group Advocates for Indigenous California Language Survival. I'd encouraged Louise to apply that first year. After all, she lived in California. (I was way out in Virginia.) After all, she was involved with the tribal council and meetings. (I was just a poet, an academic, dealing with theories about indigeneity.) After all, learning Esselen or Chumash is about a billion light-years beyond me (a woman who almost had a nervous breakdown trying to survive three years of Spanish for her Ph.D. requirements). I had a lot of excuses, and eventually Louise countered every single one. But secretly, I know my monolingual brain is completely occupied by English; I can't imagine taking decolonization to those deep dark places where Indigenous languages hide. I just hope I don't embarrass my sister.

Let me explain right here that my sister Louise is brilliant. Two years after her first Breath of Life conference, she has compiled the first Esselen-English dictionary, coauthoring it with her mentor, David Shaul. Louise accomplished this not with an academic degree, not with government funding, not with a fellowship or grant, and not with any technical support or materials other than her home computer. She accomplished this mammoth task while sitting in her living room in San Jose, sifting through research papers and copies of field notes, and with several short visits from her mentor, who was usually away working on an entirely different project. She accomplished this while running for chair of the Ohlone/Costanoan-Esselen Nation, caring for a granddaughter, husband, and elderly mother, and managing a household, both before and after knee replacement surgery!

God, I hope there's not ten different tenses.

TUESDAY

8 a.m.: coffee
9 a.m.: blessing
9:30 a.m.: homework

Oh faithful band of linguists and students who volunteer their time, expertise, and encouragement! Do you really want us to read a passage in our language out loud on the second day? I stumble over *Tanoch kalul hikpa*, "The woman sees the fish." Subject, object, verb. I thrash my way through *Iniki tanoch mashaipa*, "This woman is hungry." Demonstratives—the equivalents of the English words "this" and "that." (What is Louise doing over there? Jesus! She's writing a freaking book!) Leanne, her cheerful face bobbing from one table of fricatives and glottal stops to another, reminds us that Breath of Life does not—cannot—teach California Indians our tribal languages in one week. "What Breath of Life *tries* to do is present hungry people with the tools and materials you need to learn how to fish for yourselves."

So Leanne and her magnificent crew of volunteer linguists,

students, and museum/archive/library staff give us a crash course in how to do research on California Indian languages, with specific focus on our individual languages and the materials close at hand in California, especially at UC Berkeley. UC Berkeley, according to Leanne, has the largest collections of California Indian language and cultural materials in the world. I call them "how-to tours." Every afternoon, we visit a major collection and the tour always includes not just a general introduction to the materials, but hands-on instructions for using those materials to research a specific tribal language and/or culture. The Phoebe Hearst Museum of Anthropology. Survey of California and Other Indian Languages. An archival information site at Doe Library. The Berkeley Language Center. The Bancroft Library's extensive collection of microfilms. If my brain doesn't shrivel up first, my feet will.

Today we received special permission to view the baskets in Basket Storage. Going into the facility was like visiting our relatives in jail: sweet, bittersweet. We left purses, backpacks, food and drink outside. We donned plastic gloves. We entered a huge room full of white towers, inside of which are set deep drawers and shelving, covered with—oh, filled with—baskets made by the hands of our ancestors. Gina found one made by her grandmother. She cried. We could touch them (with gloves on), photograph them, talk to them, pray over them, sing to them. We were allowed to bring in rattles and clappers. The shaking seeds like rain, elderberry claps like thunder, and voices of our little Breath of Life tribe were springs of life in the quiet climate-controlled room. It was a heartbreaking visit. We could not take them home.

WEDNESDAY

8 a.m.: coffee
9 a.m.: blessing
9:30 a.m.: homework
10:00 a.m.: class

Every fishing hole has its quirks, little tricks to finding the best fish, special hooks that work there but not over here, and secret techniques passed down only to a lucky few. I guess it's the same with trying to learn a California Indian language: some libraries have certain field notes; others don't. One linguist's field notes are on microfilm but only at one particular branch of one particular school; another linguist's research has been processed and published as articles, but in obscure journals. Some "field notes" are actually letters and journals kept by explorers, missionaries, or entrepreneurs, scattered all over the planet in various museums, collections, libraries. Some primary materials—the actual notes themselves—are found only at a tiny nondescript storage area you'd never suspect.

But the one guaranteed thing? It's never all in one place, it's never all perfectly clear, and it's never going to be easy. Put on your hip boots and wade right in. Today, I am up to my neck in the existential *cha'a*—as in "we exist!"

So I'm not surprised that Esselen has no real verb for "to be" or for "to have." You just *are*. It just *is*. Louise tries to teach me some sleight-of-hand linguistic maneuver to get around this, but I'm thick as a brick. *Kalul yakiski-k*—"the fish (is) large" and *mawip-as saleki-k*—"the song (is) good." Somehow, the intention of "is" is communicated via this "k" sound stuck on to the end of the noun. My brain wrestles with constructing a sentence that, to my poor English-trained neural pathways, means "The fish large is." "That's it!" Louise crows, "That sounds good!"

"That sounds like Yoda," I mutter. But I'm pleased.

THURSDAY

8 a.m.: coffee
9 a.m.: blessing
9:30 a.m.: homework
10:00 a.m.: class

This year's Breath of Life class is over sixty participants, representing more than twenty-five different California Indian languages and major dialects of languages. It's one of the larger groups, Leanne says. That's a lot of Indian souls literally given the "breath of life" to take home to their communities and families.

We joke that for this week, we are all one tribe: the Breath of Life tribe, located in the Berkeley homeland. We move to our tribal rhythm: breakfast together in the seminar room, followed by sharing of our individual homework assignments and a lecture about linguistic analysis. At noon we break for lunch, then head off to various tours and little study groups scattered throughout dorms and the campus till dinnertime; in the evenings, more study groups (frequently led by our mentors and their assistants) go on late into the night. Instead of sitting around a communal fire grilling juicy salmon, we sit around dorm rooms or on outdoor benches grilling each other on vocabulary, conjugation, plurals, and the always-popular curse words.

Somewhere in the Harrington notes, Isabel Meadows remembers that Fulgencio Cantua told her, "very tasty, our language." I imagine our words being crispy or salty or smooth as a ripe fig. I like the idea that our language has flavor, texture, scent, yet can never be consumed. I tell Louise about Fulgencio's comment; she tells everyone else, and we end the evening with great smacking of lips and satisfied rubbing of tummies. "Oh, *that's* why they make those sounds, like they're savoring each syllable!" Anyone looking at us from the outside would run in the other direction.

FRIDAY

8 a.m.: coffee
9 a.m.: blessing
9:30 a.m.: homework
10:00 a.m.: class

Louise and I call each other *Ichi* now—"sister."

Louise writes beautifully in Esselen, and her speaking voice/pronunciation sounds rounded, natural. It reminds me of the way our dad used to slur his English so that the edges of the words came out softer than everyone else's. Maybe his Spanish did that too, but I never heard him speak enough of it to tell. I remember how our dad's dad, Grandpa Tom, spoke Indian in his last days, how his son, Uncle Tommy, was shocked to realize not just that this was an Indian language, but that he, too, understood it! How it came flooding back to him after six decades of dormancy: his mother tongue. We all knew that our grandmother Marquesa and her mother, Dolores, spoke Chumash together; Louise remembers playing under the kitchen table and hearing them chatter as they worked. But it never occurred to any of us that Dad and his younger brothers might have soaked up enough of that language to make any difference. As the oldest, Uncle Tommy must have heard the most, before the conversations stopped when our great-grandmother died—he was probably the only one to retain anything at all. Later, Tommy told us, he went down to Santa Ynez and spoke with some of the old folks there. *They understood what he was saying.* So was Grandpa Tom speaking his wife's language? Or was Esselen enough like Samala (Santa Ynez Chumash) to bridge the gap? Or had the family developed a kind of hybrid dialect of the two? It's one of those California Indian mysteries. And it makes me wonder if this kind of tenuous connection—literally listening under the table—is what gives Louise such fluency, as if she is coming home to a language at last, rather than learning it for the first time.

If she is coming home to the language, the language is coming home to her, too. *Lex welel*—our language—must have been lonely all this time.

SATURDAY

9 a.m.: blessing
10 a.m.: participant projects

Louise gave the blessing this morning—in Esselen.

I read my first poem in Esselen, sweated out onto the page with much help from David, our mentor, and Ruth, his assistant; pushed off my awkward tongue by Louise's determined coaching.

Did I say we were hungry Indians? We are starving! Starving for our languages.

At this morning's presentation of individual projects, I heard California Indians use their languages to speak prayers, sing songs, create original poems and stories, retell oral histories, croon lullabies to their babies, make jokes, invent picture books, caption family scrapbooks—Clara even reveled in finding a phrase that means something like "piece of shit!"

Listening, watching, I realized that virtually every aspect of culture was presented: religion, music, oral and written literatures, linguistic play. . . don't try telling a Breath of Life participant that our cultures are dead. We have become Fishers of Words, but we practice a catch and release system: snag those little silver gems, then release them back out into the wider world as quickly and lovingly as possible. Let them go forth and multiply. Whatever allegory you want to use, the work of language recovery and renewal takes patience, near-obsessive persistence, and the generosity of many.

We understand now: you just gotta know the right place to drop that line.

[2013]

HISTORY AND CULTURE—CENTRAL VALLEY AND WESTERN SIERRA NEVADA

from *First Families*

L. Frank and **Kim Hogeland**

Running nearly the length of California, two rivers give life to the great, open flatlands that lie between the Sierra Nevada and the Coast Range. The Sacramento River, drawing waters from the rugged, snowy peaks of the southern Cascades, flows southward from the Mount Shasta area to the Delta. Here it meets the San Joaquin River flowing north. These two river valleys, the Sacramento and the San Joaquin, together form California's Great Central Valley, four hundred and fifty miles long from Redding to Bakersfield and between forty and sixty miles wide.

A network of creeks and rivers, mostly flowing westward from the Sierra, feeds into the Sacramento and the San Joaquin. Within the dozens of valley and foothill microenvironments carved by these waterways, seventy-four thousand native people found food, shelter, and an eminently sustainable way of life. Throughout the Sierra foothills, where the Maidu, Konkow, Nisenan, Miwuk, and Mono people lived; in the Sacramento Valley, home of the Wintu, Nomlaki, and Patwin people; and in the San Joaquin Valley of the Yokuts and Tubatulabal, the native peoples adapted to and prospered in unique environments. While a warm and watertight house built with layers of cedar slabs around a central fire was home to many foothill people, those in the Central Valley—where cedar was unknown and in fact all wood was at a premium—might live in brush shelters during the hot summers, in capacious earthen-roofed underground houses during the rainy winters. A Konkow woman might use willow or big-leaf maple shoots for a basket, whereas a Yokuts weaver might use deer grass. People differed greatly from one valley to the next, and they rejoiced in their distinctiveness.

A typical political group in California was not a huge tribe managed by a few leaders, as in the eastern part of the continent or on the Plains, but a small, autonomous unit, often no larger than a village made up of a few extended families who shared a language dialect. The various groups just mentioned—Maidu, Miwuk, etc.—were not cohesive political entities but rather language groups. The people we are calling Yokuts, for example, had approximately sixty defined political units, each speaking a distinct dialect of a common language. Territory was often defined by a single watershed. Within each of these watersheds could be found a cultural universe of stories, ceremonies, beliefs, customs, and ways of living.

It is commonly assumed that California was a Garden of Eden and that life was easy. Yet while nature offered many and varied opportunities, wresting sustenance out of such small landholdings took knowledge, hard work, flexibility, and savvy. The many inhabitants of the Central Valley and Sierra foothill environments were tenacious people who learned to leech the bitterness out of acorns and make them a nutritional mainstay; industrious people who found a use for every part of the deer, from the heart to the hooves; accommodating people who knew how to survive in flood and in drought, who learned to trade and fight, and who, when necessary, could change and adapt. As Europeans began to arrive, first in small numbers and then, after 1848, in an onslaught, native people would recognize the bittersweet value of this adaptability.

Those who lived in the Sierra foothills and in the northern part of the Central Valley had little significant contact with Europeans until the late 1830s. But as the Spanish missions spread from southern California—Mission San Diego, the first California mission, was founded in 1769—Central Valley people living nearer the coast came to know something of European ways, especially when soldiers pursued escapees into their homelands, and when these runaway "neophytes" (recent converts to Christianity) sought refuge among them. Despite reprisals for giving shelter to escapees, many villages continued to do so, thereby receiving valuable tools for the forthcoming struggle: knowledge of how to handle horses and an understanding of European ways and especially European military tactics.

In 1834 the Mexican government formally abandoned the mission system, and some of the Mission Indians moved inland to join relatives. The populations of Californios (Mexican Californians) and Anglos continued to grow, pushing out from the coastal areas, and for the next decade there was intermittent violence in the southern part of the Central Valley as Indians waged guerrilla warfare to discourage further encroachment. The Yokuts, along with the neophytes who had fled the missions and had taken refuge with them, sometimes raided settlements for horses and cattle, and ranchers organized campaigns to recover livestock and punish the natives.

It was during this chaotic era that one of the strangest and most controversial characters in California history appeared on the landscape. In 1839, Johann August Sutter arrived in California from Switzerland by way of Hawai'i. He built a fort in what would later become the city of Sacramento and employed Konkow, Nisenan, and Miwuk people. He brought with him several Native Hawai'ians; they intermarried with the local people, and many members of the Indian community today claim Native Hawai'ian as well as California Indian ancestry.

Sutter had a reputation, at first, for treating his Indian laborers well; many went to the fort willingly. But when he came up short on workers to bring in his harvests, he would simply round up local natives and force them to work in the fields. He also trained armies of Indians to guard his fort and subdue nearby hostile villages. Edwin Bryant visited Sutter's fort in August 1846, writing that Sutter had "succeeded by degrees in reducing the Indians to obedience, and by means of their labor erected the spacious fortification which now belongs to him." Indeed, it was largely native labor that built Sutter's fort into the seat of his short-lived empire. Pioneers stopped there on their way into California, and it became a fort in truth during the Mexican–American War. And it was on another of Sutter's properties, a sawmill on the American River, that James Marshall first discovered gold in January of 1848.

The gold rush was a major turning point in the history of California—for Euro-Americans, of course, but especially for the native population. After the influx of miners and settlers that began in 1849, nothing would ever be the same again for the people of the foothills and the Central Valley. Violence, formerly erratic, now became a constant, and it was brutal. One of Tehama and Butte Counties' vigilantes, Sim Moak, described a fellow Indian fighter with "a string of scalps from his belt to his ankle." The Indians of the area were not subject to conquest or warfare, rather to massacre and attempted genocide.

Although often attributed to individual acts of unruly miners, the horrific brutalization and slaughter that happened during the gold rush and in the years that followed had widespread political and legal sanction. Under an 1850 law entitled "An Act for the Government and Protection of Indians," any white citizen could indenture the labor of an Indian child if he could prove to a judge that the child was an orphan, taken in in good conscience. The worst that could happen to someone who failed to feed, clothe, and treat the child humanely was a ten-dollar fine and the reassignment of the child to a new master. The law thus condoned the kidnapping and sale of children and young women for use as house servants and sexual slaves. This statute was not repealed until 1863, four years after Lincoln's emancipation proclamation. Anthropologist and historian Robert F. Heizer estimated that as many as ten thousand California Indians were indentured under the law's tenure.

Even the state's highest official, California governor John McDougall, called for the extermination of Indians. In his annual message of 1852, he stated that Indians were a "source of much annoyance" in California and that they would continue to be so as long as they were still present in the state. Vigilante groups, often formed in fits of revenge, idleness, or drunkenness, pursued native people even to their villages, and after shameless massacres they would present a bill for "services" to the state government, confident that their costs would be reimbursed.

On top of this, the natural environment was changing. Hydraulic mining ravaged rivers and streams and destroyed wildlife habitat. Cattle and other livestock ate and trampled the native seeds and grasses, while annual grasses and other invasive plants from Europe took over wide swaths of the landscape, virtually eliminating important sources of food. As years passed and more settlers arrived, private land ownership increased, limiting traditional hunting, fishing, and gathering. Homeless and starving, native people were now outcasts in the lands that had once supported them so well.

In 1850, Thomas Jefferson Mayfield, a six-year-old boy from Texas, crossed over the Pacheco Pass into the Central Valley with his family. He later recalled:

> Suddenly my daddy pointed over the tops of the bare hills ahead of us and exclaimed, "Look there!" And there in the distance, until then lost to us in the haze, was our valley.

> A shining thread of light marked El Rio de San Joaquin flowing, as my mother said, "through a crazy quilt of color." How excited we all were. Everyone wanted to talk at once. Then someone noticed, still farther to the east, that what we had at first taken for clouds was a high range of snow-covered peaks, their bases lost in the purple haze.

After the family settled in the Valley, Mayfield's mother died and he was adopted by a prosperous Yokuts group, the Choinumne of the San Joaquin Valley and Kings River area. In a finely detailed memoir, he recounts the intimacies of traditional daily life, then the dwindling of population and the tragic loss. He felt that he was a witness to the end of a way of life. But while a way of life did indeed come to an end, it was not the end of the Choinumne people. Like the other peoples of the region, they adapted, as they had always done, to changes in their environment. Along with other native people of the Central Valley and foothills, they worked as cowboys, farmhands, maids, and miners. Today, from Grindstone to Tule River, Greenville to Big Sandy, the many tribes are as rooted in the Valley and foothills as ever. Their presence may be as subtle as an elderly woman clipping redbud by the side of the road or as obvious as a casino marquee; their memories go back to the beginning of time.

[2007]

THE ACORN HARVEST

from *The Ohlone Way*

Malcolm Margolin

The men hunted and fished, they sweated in the sweat-house, and they cultivated power and magic to insure a plentiful supply of salmon, deer, antelope, elk, rabbit, quail, and other game. These foods were important and welcome to the villagers who added the fish and meat to their meals. But the basis of each meal was generally acorn mush. For most Ohlone groups, acorns were the staff of life, the food people ate nearly every day of their lives.

Live oaks spread throughout the Bay Area, towering valley oaks occupied the inland valleys, small groves of black oaks dotted the hills, and extensive stands of tanbark oaks covered the Santa Cruz Mountains. Each tribelet knew the location of the oak groves around them, and the oak trees' stages of development had a central place in the Ohlone mind. In the spring the people rejoiced at the bud-thickening and the leaf-burst of the deciduous oaks. Later they celebrated the appearance of the tiny cascades of pale oak flowers. As summer progressed the sight of the gradually ripening, shiny, green nuts filled them with joy and security. Throughout the year the people responded to the stately rhythm of the oaks with the greatest awareness and involvement.

With the passing of summer, hunters and medicine gatherers returned from their forays with reports on the condition of the various groves. If they reported that the black oaks were bearing heavily, the people felt great joy. If they found that the oak moths were particularly severe among the live oaks, everyone felt deep concern.

Throughout the year the people held various feasts, festivals, and religious dances, many of them tied to the biological rhythms of the oak trees. Time itself was measured by the oaks. The acorn harvest marked the beginning of the new year. Winter was spoken of as so many months (moons) after the acorn harvest, summer as so many months before the next acorn harvest. The rhythms of the oak trees marked the passage of the year and defined the rhythms of Ohlone life.

As fall approached the people looked forward to the acorn harvest. This was usually the biggest event of the year. If it was a favorable year for black oaks or tanbark oaks (these were greatly preferred to the live oaks or valley oaks), several families with "collecting rights" headed toward a grove.

It would be well into October, and the nights would be somewhat chilly. Everyone eagerly awaited the partying and socializing that would go on. Mothers looked forward to seeing their daughters who had married into neighboring villages but who would return to the ancestral groves for acorn gathering. Younger women knew that they would be wooed by men of other villages. There would be gambling, trading, ball games, feasts, and dances. Later in the year, when the various tribelets returned to their own villages, there would be time to brood upon grudges and quarrels: an unfair trade, a woman seduced, innumerable infidelities and insults—sometimes real, sometimes imagined. But harvest time was a time for joy and abandon. The branches of the trees were heavy with acorns—plump, brown, ripe acorns—and the groves of trees extended in all directions.

At night in the acorn groves the dancers dressed in their finest feathers and body paint and repeated the ancient sequence of steps. As they danced, a chorus of men chanted the word for "acorn" and then the word for "plenty," often breaking the words up into separate syllables and chanting the syllables for a time before once again restoring the words to their original forms. The feet of the dancers became one with the rhythm, while the flicker-shaft bandeaus across their foreheads waved sinuously, as if possessed with a life of their own. The people chanted and danced—not merely for a distant god or goddess—but rather for the oak trees themselves; and the trees seemed to glow with pleasure and health at the expressions of joy and gratitude that filled the entire grove.

Each morning the gathering of the acorns began afresh. It was a noisy, industrious affair that lasted for two or three weeks. Everyone participated. Boys climbed the trees to shake the branches, men knocked the acorns down with long sticks, and everywhere there were people stooping and picking over the acorns on the ground. Choosing big, firm acorns without worm holes, they snapped off the caps and dropped them into large conical burden baskets which were propped against the tree trunks. When a basket was full, it was brought into a clearing and the acorns were laid out to dry in the sun.

The Ohlones were not alone in the acorn groves. Squirrels, jays, deer, and of course grizzly bears also came to the groves to gorge themselves in preparation for winter. Acorn woodpeckers were especially busy and prominent, inserting acorns into holes they had drilled in certain trees. Larger trees might have thousands of little holes, each with an acorn fitted tightly into it. The Ohlones laughed at the acorn woodpeckers, perhaps because they felt a kinship with this curious bird who like them gathered acorns and stored them for the coming year. Spirits were high, especially in years when the acorns were plentiful.

Eventually the harvest ended. Every family had collected enough acorns. The people lingered around the acorn camp for a few more weeks, but the party mood was fast disappearing. It rained more frequently now, and the harvesters felt that it was time to head back to their permanent winter villages. It was time to repair bows and arrows, time to make new baskets, nets, knives, traps, beads, stirring paddles, and brushes. Family after family drifted away, and the acorn camp gradually broke up.

Back at their villages the people relined the hampers with mugwort and other aromatic herbs to repel insects and keep the acorns from molding. They rebuilt the acorn granaries—large, basket-like structures on stilts that stood outside the huts. They filled the hampers and the granaries with fresh acorns. The rains began in earnest now. Life became settled. Winter was upon them—a time for dancing, retelling myths, gathering shellfish, and (for the men) the daily ritual of the sweat-bath. Soon the acorn harvest would be only a memory.

On those rare years when the acorn harvest failed, the people gathered buckeyes instead. Acorns were not absolutely essential to life, only to a proper life. And with the hampers and granaries filled with acorns once again, a good way of life was assured for another year.

The preparation of acorn mush was a woman's daily occupation—almost as regular and predictable a part of life as the rising of the sun. Each day a woman removed several handfuls of acorns from her storage baskets. She hulled them one at a time by placing them on an anvil stone, hitting them with a hammer stone, and peeling off the shells. Then she put the kernels into a stone mortar or sometimes a mortar basket (a bottomless basket glued to a rock). Sitting with the other women of the village, she pounded the acorns with a long pestle, pausing now and then to scrape the acorn flour away from the sides of the mortar with a soaproot fiber brush. Then she pounded some more. The rhythmic thumping of the women's pestles filled the air. For the Ohlones this was the sound of their village, the sound of "home."

After pounding, a woman put the flour into a shallow sifting basket which she vibrated rapidly back and forth to separate the fine flour from the coarse. Putting the fine flour aside, she returned the coarse flour to the mortar for still more pounding.

The flour was now uniformly fine, but still far too bitter to eat. The woman next scooped out a hole in the sand near the creek, lined the hole with fern leaves, and emptied the flour into the hole. (Some women preferred to use openwork "leaching" baskets which they similarly lined with leaves.) She then poured large quantities of water over the flour to leach out the bitter tannin. If she was in a hurry and firewood was plentiful, she used hot water. Some acorns, like those of the valley oaks, had little tannin; they leached out quickly. Others, like live oak acorns, took considerably longer.

After the leaching came the cooking. A woman placed the flour and some water into still another kind of basket—one so skillfully made that it was completely watertight. Since she could not place the basket directly onto the flames, she heated some round stones in the fire. When a stone was hot she removed it from the fire with two sticks, dipped it quickly into some water to wash off the ashes, and dropped it into the acorn mush. She stirred constantly with a looped stick or wooden paddle to keep the hot stone from burning a hole in the basket. She then added more stones until the basket was perhaps one quarter filled with stones, and she kept them all moving and rolling until—after only a few minutes—the mush was boiling. In Bayshore villages that were built on alluvial soil, stones had to be carried in from far away; and good cooking stones—ones that would not crack when heated—were highly valued.

When the mush was fully cooked, the woman served it, sometimes in a watery form as a soup, often as a thick porridge. If she wanted to make acorn bread, she boiled the mush longer and then placed the batter into an earthen oven or on top of a hot slab of rock. Acorn bread (described as "deliciously rich and oily" by early explorers) was a favorite Ohlone food—a food to be taken on trips or to be shared at the many feasts and festivals throughout the year.

Acorns were a crop ideally suited to the Bay Area, and indeed to most of California. Unlike wheat, corn, barley, or rice, acorns required no tilling of the soil, no digging of irrigation ditches, nor any other form of farming. Thus, while the preparation of acorn flour might have been a lengthy and tedious process, the total labor involved was probably much less than for a cereal crop. Yet the level of nutrients in acorns was extremely high—comparable in fact with wheat and barley. What's more, acorns were extremely plentiful. Frank Latta, an amateur ethnographer who spent a large part of his life studying the Yokuts, estimated that an Indian family consumed from 1,000 to 2,000 pounds of acorns a year. Granted that an Indian family tended to have more members than our own, nevertheless this is still a large quantity of acorns.

The extraordinary virtues of the acorn help explain why the Ohlones and other Central California Indians never adopted the agricultural practices of other North American groups who raised squash, corn, and other crops. Lack of agriculture was not the result of isolation, conservatism, laziness, or backwardness, as some people have suggested. The truth is far simpler: Central California Indians did not adopt traditional agricultural methods because they didn't have to. Acorns, along with an extremely generous environment, provided them with a more-than-adequate diet.

[1978]

BREAD

from *Enough for All*

Kathleen Rose Smith

ACORN BREAD

With the destruction of the seed-bearing wildflowers used for *yuh·u*, acorn is the one carbohydrate-rich Native plant food that is still eaten by California Indians today. Many different kinds of oak trees grow in my ancestral homeland, but the only ones I have heard any of my relatives talk about using for food are black oak (*yohškʰle*, or *Quercus kelloggii*), coast live oak (*šaʔč̓ikʰle*, or *Quercus agrifolia*), Oregon oak (*wi·yikʰle*, or *Quercus garryana*), and blue oak (*Quercus douglasii*). Another tree with acorns that we eat is tanoak (*šiʔč̓ikʰle*, or *Lithocarpus densiflorus*). We consider it to be an oak, but botanists do not and instead put it into another genus. Today, tanoak is our most important source of acorns, but that wasn't the case in the past. Black oak was and is still favored by some.

Acorn soup or mush (*thoʔ·o*) is the plant food most associated with California Indians. California Native people from every part of the state still enjoy having thick *thoʔ·o* at home and during public ceremonies. One can find many written accounts on how to prepare and boil it. Depending on the amount of water used, it will be thick, like a mush, and can be eaten with two fingers, the middle and index fingers; or with more water added, it can be eaten like a soup, with a spoon.

My mother cooked acorn in a stainless steel or porcelain pot on her stovetop, stirring her acorn-flour and water mixture until it thickened, and adding more water, as needed, to make it less thick. Never use an aluminum pot, as this will react with the tannic acid in the acorn.

The book *It Will Live Forever* (Heyday, 1996) has one of the best accounts I know of about how to process and boil this food in a basket the way the Miwuk/Paiute people of Yosemite do. Basket cooking is done outdoors, as was all the cooking in the old days.

Instead of describing stone-boiling, I want to describe the lesser-known method of cooking acorn: baking acorn bread (*si·lun*) underground in an earthen oven. Today, acorn bread is generally baked in a conventional oven, but the only way I know how to bake it is the way my grandmother Rose Bill cooked it, in an underground oven. Just as acorn mush stone-boiled in a basket tastes better than that cooked on a stove, so does *si·lun* taste better when baked in an earthen oven.

Even though acorn bread can be made from many different kinds of acorns, my grandmother Rose Bill made hers from black oak acorns. In the Dry Creek Pomo language we call both acorn bread and bread made with wheat flour *si·lun*. *Si·lun* is the general term in Dry Creek Pomo for acorn bread. The one I make, from black oak acorns as Rose Bill did, is called *k^h·a·ṭo*.

When gathering acorns (*biʔdu*) for *si·lun*, we don't use the first ones to fall from the trees for food. They fall early because of some flaw or other. The good acorns will start to fall from the trees later, helped by a gust of wind. To tell which acorns are good and which are not, look at them. Feel them. The heavy acorn has a fully formed nut inside the shell. The lightweight one does not.

After gathering, sort out any imperfect acorns. Make sure none have insect larvae inside.

Dry immediately. Spread out your acorns in a flat, clean, dry place. Otherwise the acorns will get moldy and inedible. Oaks and tanoaks don't always produce acorns every year. Sometimes it takes two years or more before another crop is produced. Store the acorns shelled or unshelled.

I don't often cook acorns—only on special occasions—so I keep those I have in their shells until I need to cook them. When dried and stored properly, healthy, ripe acorns can be kept for years before eating.

Crack the hulls of dried acorns with a hammer or stone, hitting them lightly enough that the nutmeats stay intact, then remove the hulls. Clean the nutmeats (*maʔ·a*) by next removing all of the red skins that cover them. Those of tanoaks and coast live oaks fall right off, but you will need to winnow or scrape the skins off black oak acorns, after splitting the nuts with a knife wherever they have a crease.

We reduce the cleaned nutmeats to a fine powder by pounding the nuts in a stone mortar (*kʰaʔbe·tʼle*) with a stone pestle (*dok·o*). Pomo acorn mortars have only a shallow indentation, because a *k̓ol·o* (pounding or hopper basket) sits on top of the stone. (When I was growing up, I always heard the mortar rock referred to as *k̓ol·o*. But *k̓ol·o* is the word for the pounding or hopper basket, which is very sturdy and open on the bottom.)

Gramma made her own mortar and pestle out of stone, shaping them with a very strong metal hatchet. Once I tried to sculpt a pestle out of basalt using an inexpensive, imported hatchet and ended up destroying the hatchet blade in about a half-hour with no discernible change in the potential pestle stone. Sympathetic others have since given me their unused stone mortars and pestles. I use these stones to pound up acorns and peppernuts.

We put a small amount of hulled nutmeats in the bottom of the mortar, then lift the heavy pestle to shoulder height and guide or drop it against the acorns in a comfortable cadence, adding more and more nutmeats to the mortar until enough has been processed into flour. Care was and is always taken during pounding to make sure that the two rocks never touch.

Today, the nutmeats are most often milled into flour with some kind of electric mill, usually a coffee grinder. Before those were available, hand-cranked grinders were used.

To finish making the flour, sift the meal with a metal sifter to separate the fine from the coarse particles, which must be further pounded or ground.

I've been told that for baking, the acorn flour was mixed with red clay (*ʔam·aṭ̓·a*) and did not need to be leached to remove the tannic acid, but I leach it first by running or pouring water over the flour until the bitterness is removed. I do this at home by lining my twined work basket with a clean cotton dish towel. I spread the acorn flour evenly on the cloth and slowly run water from the tap onto the cloth, making sure the running water is spread evenly over all of the acorn. In order to know if the bitterness has been leached from the acorn, it needs to be tasted from several different places. When it has been leached to your satisfaction, the acorn is ready to cook.

For the oven, dig a shallow, oblong hole about two feet deep and wide enough to hold the bundle of leached, damp acorn, shaped like a loaf one and a half to two inches thick. Wrap this loaf in several layers of the fresh leaves of soaproot (*haʔ·an*, or amole), wild grape (*šic·un*), big-leaf maple (*kal·an*), or woodwardia fern (*ʔahkʰamʔoda*), and then a wet gunnysack.

Make a fire with hardwoods—madrone (*ḱabʔaḱ*), or manzanita (*ka·yekʰle*) if possible—and allow it to burn until the wood becomes hot coals. Softwoods won't work, because they turn to ash too quickly.

According to my mother, her grandmother Juana Cook lined her underground oven with rocks (*kʰaʔbe*), then shoveled hot coals (*mahsiy*) over these. Atop this she placed the uncooked, leached acorn, wrapped in fresh soaproot leaves and wild grape leaves. Then she shoveled more hot coals atop this. Finally, she sealed the oven by shoveling earth or sand atop the coals, so they were smothered but remained hot (*ʔoh·o*). At dusk she left the bread to bake overnight, for about twelve hours, removing it from the oven in the morning.

When removing the bundle, be careful to keep the soil or sand from falling into the food, and be careful not to get burned from touching the still-hot rocks and coals. Some of the outer leaves will be burned, but when properly covered, the acorn bread will be steamed, and the beautiful color of rich, dark chocolate cake. Some have even said it tastes a little like chocolate cake.

My old people used this kind of underground oven to cook a number of different foods, including fish, shellfish, meat, and the bulbs ("Indian potatoes") that we called *hiʔbu*.

DRY CREEK POMO WHEAT BREAD

My relatives consider bread made from wheat or corn dough and cooked on hot coals to be as traditional as that made from acorns. We have three types of wheat or corn flour bread: wheat dough with leavening baked in an oven, or *pan*, a Spanish word; tortillas, or "torts," wheat or corn flour dough formed into thin disks and cooked in a flat pan on the stovetop; and wheat dough without leavening roasted on hot coals or in an oven, *si·lun* in my mother's Dry Creek language or *tuptups* in my father's Bodega Miwuk language.

It's especially dramatic to cook *si·lun* on hot coals. Manzanita and madrone make the best coals, although other hardwoods may be used if these are not available.

Make the dough by mixing white flour and water together, then knead. Form the kneaded dough into fist-size balls. One by one, flatten the dough balls. Then, with a piece of flattened dough between your hands, use a clapping motion while rapidly turning your wrists back and forth at 90 degree angles until you have created a disk of dough up to twelve inches in diameter and a bit thicker than a store-bought flour tortilla, ready for roasting.

My mother made hers the same size as the cast-iron flat pan she cooked her torts on, but it takes practice and skill to make them that big. She almost never used a rolling pin, and if she did, it was only to get the process started, never to complete it. The only time I remember my mother using a rolling pin to fully flatten her dough was to make pie crusts.

All of my old people roasted their *si·lun* on red-hot coals. They watched it closely so it wouldn't burn. When one side was cooked, they flipped it over with fingers, a stick, tongs, or any other available tool to cook the other side. When the bread was finished, there were no ashes in it, and it was puffed up slightly from the steam created by the moisture in the dough.

Serve it immediately, or wrap it in a cotton dish towel so it won't get tough while cooling.

Today, *si·lun* might be used in a "wrap" sandwich, because it's great to eat with cooked, crisp seaweed wrapped inside, or a slice of cooked abalone, or beef (usually flank), or sliced, fried russet potatoes. We call beef *behše,* which literally means "deer meat." It also means "black-tailed deer."

[2014]

ROUNDUP AS IN DAYS OF OLD

from *Bird Songs Don't Lie*

Gordon Lee Johnson

Buick-sized boulders, high chaparral, and ancient oaks stud the hills and ravines of the Cahuilla Indian Reservation near Anza.

In a drought-thinned pasture about four hundred yards south of the Clarke family place, a half-dozen or so riders work their way behind the small herd of about sixty. They attempt to slowly move the cattle, in a tight group, toward the corral, where they'll get vaccinated and where spring calves will get branded.

But it's not so easy. Jittery and rebellious, animals break through gaps between riders, juking like halfbacks to head downfield. Cattle-wise quarter horses wheel in chase, hooves digging in, strides lengthening to turn the fleeing beef.

You can hear the yips and hollers of riders brandishing ropes, waving hats, hoping to enforce order. You can hear the cattle snorting and bellowing, unwilling to go meekly.

From folding chairs up near the house, Patsy Liera, seventy-five, and Virginia "Ginger" Liera, eighty, watch the cowboys with a smile. The sights and sounds are all too familiar. As little girls they watched their father and uncles and other local cowboys do the same. And once old enough, they too were atop horses chasing cattle.

"It was a fun way of life," Virginia says.

For nearly a hundred years, the Clarke home has been the site of an annual roundup and branding. At one time there were probably a half-dozen Cahuilla families who raised cattle and had big roundups. While several families still raise cattle, the Clarke-Liera roundup is the last to operate on this scale.

"My dad did it. My grandfather did it. I'm not going to let it die with me," Gerald Clarke says.

Gerald's first cousin, Robert Liera, agrees. Family members share ownership of the herd, and the whole family contributes to the roundup. The night before, a pit is dug and bundles of beef and a couple of turkeys are thrown onto coals, covered, and left to cook overnight.

The kids and other family members all pitch in. Beans and stews and salads are made. Patsy herself made sixty tortillas Friday night.

Even weewish, a traditional but labor-intensive Indian staple made from acorn flour, is prepared. Gerald's daughters helped shell and grind the acorns.

It takes some doing, but most of the cattle are eventually driven into the corral and the gate is closed.

A couple of runaways go "na-na-na" out in the pasture. "Yeah, they're laughing now, but they'll be first to go to market," Clarke says. "Cows like that rile up the others."

Cowboys, and one cowgirl, use their horses to separate out the adults, aiming them through a chute where Gerald jabs them with a big hypodermic full of medicines to keep them healthy.

When Clarke isn't cowboying, he's an artist and is head of the visual arts department at Idyllwild Arts Academy. When Robert Liera isn't cowboying, he works helping to keep the Pauma casino running smoothly.

One by one, each calf is roped, then stretched out to get earmarked, inoculated, and branded. Branding irons are heated in a fire. And all twenty-five calves get their mark.

Family and friends help with the work. It takes some doing to drop a squalling calf on its side and hold it there while it gets doctored and branded.

But once the work is done, the feasting starts. The feed is part of the tradition, Patsy says. They put on a big spread back when she was little, too. Her uncle, John Lubo, would grow grapes and make wine. The wine flowed with dinner.

It's always worrisome how the meat will turn out. But when the burlap is removed from the bundle, and the aluminum foil is slit open, sweet steam rises from the beef stewing in its own juices. And you know it's gonna be good.

Prayers are offered, and a hundred or so people sit down to eat a meal that could have been served a hundred years ago.

[2018]

SONG: OVERCOMING THE LANGUAGE BARRIER

from *Flutes of Fire*

Leanne Hinton

In California, the border between the United States and Mexico is clearly visible in satellite photographs. You can see a startling boundary line between the green crops of Imperial County, watered by the mighty canals that empty the Colorado River, and the brown fields of Baja California, where, due to the barriers of international politics, the canals never reach. On the ground, barbed wire fences, metal walls, and armed guards make the location of the border obvious.

From the point of view of Native America, this boundary is arbitrary and alien. It clearly defines the division between the dominance of Anglo and Hispanic peoples, and the English and Spanish languages, but it simply runs right through the middle of American Indian linguistic and political divisions. Relatives are separated from each other by that border. The Kumeyaay language, which is spoken by communities both north and south of the border, is officially called Diegueño because they are the people who were at Mission San Diego back when California was part of Mexico and the border did not exist. It is not possible to write about the Native languages of California and ignore Baja California.

Once, some decades ago, I went with a group of Kumeyaays and other friends from San Diego to visit the Kiliwa people in Baja California. The Kumeyaay group included such illustrious people as Rosalie Pinto, a singer and medicine woman, and Delfina Cuero, narrator of the book *Delfina Cuero: Her Autobiography* (Shipek 1991). Rosalie was the motivating force for this trip. Energetic and intense, full of intellectual curiosity, she wanted to visit the Kiliwas because she had heard they spoke a language related to Kumeyaay, and she was interested in their history of isolation and traditionalism.

The Kiliwas live in the Arroyo León, located in the foothills south of Valle Trinidad in the heart of northern Baja. Nowadays, the paved peninsular highway goes through Valle Trinidad, cutting away its previous solitude. But at the time of our visit, the Kiliwas were very isolated, both geographically and socially. Their dealings with Mexican institutions had not been particularly happy, and it was a constant battle to keep their land base from being eroded by the surrounding interests. During the Mexican Revolution (1910–20), Kiliwa men were known as great fighters, but over half died in a massacre in 1911, and those who remained fought with a radical fringe group that never gained any power in the new government, leaving the Kiliwa families with neither recognition nor reparation. Embittered, and ignored by the rest of Baja California, the tribe was alienated both socially and economically from the Mexican mainstream.

Some people left to work in the towns, but those who stayed in the traditional community lived almost completely without money—they built thatch homes, depended largely on wild foods, and, for the most part, spoke no Spanish. At the time of our visit, there were only nineteen Kiliwas in Arroyo León, and only a few spoke Spanish fluently. From the vantage point of our overpopulated cities here on the other side of the border, it boggles the imagination to think what it must be like to have only eighteen other people in one's entire social universe to communicate with.

But wait. Did I say communicate? One of the many things I learned on that wonderful journey was how many different ways there are to communicate. And what I learned most stunningly was how important music is as a form of communication.

Speaking presented an interesting translation problem. The visiting Kumeyaays, from north of the border, knew English but no Spanish, and none of the Kiliwas knew English. Some of the Kiliwas and one or two of the English speakers spoke some Spanish. When the Kumeyaay elders wished to say something, they spoke in the Kumeyaay tongue, which one of the younger Kumeyaays translated into English; someone else then translated that into Spanish, and finally one of the Kiliwas who understood Spanish would complete the translation in their language. Who knows how many accidental transformations of the original meaning happened between the first and last person!

But maybe the minor mishaps of translation through four languages weren't all that important, for most of the talk was formal and polite, and the main message was surely understood: I respect you, I feel kinship with you, I am glad to be here with you. Also, the people didn't spend all that much time trying to talk to each other. Most of the time they spent together relied on other forms of communication: gestures, smiles, touch, eating and drinking together, dancing and singing.

Singing together. These two tribes shared no language in common, and most of the individuals who were at this gathering had never seen each other before, yet they knew many of the same songs. And the songs that weren't known to both tribes nevertheless belonged to genres known to both, so catching on was easy.

All night long the singers from the two tribes sang the Bird Songs—songs that tell of a migration at the beginning of time. All night long the party formed their opposing lines (men on one side, women on the other) and danced back and forth beside the fires and lanterns out there under the summer stars in a black, black sky.

The Bird Songs are among the great song cycles of the area that depict epic journeys and great moments of creation, and they are not just for socializing. They are for ceremony, and especially for funerals. It is hard work being a singer, and if you are called to sing at an event, you must go. For a funeral, you must sing all night, sometimes for as many as four nights, to sing the departed soul on its path. They are beloved songs, and even just singing for bonding, as the Kumeyaays and Kiliwas did that night, is profound in its own way. You can't help but realize, as you are dancing back and forth, vibrating with music, that this form of intertribal communication has been important for thousands and thousands of years—song overcoming the barriers of language and creating unity, asserting kinship, passed from one community to the next by decades and centuries and millennia of intertribal gatherings.

We see it going on all over Native California. The Bird Songs themselves are sung throughout Southern California, by people of many different linguistic heritages, including Kumeyaay, Quechan, Mojave, Cahuilla, Cupeño, Luiseño, Serrano, and Chemehuevi. In Chumash country, along the Santa Barbara coast, there are records from Mission days of gatherings involving tribes from all over Southern California, and even as far away as Tucson and northern Mexico, and we can assume songs were traded there as well.[1]

Today we can see the use of song in intertribal communication at powwows in California's urban centers, which are attended by people from tribes from all over the country. The same kind of unification through song has been going on for centuries through the Deerskin Dances and Brush Dances of northwestern California, where Yurok, Karuk, Hupa, and Tolowa people traditionally come together; and in the Bear Dance of the Maidu, Pit River, and Northern Paiute tribes in eastern California—all tribes separated by language but united by song.

Many song types are universally known across large geographic

1 José Ignacio Rivera, interview on KPFA, September 1993. Rivera is a historian, educator, and former director of the Tohono O'odham Nation Cultural Center and Museum, Tohono O'odham Reservation, Arizona.

areas by people who speak different languages, and songs can travel fast from group to group. They can be traded just about as easily as a basket, or a bundle of corn, or a string of dentalium shells. Native people all over California know the songs of many tribes besides their own, and they can sing them well. Some songs became widespread so long ago that no one knows which tribe they started with. Others, traded perhaps a hundred years ago or less, are of well-known origin from a specific tribe, often with a fine story attached as to how those songs got to the communities that now sing them.

The best story I know about song travel is one the Havasupais tell about their Horse Songs. In the winters, the Havasupais would camp on the plateaus above their summer canyon home, and one time in the early nineteenth century, some Navajos raided the Havasupai camp and carried off a baby boy. A Navajo family adopted that boy and raised him as their own. When he became a young adult, some Hopi people came to tell the boy about his origins, and he decided to go home to his people. In the dead of night he took his adopted father's best saddle blanket and saddle and rode off on his best horse. When he arrived at the Havasupai camp, he dressed and rode like a Navajo, and knew only the Navajo language. This was a dangerous moment: if they thought he was a Navajo enemy, the Havasupais might have killed him then and there. But when he saw his people, he just sat on his horse, folded his arms, and bent his head down and wept. Seeing this, the Havasupais knew him for a long-lost relative and took him down off his horse and welcomed him. He lived with them the rest of his life. One of the gifts he brought for the Havasupais was a set of songs, changed now but still recognizable as being from the Navajo Blessingway song cycle. He had not only brought the Navajos' best horse but also their best songs. The Havasupais have sung them ever since, and they call them the Horse Songs.

Now that English and Spanish serve, respectively, as a lingua franca in California and Baja California, spoken communication between tribes is not as limited as it once was. But it is easy to imagine the old days, a couple hundred years ago, when a visit between tribes was like the meeting between the Kumeyaay and the Kiliwa—a very special time, where feelings are warm and words are few, and the singing can flow and flow.

This is one reason, no doubt, why so many Indian songs have no intelligible words. Words are barriers to unity; words separate people, sorting them by language and by opinion. But music unifies. Songs without words are vocal music in its purest form, music that brings people from different tribes together, brings out their fundamental unity, and communicates that important message far better than language ever can: I respect you, I feel kinship with you, I am happy to be here with you.

The trip to visit the Kiliwa people took place almost half a century ago. Many of the people who traveled together from California, and those in the Kiliwa village who welcomed the travelers, have passed. But the Bird Songs and other song cycles are still thriving in Southern California and beyond. California Indians worry about the survival of the Bird Songs, but they continue to be reclaimed by young people each generation, and they are still strong. New singers grow up hearing the songs and become inspired to learn them themselves. Singing teams take them on and train them, and new singing teams form. There are giant conferences and contests where Bird Singing teams compete. The public can even access recordings of them on YouTube—just search for "Kumeyaay Bird Songs" or "Cahuilla Bird Songs" or "Mojave Bird Songs" or any other language of the Southern California homelands.

These songs help people maintain and revitalize their cultural traditions and their languages. I end this chapter with two statements by current Bird singers.

STANLEY RODRIGUEZ, KUMEYAAY SINGER

There may be only a few words in those Bird Songs and other sets of songs we sing—but there's a whole story that goes with it. Put it all together and that's our history. And it's not only our history, but it teaches us how to conduct ourselves, with other people. . . .

Now many [of those songs] have gone dormant. It doesn't mean they're lost. It means they can come back. And there have been people who have stepped forward and have worked on bringing those song cycles back, doing the best that they can. And this is something that brings hope to our people. And when we talk about it at Kumeyaay Community College, these things that we want to do, we call it decolonizing. It's our right to be Native. It's our right to sing our songs and to know our history [through the songs].

—excerpt from a talk by Stanley Rodriguez,
Kumeyaay Lecture Series: Songs of Knowledge,
www.youtube.com/watch?v=mekTcjztNXk (4:26–5:56)

ANTHONY J. ANDREAS III, AGUA CALIENTE BAND OF CAHUILLA INDIANS, BIRD SINGER

The Bird Songs come from our oral history, of our creation. The people, they were lost, so they began this massive march, searching for their home. They came to the San Jacinto Mountains here, and they could feel that their home was on the other side. They prayed to their God, they wailed, they cried out, and he imparted to them the Bird Songs. . . .

My father revived the Bird singing here for our tribe. It was dead, no one sang the old Bird Songs anymore. My father reached out to an elder [named Joe] and asked him if he would teach him the Bird Songs. You know the story goes that Joe said, “Come back tomorrow,” and my dad would come back the next day, and he’d tell him again, “You know, let me think about it a little more, come back tomorrow,” and finally he ended up saying, “Okay, I’ll teach you, but it’s going to be a commitment.” And he taught my father all the old Bird Songs. He incorporated us kids into the Bird singing, and my sisters into the dancing, and then my uncle joined in, and then pretty soon it was revived again. We’ve actually found a piece of our culture that we can actually hang onto, that we’re not going to lose anymore.

We started in the same place we left: in the beginning. People searching and longing for home. This giant mountain was too big to cross over, and as they sang the Bird Songs, and actually they were changed into birds and they flew over, and we became human again. That’s what the Bird Songs mean to us. It helped us find our home.

—excerpts from “Anthony’s Path,”
produced by the Robert Wood Johnson Foundation;
posted online June 13, 2017,
www.youtube.com/watch?v=d_Z9wSMNkA0

[1994/2022]

EN LA NOCHE— IN THE EVENING

from *An Indian among los Indígenas*

Ursula Pike

Two weeks before training ended, I turned twenty-six. Laura asked where I wanted to celebrate, and I chose Tio Lujo's current site. We weren't sure where Tio Lujo's Bar would be from one weekend to the next. It moved to different spots throughout Cochabamba every few weeks. But the Westerners and expats in town always managed to find it. Information about each new location was spread between rooms at the cheap hostels and restaurants recommended by the travel guidebook everyone carried. *Tio*, which means uncle, ran the bar and was from Argentina, Chile, or one of those other South American countries that didn't seem part of the Third World. His black-rimmed glasses were thick and would have looked ironic in the United States, but in a country where few people could afford glasses, there was no irony. The bar had small tables lit by candles, Spanish music playing on tinny speakers, and a menu of food that was familiar but not very tasty. I never found out why the bar moved around, but suspected it was poor management due to too much Bolivian Marching Powder. Bolivia was full of people from around the world who came specifically for the high-quality, cheap cocaine. *Lujo* means luxurious, and no matter what building the bar ended up in, the beers were always more expensive than anywhere else in the city. The bar probably had some other official name, but we called it Tio Lujo.

From the cab we took to Tio Lujo's, we could see the streets filling up with people walking to the Festival of Urkupiña. Devotees of the Virgin Mary made the pilgrimage on foot to the mountain where she had appeared. It was still winter in the Southern Hemisphere, and the pilgrims wore layers of jackets and scarves.

The first round of beers arrived at the table. I hoped someone would bring up the film we all watched during training that afternoon. *Blood of the Condor*, or *Yawar Mallku*, was a 1969 Bolivian film about Quechua villagers and an agency called the Progress Corps. Before starting the film, the training director said, "This movie changed the history of the Peace Corps in Bolivia." All twenty-six of us sat in the large meeting room, which smelled of rice and meat because it was also the lunchroom. We were two weeks from our swearing in—the moment when we held up our hands and promised to represent the United States as Peace Corps volunteers.

The black-and-white film opened with a Bolivian couple in a small earthen-walled room. The wife was young, had smooth skin, and wore a serious expression, but the husband was weathered, and slurred his words. They argued about the death of their children, and the husband blamed the wife for not having another baby. Every word they spoke was in Quechua. I had never seen an entire film in an Indigenous language, and I perked up every time I heard a word I recognized—*warmi* (woman) and *wawa* (baby).

Then the volunteers from the US showed up. Their Spanish was laughable and barely understandable. One woman wore Jackie O sunglasses and pedal pushers. We laughed. Nervously. Those ridiculous people were supposed to be us. I looked around the room. A woman nearby squinted at the screen.

"We, of the Progress Corps, have come here through many sacrifices of our own so that you can develop," the head of the group said to a line of silent, staring village residents. He was a barrel-chested man wearing the same button-up flannel shirt in every scene. He puffed on a pipe as he spoke with controlled condescension to the Bolivians. Boxes of donated clothes were offered to the villagers, who reluctantly accepted the gifts. I thought of the US soldiers who gave blankets infected with smallpox to Native people, and wondered if the filmmaker was saying something about poisoned gifts. Some of the people in the room were paying attention, but more than a few had dozed off. *Are they seeing what I am seeing¿* Maybe this was my paranoid Native imagination.

The line about the sacrifices the volunteers were making for the betterment of the Bolivians sounded a little too familiar. No one had stated it so plainly, because our "sacrifice" for the sake of the Bolivians was assumed. Peace Corps volunteers were the most noble motherfuckers on the planet, or so we were told. The more that personal comforts were forgone, the further away we were from a city, from electricity, from toilets and running water, the more valuable was our sacrifice. That sentiment was as true thirty years earlier when the film was made as it was that afternoon in the cafeteria.

In the movie, the women in the village were never able to get pregnant again after visiting the clinic run by the Progress Corps. The film ended when the villagers discovered that the volunteers were "sowing death in the bellies" of the women of the community. It was an allusion to the forced sterilization of the Indigenous women. The North Americans were pulled away into the darkness by the villagers, never to be seen again.

"Remember, this was not based on a real incident," the training director said as he switched off the television. He explained that the movie was shown widely throughout Bolivia in 1970, and it wasn't seen as fiction. Peace Corps was asked to leave the country by the Bolivian government partly because of the reaction to the movie. Twenty years later, the organization returned, thanks to a government that was friendlier to the United States.

"Do they really think Peace Corps did . . . did this to women¿! Is that how they see us¿" a woman in the front row asked, her brow crinkled in confusion. Forced sterilization seemed beyond her comprehension. The training director assured us that it never happened and that Peace Corps never operated clinics.

While watching the film, I thought about my mother getting her tubes tied the year I was in fourth grade. I didn't know the term *tubal ligation* at the time, but that's what it was. Her baby-making days were over. She wanted me to know she was choosing it. The afternoon my mother went into the hospital, I stood on the playground imagining giant tubes like multicolored hoses snaking out of her, while a white doctor struggled to tie them together. A few months later, she enrolled in community college.

I was surprised that the other volunteers didn't seem to know that forced sterilization was an actual practice. It wasn't just a perfect metaphor for the genocide Indigenous people had experienced but an actual crime committed on Native women up until the 1970s. In North America, one in four Native women were forcibly sterilized. Full-blooded women were targeted first.

Although I knew that the Peace Corps had never sterilized women, I wasn't surprised that Bolivians were suspicious of the organization's actions. In a world where Indigenous people had been taken advantage of by foreigners and every few decades a new generation showed up promising to help, of course they wouldn't trust volunteers from the US. But I didn't say anything. That evening as I changed my clothes to get ready for my birthday celebration, I wondered what the other trainees would have thought if I'd said I understood why the Bolivians believed the film to be true. Would they see me as unsophisticated and backward? I knew no one would bring up the film on this night of celebration with a handful of days between us and the beginning of our service.

From the inside of the bar, I saw that the number of people in the street walking to Urkupiña had doubled in the short time I had been sitting drinking my beer. Laura sat in the seat next to me, and someone said, "Happy Birthday." I thought about bringing up the movie, but what kind of party would it be if I talked about something as horrible as forced sterilization¿ Laura and I huddled in a corner with a bottle of wine. My time in Kantuta had been demoralizing, but she had had a blast during her visit to southern Bolivia. She had already put a deposit on an apartment. I drank my wine and hoped that I didn't look as dejected as I felt. The bar filled up with volunteers in town for trainings who had heard about the party. I knew it wasn't really for me, but I loved that my party was becoming a big event.

"Hello, who is that¿" a woman behind me said, and I looked up to see a scruffy guy with a battered leather hat walk in. It was Daniel, the volunteer from Kantuta who had warned me to stay away. With yellow hair, blue eyes, and dimples, he looked every inch the Southern California surfer dude that he was. I assumed he had no idea who I was, and hoped I wouldn't have to speak to him.

"This must be the birthday girl," he said and wrapped me in a hug. He knew who I was and that I was moving to Kantuta. He had heard about me puking out the back of the sugar cane truck, thanks to Nina. I smiled and tried to think of a witty response, but he disappeared back into the crowd. Laura and I laughed as he stepped away and I was handed a shot glass full of Bolivia's finest *singani*.

At some point I had had too many drinks and knew I needed to leave the building. I didn't want to cry on Laura's shoulder and tell her how much I was going to miss her. Saying no was difficult for me, but I knew I had passed my limit, so I sneaked out the door. I did this anytime I was too drunk to pretend that I was having a good time. Sometimes I needed to be alone. I peeked behind me and was both relieved and heartbroken that no one was coming to save me.

Stumbling out into the street, I bumped into a woman who was heading to Urkupiña. It was nearly midnight, but the wide main boulevard was now full of people. Dogs hiding behind fences barked. Many of the people were carrying toy cars, fake money, and tiny houses. Earlier that night, a taxicab driver told us they were replicas of what the people wanted. When festivalgoers arrived at the hill where the image of la Virgen had appeared, a *yatiri* would bless the replicas, and the people would leave them in hopes of having their specific request filled. The mixture of Indigenous ceremony and Christian icons made me think of the prayer said before powwows I'd attended, thanking Jesus, the Creator, and all our ancestors. I wished I had something a *yatiri* could bless. What could I place on the hill that would help me be the opposite of the smug volunteers in the movie? The three months of training that was about to end had improved my Spanish, taught me a little bit of Quechua, and burned into my mind the shape of Bolivia on a map. But I had no clue as to whether I could help Bolivians. No trinket represented the knowledge I thought I lacked or the experience I hoped to have in Kantuta.

[2021]

BLACKBERRY BRINED SMOKED SALMON

from *Chími Nu'am*

Sara Calvosa Olson

"Did a bear write this recipe?" you might ask. No, but bears know how to live.

This is best prepared in late summer when the blackberries are bursting with sun-ripened sweetness. As for the smoke, I use an electric smoker with a thermometer so I can keep an eye on the temperature and ensure that we're smoking low and slow. I also throw a serape over it to keep it nice and warm because my smoker is very old and rickety. You can use any kind of wood chips you prefer. I used pecan wood, but traditional alder wood, mesquite, applewood, or cherry would be fine alternatives. As you get into smoking, you'll discover which woods pair best with different proteins. This recipe can be pressure-canned (I like to stuff blackberries into the jar before canning) or it can be eaten immediately.

Wild blackberries or blackberries from a farmers' market will give you the flavor that we're looking for. Supermarket blackberries taste like exhaust pipes and unfair labor practices. Most of the wild blackberry patches we come across these days are an incredibly hearty introduced species that is native to Armenia and Iran, *Rubus armeniacus*. It was inaccurately christened the "Himalaya" blackberry by Luther Burbank, a backyard botanist and part-time eugenicist from Sonoma County, in the late 1880s. He sold the blackberry in a catalog to other settlers, and with the help of birds and other berry-hungry fauna, this plant spread itself far and wide, out of control. Our own California native Pacific blackberry, *Rubus ursinus*, with a more delicate and trailing bramble, did not stand a chance against the aggressively thick canes and roots of its Eastern cousin and continues to decline in habitat. You can find huge brambles of Himalaya blackberries nearly everywhere in California, especially near water sources. The berries are large, juicy, and undeniably delicious, but they do not belong here, and it's best to cut them back or remove them so they are not outcompeting our little Pacific berry for resources.

But hey, there's no denying the value of a good berry patch. I have so many memories intertwined with the musky sweet smell of blackberry patches.

2 cleaned and deboned fillets of salmon, cut into strips width-wise
1 to 2 cups lukewarm water
1 cup maple sugar or honey
¼ cup salt
2 cups wild blackberries
1 cup pecan chips (if using an electric smoker)
Nonstick spray

Store for use throughout the year.

Prepare your fillets, making sure they're nice and clean and free of any pin bones. When you're filleting a fish, the most important thing is a sharp knife. If your fillets come out sloppy, don't worry; it just takes a lot of practice. Mine aren't winning any prizes either.

In a large bowl, mix together the lukewarm water with the maple sugar and salt, and stir until the salt has dissolved. Add the blackberries and smash it all together. Place the salmon strips in the bowl gently so you don't tear up the flesh and, using your hands, submerge the fish completely. Cover the bowl with plastic wrap and refrigerate for 8 hours or overnight.

Take the fish out of the bowl and put the fillets on racks, skin side down, on top of a baking sheet. Let them come to room temperature for 2 to 4 hours so some of the water from the brine evaporates. This helps develop the pellicle on the outside.

You're going to want to smoke this low and slow, so prepare your smoker the way you normally would and if you're new to smoking and have an electric smoker, soak your chips for a few minutes and then set them inside the smoker and plug it in. You'll want to smoke the fish for at least 8 hours at 140 to 150°F, depending on the texture you like for smoked salmon. The longer it smokes, the drier it gets. You want to be sure to get to an internal temperature between 130 to 140°F. Fish can be packed in jars and pressure-canned for pantry storage for up to 1 year or kept in the refrigerator for 1 to 2 weeks.

[2023]

IF OPRAH WERE AN OAK TREE

from *Becoming Story*

Greg Sarris

I am learning about "sudden oak death." Specifically, I am learning to see it outside my window: I understand the crimson-colored bleeding canker on the trunk of the magnificent three-hundred-year-old live oak in the middle of my garden indicates lethal infection, presages the tree's imminent death.

My first thoughts are selfish: I will have to cut down the tree. That is, I will have to pay someone to cut down the tree, otherwise risk an enormous corpse crashing atop my kitchen. Below my yard, bordering my neighbor's property, a live oak, equal in size and splendor to this one, died last summer, costing nearly two thousand dollars to cut down. I shared the cost with my neighbor. I will have to foot this bill alone.

Then there is the aesthetic concern, also selfish, I suppose. My home, whose modern architecture was crafted around these Sonoma Mountain ancients, which were expected to outlive the home's residents, if not the house itself, will look completely different without them.

The home's rectangular structure, meant to look integrated with the forested landscape, will appear instead an obtrusive brown box of metal and glass plunked against a naked hillside. The native ferns and grasses, dependent on the tree's shade and acidity, will give way to non-native species, including, for example, the oatgrass and numerous varieties of thistle that commonly flourish on the dry, open hillside here.

All of the live oaks around my home—indeed in the entire region—show signs of infection, if only foliar lesions, the first, and omnipresent, indication of the disease's presence. In any given stand of infected live oaks the mortality rate is presently 40 to 80 percent. Will I have two trees left? One?

The history of sudden oak death (SOD), and the scientific community's frustration with it, not to mention the ongoing devastation, sounds a lot like the AIDS story.

In May 1997, Marin County homeowners noticed live oaks beginning to die in their gardens. Two years earlier, in April 1995, the UC Cooperative Extension office in Marin had been asked to investigate an unusual dieback of more than a dozen tanoaks bordering a creek, and in June "a shocking number" of dead trees, described by Pavel Svihra in his case study of SOD, was noted on the slope above the creek and along the crest of the hill. The dying live oaks, reported in 1997, showed symptoms similar to those of these tanoaks, and scientists suspected the same causes—prolonged drought from 1990 to 1992 followed by very wet years in 1993 and 1994, which might have reduced the trees' vigor, making them susceptible to infestations of various fungi and bark beetles, none of which normally kill healthy trees.

In June 1998, the word "epidemic" was used—live oaks, tanoaks, and now black oaks were dying from Mill Valley to Novato. By 1999 tens of thousands of trees in Marin and Sonoma Counties were infected. By the year 2000, when David Rizzo, a UC professor, isolated the pathogen now believed to be the primary causal agent of SOD—a heretofore unknown fungus of the Phytophthora genus, termed a year later *Phytophthora ramorum*—the disease was present in twelve California counties, most notably in Marin, Santa Cruz, and Sonoma. Today it is found in an additional thirteen species from ten plant families that act as hosts—redwoods and rhododendrons among them. So far, the disease appears fatal only to the three oak species—live oaks, tanoaks, black oaks. Yet as Pavel Svihra notes, "There are no measures available that will alter the underlying disease [*P. ramorum*]."

My Coast Miwok ancestors depended on oak trees. Acorns were for us, and for all central California tribes, what rice has been for China and wheat for Europe. For ages, acorns fed some of the densest pre-contact populations in the New World. Acorns from live oaks proved the most difficult to harvest and store, and yielded a meal, or mush, that was greasy, though good for making bread.

Tanoaks provided the acorns of choice. Coast Miwok and Southern Pomo located inland traded with those on the coast for access to the trees. The tanoaks have been the hardest hit by SOD, with 90 percent of the stands in many areas decimated. The moist coastal climate, which the tanoaks prefer, affords, unfortunately, the best condition for the reproduction of the pathogen *P. ramorum* and its spread to the trees, which our northwestern neighbors, the Kashaya Pomo, simply called *cisq qhale*, beautiful tree.

My home sits less than a quarter mile from the site of the Alaguali village. Friends' ancestors come from Alaguali. (My ancestors hail from nearby Petaluma and Bodega Bay.) I imagine these ancestors, women with tattooed chins, men sporting seal bone nose plugs and finely chipped abalone pendant earrings, raking with hand-crafted wooden instruments the old leaves and worm-infested acorns from under the tree outside my window, halting the spread of worm and other parasite infections that would tax the health of this wondrous individual. With obsidian-bladed knives they cut suckers around the tree's base and on its gnarled trunk. Every five to ten years they set fire to the area, burning undergrowth that would sap nutrients from the soil, and at the same time replenishing the ground with ash, which the tree desperately needs and depends on. That was about two hundred years ago, when the tree was one hundred.

Then the Europeans—the tree witnessed the first Spanish livestock, herds of curly-horned cattle and spotted horses that roamed into these hills from the mission plantation in Sonoma and from as far away as the mission in San Rafael. These animals carried foreign seed in their dung: oatgrass, mustard, and thistle replaced pepper grass and showy clover on the sunny slope beyond the tree's canopy. And, as I mentioned before, the padres imposed—and were insistent upon—a ban against controlled burning, as they wanted the grass for their livestock, and at the same time they also ordered a ban against bathing. Did the dense clusters of pinprick leaves register a pneumonic cough, perhaps feel the heat of a human's death—presaging fever?

General Vallejo and his army of Mexican soldiers who secularized the missions and established the extensive ranchos intensified the simultaneous destruction of Coast Miwok lifeways and the aboriginal landscape. Among other disruptive acts, the American settler named William Bihler bombed with dynamite the southern end of Tolay Lake, a sacred place for the Coast Miwok, draining the lake of water, rendering a dried lakebed suitable for planting wheat and corn. Certainly the earth trembled with the blasts. Blasts, blasts, blasts . . . This tree outside my window felt all of them, shuddered, with dynamite and gun blasts alike, dynamite imploding entire hills, blasting enormous crater-like holes in the mountain, gun blasts dropping the last elk, pronghorn, grizzly bear and black bear; shovels, then drills, digging into the earth for water; thudding tractors, more dynamite, carving up the mountainside, flattening ridges for roads, then paving the roads; oh, and lest I forget, no doubt an enormous steel crane, an unearthly monster, driving piles into the ground for the foundation of this house!

I marvel at the history I imagine recorded in the tree's life. I think of a young couple taken from Alaguali, my friends' ancestors, baptized by the Spanish padres as Isidro and Isidra. Did they miss the tree? Enslaved at the San Rafael mission, did Isidro and Isidra look up one late autumn afternoon, him tending cattle, her ironing the padres' vestments, and wonder if there was anyone still who might rake the leaves and wormy acorns from under the tree? Did the tree miss their songs, and the click and the *sh* in the words of their conversations? Does it understand Spanish or English? This tree and its ancestors for ten thousand years heard only Coast Miwok and Pomo languages from humans. Forget ten thousand years, think time immemorial for my people.

Once Indians on foot came up and down this spirit- and oak-filled mountain, and now I, an Indian tribal chairman, come up and down the mountain at least once a day in a car (never mind that it's a Prius), along with a couple hundred other people, all of them up and down the mountain in their cars too. This heady notion of history I glean from the tree's point of view—a lofty vision of time—distracts me from my baser preoccupations with money and aesthetics regarding the tree's impending demise. Even as I implicate myself—my home, my driving up and down the mountain—as part of a story that hasn't related a necessarily pleasant experience for the tree, I congratulate myself for knowing as much . . . that is, until I recall what a short chapter of the tree's history I have a sense of.

Time immemorial? The oak trees, along with their bay laurel neighbors, have been here forty million years.

I remember being startled by screaming—cheering?—coming from the TV set. It was Oprah, or rather, her audience. Oprah was giving each of her perfectly coifed, perfectly thirtysomething guests one of her "favorite things." In this case it was a kitchen utensil. What, a blender? A juicer? As if she had spent a lot of time in her local appliance store, or even her kitchen, testing such things.

Okay, I admit it. I was watching Oprah. At one o'clock in the morning, after a long day of writing, teaching, and overseeing the daily operations of my tribe, I turned on the TV, mostly to see the news, but flicking the channels, I found, or landed on, Oprah, a repeat from a 4:00 p.m. broadcast a decade ago. She still fascinates us. Why is everyone hooked on Oprah?

We care about her "favorite things"—foods, clothes, vacation spots, furniture, kitchen appliances, books, cars, celebrities, you name it. We care about what her interior designer can tell us about chintz and color schemes, and what her makeup artist can tell us about lip gloss and face creams. We care what her psychologist says about our problems. Did we know we had such problems? And of course we care about what her favorite poet, Maya Angelou, says about our souls. We care about Oprah. Who doesn't know the story of the poor girl from Mississippi who became the most powerful woman in show business? Doesn't her story prove that all of us can overcome personal obstacles? We care about her weight issues. We care about her daily life. Have you called the number where you can listen to "private conversations" between her and her best friend Gayle? Oprah's social and political causes become our own. Have you donated to Oprah's Angel Network? Her heroes become our heroes. For example, the young girl (on the repeat show two nights ago), who saved her mother from a bear attack in her living room, and the fireman in Hawaii who saved a girl after her car had plunged into the ocean and was five feet under water. Real life stuff, fantastic or ordinary, we watch it on Oprah. And if you miss Oprah on TV, perhaps because you don't watch TV, you will see her in the supermarket. Whole Foods or Safeway, doesn't matter. Her *O Magazine* is prominently displayed alongside *People* and *Star*. It's always Oprah on the cover, because, as her best friend Gayle once said, "People want to see Oprah." Is it possible to *not* see Oprah?

I rushed to the TV to see what Oprah was giving away. Toothpaste coating my mouth, eyes frozen on the screen, I no doubt resembled a rabid animal. Too late; Oprah, happy as a lark, had already moved on and was cooking something with a special guest chef. Would each of her audience members get a frying pan? Frustrated—both for missing what it was she gave away and for caring—I flicked off the TV.

Later, I heard the tree scraping against the house. Wind; I would have to sweep leaves in the morning, a chore compulsive sorts like myself don't like to think about before bed. Then a second thought: before long there would be no leaves to sweep.

Is there any chance the tree will survive? Can we find a cure? Could Oprah help?

Better yet, what if Oprah were an oak tree? The oak tree outside my window, for instance.

Each weekday, Monday through Friday, promptly at 4:00 p.m. on CBS, you would see on *The Live Oak Show* the tree outside my window. Featured in the middle of your screen would be the oak tree, long shots, close-ups, and numerous profile shots, the camera cutting back and forth from the tree to its various guests, the vast majority human, most of whom would be talking about the tree. Of course there would be shows that featured psychics, mediums who claim to channel the spirits of the trees, who would talk on camera *with* the tree. As certain guests discussed the tree's physical properties, the camera would pan from the gnarled trunk, properly called a bole, as the audience would be informed, to the myriad branches and onto the curled prickly leaves. During a special fall-season show featuring acorn harvesting techniques, the camera would zoom in on hands collecting nuts off the ground and, later on the same show, provide close-ups on proper rakes and clearing techniques for clearing away from under the tree the old leaves and the wormy nuts that had been left behind during the collecting phase. That show would end with a tight low-angle shot of the pile of debris burning—a voiceover reminding us that ash is good for the tree. The programs that cause the most angst in viewers (even as they are the programs with the highest ratings) have to do with the tree's health status. Mid-season, during a program on foliar lesions, the frame would zoom in on numerous leaf samples, and special cameras would catch microscopic cellular activity, including the presence, or not, of that life-threatening pathogen *P. ramorum*. The next season would premiere with a shot of the bleeding canker, a painful sight no one can forget—viewer discretion advised—an image that keeps viewers hooked the entire season. Will we get to see the canker again? When? Will it be worse? Better?

There would be a show about the tree's "favorite things": ash and other nutrients that enhance its ability to fight disease; methods of pruning that enhance its beauty and overall vitality, using (of course) its favorite shears, modeled after indigenous tools that prove the least painful or disturbing to the tree; birds—chickadees during the winter months, and sapsuckers, finches, and sparrows during spring and summer, with flickers, jays, and pileated woodpeckers in the fall—all of which help control parasites harmful to the tree; acid-loving flora, ferns, and such on the ground below the tree; native grasses and bulbs beyond the tree's canopy (pepper grass, various clovers, bluedicks, and poppies that maintain the local terrain by assuring, among other things, adequate water retention); rain free of acid; air free of pollutants; stable weather patterns.

One show would be devoted entirely to scientific research on SOD. We would learn about whatever progress is being made on the disease, new discoveries about its life cycle, and methods of transmission, and there would be an Angel Network of sorts, let's call it the Oak Tree Spirit Network, that we could donate to for further research. Another show would feature the tree's cousins, its immediate live oak neighbors, as well as its distant relatives, black oaks and white oaks, the latter, interestingly enough, *not* killed by SOD. Tanoaks, which live farthest from the tree—rarely, if ever, on Sonoma Mountain, but west, along the coast—are also the most distantly related of its oak relatives.

A series of shows lasting an entire week would follow a team comprised of scientists, politicians, and Coast Miwok and Southern Pomo descendants as they journey up the mountain on foot to the tree. Scientists would point out copses of live oaks, noting infection rates as well as native and non-native plant and animal species and the likely impact of climate change on the ecology of the region. Politicians would take notes, commit to more funding for research on SOD and on climate control, understanding that a warmer climate challenges the well-being not only of the ancient oaks—in particular the tree outside my window—but of all life as we know it on Sonoma Mountain. After all, climate change creates conditions for new pathogens like *P. ramorum*. The Coast Miwok and Southern Pomo descendants would repeat the ancient adage that people cannot forget the tree lest the trees forget the people, and, once the party reaches the tree, these aboriginal descendants would speak to the tree in their revitalized native languages. A fire is burned under the tree, mimicking old controlled-burning practices, as an offering to the tree, and the scientists point out that temperatures above 95 degrees Fahrenheit kill *P. ramorum*. Finally, everyone enjoys a taste of mush or bread made from the tree's acorns. It is a cannot-miss *Live Oak Show* week.

On the cover of each *O Magazine*—that is, the oak magazine—would be a flattering picture of the tree: in spring, the tree against a landscape lush green with assorted golden poppies and purple lupine; in summer, the tree, stately, against the warm, sun-dried slopes; in fall, with Native baskets, used for harvesting, at its base, the rich designs and earth tones of the baskets complimenting the tree's colors and textures; in winter, the tree glistening wet, ferns, glistening likewise, below it.

Saturday Night Live would make fun of the oak tree, with skits imitating various memorable episodes, like the one that featured Brad Pitt and Angelina Jolie talking about the seedlings they adopted. Social critics would point out that many of *The Live Oak Show*'s sponsors were not fully politically correct in terms of fair trade and labor practices, not to mention the toll the magazine's enormous subscription rate takes on the forests in Canada and South America, and the outcry would prompt the sponsors to clean up their act, and the magazine itself would convert to being published solely on recycled paper.

Thinking critically about its popularity, the show would feature a program exploring the tree's celebrity. What makes the tree so popular? Why are we hooked on that specific tree outside my window? The most simple and obvious explanation, used by psychologists, is that the media, and specifically its ability to mass-produce images of the tree, forces us to become familiar with it. It becomes commonplace, as well known as a member of our immediate family. We see it as often as the people we live with, and, if we pay attention—that is, if we watch the television show with even a modicum of ardor or regularly read the magazine—we may know more about the history and daily life of the tree than the people in our own households. Or at least we think we do. Other psychologists and media experts would point out the irony that the tree's celebrity is simultaneously based on, and maintained by, the fact that it is on TV, and that, in fact, we don't know it at all, or only to the extent producers and such want us to know it. Bottom line: The tree outside my window *can't* be likened to the tree outside your window, for then it would become truly commonplace and no longer of such intense fascination.

The irony, understood by anyone with an interest in the workings of mass media, seems symptomatic of the larger culture and history of which it is part. In an ironic yet very noticeable way, we don't *know* our own homes. We may occupy our homes, our neighborhoods, our bioregions, our watersheds, whatever, but we are simultaneously separated from them, not engaged with them. Thus, we are strangers where we live. We are here but not here, home but not home. At some point, all of us, Native and non-Native, developed, or perhaps accepted as a result of military defeat and colonization, a culture characterized by this condition. Aboriginal people—let's start with the Israelites—were removed from their native land, or home, and enslaved and then freed, finding themselves in a place with only a *promise* of land, or home, once again. This story has played itself out multiple times, replicating a pattern that has disengaged so many people from their native homes that now the vast majority of the human population finds itself in this condition. Certainly, there are variations in the story, and different Native people cling to land-based lifestyles and traditions with varying degrees of success. But, for the most part, we have effectively become strangers where we live, at least from an aboriginal land-based point of view. We may no longer look specifically for a promised land, with or without our tribe, but the act of looking for home—call it security, if you wish—is the same. We set our gaze elsewhere. We think more money, a bigger house, more cattle, a script that will sell, whatever it may be, will get us *there*. Often governments and historical circumstances provide no alternatives, if they even allow us opportunity to pursue such things, but the trick—and the truth—is that as long as we remain separated from our home, not fully engaged with it, looking elsewhere, we will always be insecure. It will feel natural to see, perhaps dream, of home and security down the road, next year, in another life. It will feel natural to look at the tree on TV and not at the one outside your window. The tree on TV will be real to us. We've learned to look that way.

Could *The Live Oak Show* be popular because environmentalism is popular? I'd like to imagine so. But to what extent, then, does environmentalism remain an idea and not something lived? The tree's survival, not to mention our own as a species, depends on our living connectedness with the world, and most importantly with the local world, our home. The danger of seeing only the celebrity tree is not only that we don't see the tree outside our window but that we don't see our relationship to that tree, how our lives, and the decisions we make, impact its well-being. A celebrity culture—let's say any culture disengaged from its home—is in many ways a blind culture. If we don't see the tree outside our window, if we are not truly at home in our home, how can we understand our connection with it? How can we know to be responsible? This blindness, in fact, helps maintain the disconnection that maintains, in turn, the blindness—a very dark circle, a patch over our eyes.

Looking at the tree outside my window offers vision. It suggests a history I am implicated in and inextricable from, not just in terms of my Coast Miwok ancestors but now, while the tree and I are alive in the same home. My car trips up and down the mountain contribute to poor air quality, as does anything I purchase in the grocery store or local mall that requires the burning of fossil fuels, whether strawberries from Watsonville 120 miles away or a pair of tennis shoes made in China. What I plant under the tree, or near it, the amount of water those plants require, also affect the tree's well-being, as do the types of fertilizers I use. My neighbors, too: whatever they plant, whatever livestock and pets they own, affect the tree. The Angus cattle in the nearby hills continue to spread exotic seed. Sulfites used in the non-organic grape vineyard down the road waft in the air and poison the groundwater.

Domestic cats—two live next-door—kill birds that clean the tree of parasites. Dogs—there's an adorable yellow lab in the yard two houses down—can spread viruses that kill the native blue fox, the predator so necessary for the containment of squirrel populations. Too many squirrels deplete the tree of acorns. Never mind that without acorns the tree won't be able to produce seedlings—what if one day I needed those acorns for food?

This tree engages me with my world. Vision and connection. It's still giving, the ancient oak. I sense irony in this, and something at once sad and beautiful too, and urgent.

This morning I went out to rake leaves. The tree these days is dropping quite a few of them. The mid-April sun was warm. The gentle slopes in the distance were bright with buttercups and purple lupine. But, alas, when I turned back to the tree, bamboo rake in hand, there was the large gnarled trunk, the bleeding canker at its center, startlingly crimson in the light. I wanted to turn away, move to the other side of the tree where the canker wasn't visible. Oh, where were those yellow and purple hills? But too late. I'd seen what I'd seen. I felt depressed. My thoughts over the last few days appeared banal, plain stupid, particularly the notion of Oprah as this tree. Stupid metaphor. But this tree—the ugly canker—was important, wasn't it? Couldn't I find a more meaningful way to write about it? It was, after all, talking to all of us; it was our canary in a coal mine. Then the tree made me laugh out loud. Silly English professor, with your metaphors and meanings, good God. Canary in a coal mine? Why not the tree in front of me?

[2022]

MAKING HISTORY

INTRODUCTION

from *Inlandia*

Susan Straight

We had forests. As a child, I read of Sherwood Forest in England, where men could be lost to sight for years; of haunted woods in Europe, like those where my mother was born, where wolves and witches and darkness reigned amid the huge firs; of rain forests in South America where birds and monkeys screamed amid the dripping branches; of the chestnut and hickory and dogwood of Appalachia and the wilderness of trees in the great eastern forests of America.

And though no one knew it, in my part of Southern California, the inland reaches of terrain where most of us see only smog-shrouded hills and dried wild oats and mazes of freeway, we had magical, mythical woods as well—thousands and thousands of acres planted in orange and lemon and grapefruit trees that covered much of Riverside and San Bernardino and Redlands. Apricots and olive groves in Hemet, the date palm groves in Mecca and Indio, walnut trees in Elsinore, and cherries and apples in Cherry Valley and Oak Glen. Between them, in the wild San Gorgonio and San Jacinto Mountains, on the rolling hills of Temecula, we had pines and oaks that had lived for centuries. Along the riverbeds were cottonwoods and willows, and in the desert Joshua trees made their own eerie forests, and smoke trees rose from the sand. All my life, here in this place, we have had our own myths and legends and stories, but they were not heard very often outside in the world.

I live in a house three blocks from Riverside Community Hospital, where I was born, where my brothers, my ex-husband, and his siblings were born, and most of our friends and all of our children.

I have always lived here, except for my college years, and I have seen nearly every mile of land in the region which this new anthology calls "Inlandia." When I was a child and people from elsewhere asked adults about where we lived, I remember hearing again and again that we were an hour from the mountains, an hour from the desert, an hour from the ocean, and an hour from Los Angeles. And I always thought, when I was a child, But why would we want to leave?

We had everything, in my eyes. The endless forests of cultivation, the lush wildflowers of the desert in spring, the date groves and pine forests. Trout from mountain lakes, lemons and oranges and avocados all winter, and as children we didn't care when smog veiled the hills in the summer. We mined the foothills near our house for fool's gold and rose quartz, and then we lay panting in an orange grove, and swam in the swift waters of the canal, where grass waved on the bottom as though in a true stream.

In fact, I realized as I grew older, everyone wanted to come here, to the inland region. Everyone's parents had come from somewhere else. My own mother was from Switzerland; her parents had moved from their small valley to seek their fortunes. They did not find them in Ontario, Canada, or northern Florida, but then they saw the ultimate pictures of prosperity and success, the land of milk and honey as represented in decades past: the postcards of purpled, snow-covered mountains in the distance, and orange trees in the foreground, all golden in the sun.

That is truly what we saw, growing up here, all winter. It was paradise, though I have since learned that the rest of the world might not recognize it.

In elementary school and junior high, I found that nearly everyone's parents had immigrated here—from Louisiana and

Oklahoma and Mississippi, from Michoacan and Zacatecas and Guanajuato, from the Philippines and Germany and Japan. I had friends whose fathers were military men and whose mothers were immigrant brides from those countries. I had other friends whose fathers were military men and who'd returned to the South and vowed never to live in poverty and segregation again. All settled in Riverside, in San Bernardino, in Victorville—wherever there were military bases. And their children grew up in the Inland Empire—a new people. They played with the children of the Okies who'd broken down here, with my mother-in-law's people, who'd broken down in Calexico and whose sons became some of the first black Border Patrol agents.

I lived in a neighborhood called Okietown for the first three years of my life, and then my mother married my stepfather, who had also found his promised land here, having left New Brunswick, Canada. We moved to Riverside, and they have never left.

We ran freely as children, to the foothills and groves and river, and my parents, who loved this landscape with the passion of those raised in snow, took us camping everywhere. We knew every mile of Inlandia.

The dinosaurs of Cabazon, where people could eat hamburgers inside the head of a brontosaurus. The date palm groves in Mecca and Oasis and Indio, where even the names were exotic, and where I stood under the gray-green fronds arching above me, touching the etched trunks and the golden sprays of dates cascading overhead, and knew it was really a cathedral. The heat was so intense, and the cicadas' song filled my forehead, and the smell of water in the irrigation furrows was silver. On the way home, we got date shakes in Indio and watched the famous movie—*The Sex Life of the Date*.

I love every mile of my homeland. The fields of watermelon and cantaloupe in Blythe and Ripley, where my foster brothers and sisters came from. The savanna-like golden grasses in the Temecula Valley, with the oaks gathered like black clouds in the distance. The steep entrance of the Cajon Pass, where the mountains are purple in winter dusk and the wind is so fierce it will throw trucks like toys. The dunes outside Palm Springs and Whitewater, where the sand is white and soft as cake flour, and the smoke trees rise like ghosts in the distance. (My ex-husband once worked at a juvenile correction facility in Whitewater, and when Los Angeles boys tried to run away, he followed them in that desert, as they trudged with suitcases and radios through the creosote and rabbitbrush and hot sand, until they gave up in what they considered a particularly impersonal hell.)

I love the tiny communities that only we in this place know—Rubidoux, named for a pioneer of the area, and Belltown, where our cousins live near the Santa Ana River; Agua Mansa and La Placita, where New Mexicans came to grow grapes along that river and build adobe houses, marked now only by a cemetery and a few scattered homes; the old Cucamonga, where vineyards flourished and my parents bought wine; and Muscoy, on the outskirts of San Bernardino, where my brother liked to check out fighting roosters.

For twenty-five years I have written about this region and tried to infuse my work with love and desire and the fierceness we retain in these small places where people loved their own with the vehemence, the stubborn and suspicious and inventive qualities required to survive in this part of Southern California. It was a place where the land and sun and smog and violence and people could be forbidding, but the same land and sun and people offered survival and love and tungsten-hard loyalty to each other.

And for all these years, I have wanted to see my place represented in literature, in a wide-ranging collection of all the communities and voices and landscapes I've known.

Here it is.

The oranges, the Washington navel and Valencias I've tasted all my life, the ones my brother grew for many years, descendants of the tree which I drive past often and always nod to in obeisance. They are here, in John Jakes's excerpt and in the narratives by Harry Lawton and Mary Paik Lee of those Chinese and Korean men and women who harvested the fruit.

The legends of Tahquitz, the angry god whose stories I heard as a child when I was afraid to hike in his canyon above Palm Springs, and the stories of Mukat and his children, who lived in the desert. Malcolm Margolin's account of the expulsion of the Cupa people from Warner Springs, less known than the famous tale of Ramona, but sadder to me because I knew Gordon Johnson, a descendant of one of the women wailing as she left her home. Johnson's stories of humor and heartbreak on Pala, where his ancestors persevered, bring the story full circle.

The forbidding, alluring desert is here, in Erle Stanley Gardner's excerpt: "I went to sleep with the sand making little whispering noises that sounded more and more like words." I have heard so many times those whispers, in Cabazon and Palm Desert, and have been trapped in a truck while the raging winter sandstorms blasted the paint off the hood. Erle Stanley Gardner wrote in the inland area, sometimes at the Mission Inn, where Carrie Jacobs-Bond wrote her poem included here, and where I wrote parts of all my novels.

Sometimes I believe we have an advantage here in our land, because even the very words used to describe us are lovely: pomegranate and pyracantha, bougainvillea and jacaranda, granite and ghostly coyotes and eucalyptus. Even our smog makes the sunset vivid as dangerous passion.

The writers I read for inspiration as a young author are here. I always admired Laura Kalpakian's fictional St. Elmo, her creation of a place much like San Bernardino, and how, as the excerpt in this anthology shows, she knew the people here so well. Route 66 was a mythical place in our history, and no one wrote about it like John Steinbeck; not until I read *The Grapes of Wrath* did I understand the refusal of many of my elderly neighbors to get rid of a carburetor or radiator or even an old tire.

Recent statistics reveal, several years in a row, that the many disparate communities of my city, my region, my landscape—once fairly small in population—have been transformed into the fastest-growing counties in America. Hundreds of thousands of people, drawn by affordable housing, have left Los Angeles and Orange and San Diego Counties to move to this area.

The new voices in *Inlandia* represent the best of my hopes and dreams and literary desires, the eloquent renderings of how the old worlds and new have collided and melded in this place like no other. Alex Espinoza has made his native Colton into Agua Mansa, a tender and heartbreaking and hopeful place. The Riverside landscape of Michael David Egelin, the Highland of Keenan Norris, the Blythe of E. J. Jones, and the Salton Sea of Gayle Brandeis are all places I have always wanted to see in print, the mirages and neighborhoods and voices I missed before.

When I left Riverside to attend university in Los Angeles, I was already fully formed, stubborn and fierce and suspicious as my inland compatriots. As I'd expected, my universe was ridiculed. "You're from Riverside? The Inland Empire? What do you have out there? Cows? Oranges, right?"

To answer the people from Pasadena and Los Angeles and Orange County and San Francisco, I had many responses. My land has had the distinction of being the capital of many things in the past—arson, smog, urban sprawl, methamphetamine, biker gangs, and yes, citrus and dairy. We have always been a rural place where people grow things to make their fortunes, and sometimes they grew hamburgers and Hell's Angels, as in Eric Schlosser's examination of the MacDonald brothers and San Bernardino. M. F. K. Fisher gave up on growing anything but haunting memories. People grew desire for gold, they grew insane. I knew the Harada house, where a Japanese American woman grew courage.

Now many of the groves—walnuts and apricots and oranges—are gone. Now people in this region grow houses, and mortgages, and more and more children.

But in the past, sometimes people who came to inland Southern California grew nothing but false hope.

In college, as a seventeen-year-old freshman, I was assigned to read Joan Didion's essay "Some Dreamers of the Golden Dream." Her depictions of inland life were stunning and at the same time painful to me. "This is a story about love and death in the golden land," she begins, and describes what was to most people "an alien place . . . a harsher California . . . this ominous country." I had never read a phrase like "talismanic fruit," and I stayed up all night with my fingers turning the pages, knowing she was exactly who I wanted to be, that I wanted to write like that. But I had never seen anyone examine my own world, the Santa Ana winds, the lemon groves bordered with river-rock walls, and it was through those words that I now learned how others saw us: "the country of the teased hair and the Capris and the girls for whom all life's promise comes down to a waltz-length white wedding dress and the birth of a Kimberly or a Sherry or a Debbi and a Tijuana divorce and a return to hairdressers' school. Here is where the hot wind blows and the old ways do not seem relevant, where the divorce rate is double the national average and where one person in every thirty-eight lives in a trailer. Here is the last stop for all those who come from somewhere else, for all those who drifted away from the cold and the past and the old ways."

I lay awake all night, thinking of my friends and their parents. My future husband's parents, who fled Mississippi and Oklahoma but who'd brought their cooking and voices and ways with them. My neighbors, born in Japan and the Philippines and Germany, now married to white and black and Mexican American servicemen, whose children I had always known. My own mother, who had left the cold behind and whose husband left her amid a dust storm in Glen Avon with me at three and a new baby, when the dirt sifted under the windowsill and covered everything.

I went home the next day and tried to tell my mother about the piece, and about writing, and about how it made me feel. Didion had said, recalling one of our great scandals, "Here is where they are trying to find a new life style, trying to find it in the only places they know to look: the movies and the newspapers. The case of Lucille Marie Maxwell Miller is a tabloid monument to that new life style." My mother frowned and said, "Lucille Miller? Oh, your Aunt Beverly lived on her street. The one who killed her husband. Beverly always said that woman was capable of murder."

I didn't know what to feel then. I was one of those people Joan Didion knew everything about. I drove to Ontario, the neighborhood in the essay, where my father and his siblings had struggled to survive when their parents, who'd immigrated from Colorado, left them. To Fontana, where my grandmother worked at Kaiser, the now-closed steel plant which was our lifeline. To San Bernardino, where my mother had her first job. To Muscoy, a tiny place of dirt roads and clapboard houses where my stepfather had bought a one-room shack with no bathroom. His first property. I drove home to my neighborhood in Riverside, which made the places in Didion's piece look good by comparison.

I wanted to someday know the code of her elegance and precision and genius, the prose I admired so much, but I wanted to read about my dreamers in their smog-shrouded pale asphalt streets, in their orange groves where the white blossoms fell around us like stars when the sun was going down, in their canyons where the gods of the mountains, like Tahquitz, waited for revenge, in their silver-hot vineyards and the date groves of Mecca where dark men cut grapes and put paper bags around the date clusters.

And now it is here. Inlandia.

[2006]

PREFACE

from *Deep Oakland*

Andrew Alden

People are naturally drawn to natural things. Given a chance, they're ready to listen to birds, to reckon trees, to attend to all kinds of living creatures. Many are called by the clouds and winds and stars. Fewer are drawn downward: listeners to landscape, reckoners of rocks. Nevertheless, we're all shaped by the geological as well as biological forces of the Earth.

Every city sits where it does for geological reasons, which may include the availability of underground and surface water, ready access to natural sources of wealth, terrain suitable for rail lines and highways, navigable rivers and ports for shipping, amenable climate and exceptional scenery.

Regarding a city in terms of its geology—seeing it from the ground down—is not the usual way. Until well into the twentieth century, geologists weren't consulted before cities were founded. But sooner or later, growing cities hit limits imposed by their geology, and how they respond affects whether they thrive or founder. The longer I explore Oakland, the more I see how its unusually rich geological setting steered its history and constrains its prospects.

Beyond Oakland's value as a case study, if you're here, you're in the midst of an underappreciated teaching tool, a textbook for a wide range of geological concepts. It has features its managers might better heed and others its residents might treasure.

When I say the word *geology*, most people think I mean rocks, but it's about much more: the work of streams, the formation and movements of sediment, the rise and fall of mountains, the changes of living things as age succeeds age. By geology I really mean how the Earth works—how *planets* work. Geology is the study of worlds made of rocks. The Earth is active, geologically alive, and every place on it takes part. Geology opens one's eyes to a secret world that lies beneath and all around us. Knowing some geology is like having a key to the house that opens up a vast extra room. Here I hope to introduce the ways of Earth to you.

Why does Oakland geology matter? Every town and city has its own geological setting. Oakland is a special city that owes its origin and character to a remarkable setting, making it not just a beautiful place but a good one to learn the basics of geology. The Oakland Hills tempt me every day to visit them, and when I do they dazzle me with views as well as rocks. By my estimate, Oakland has more kinds of rock—red, white, blue, and green—than any other city in America. That's my idea of a tourist attraction. Once acquainted with the subject, anyone can turn to their own hometown and see it with new eyes. Turning on one's geologist eyes is something like snorkeling: the surface world with all its sound and motion drops away, and an entirely different world swims into view.

Oakland has always been praised as a beautiful place, its range of high hills descending in a wave to a wide coastal plain. But since the day the original inhabitants, the Ohlones, were joined by outsiders in 1770, this place has differed with each set of eyes that beheld it. The Americans who founded the city exploited the natural resources of its core territory from the start: timber, firewood, water, soil. As Oakland grew, they found more natural assets in the surroundings to turn into money: clay, stone, gravel, seafood, sulfur. Each of these resources has a connection with our distinctive geology. Each in its turn was consumed, gratefully but imprudently, until it was exhausted or made uneconomical by sources in more distant places. The local resources that survive—the landscape, the views, the light, the air—are inexhaustible and precious, and these too have their place in the geologist's view of Oakland.

It's a truism among people who work on sustainability that our actions should consider the effects on the seventh generation to come. Oakland was founded in 1852, and for me that's close enough to seven generations ago. Therefore it's time to consider the consequences of the city's first decisions as we look seven generations ahead.

Oakland has gone through four epochs of human history, which I define here in strictly local rather than regional or national terms. The Ohlone period, named for the tribal peoples who were the first to belong to this land, began late during the last ice age and ended in approximately 1800. The Spanish period began locally with the forced removal of the Ohlones, shortly after the first expeditions from New Spain in the late 1700s. The Mexican period began with independence from Spain in 1821. For convenience, I refer to US citizens and residents as "Americans." The American period began in 1850 and continues to the date of this writing. Oakland is an American city, but it contains significant populations representing all three previous periods that make up part of our special sauce.

The history of California is marked with violent acts. They're important to recognize. Briefly put, the Spanish crown basically enslaved the local tribes and separated them from their land under the auspices of the Catholic church. The government of Mexico then dispersed their land to private hands, spawning a short-lived rural aristocracy of Mexican ranchers whose free-range livestock had it better than the remnant tribespeople who worked for them unpaid. The United States seized it all as a war prize, turned the best parts into gold and neglected whatever didn't measure up to that standard. The original peoples of California were subjected to actions, both legal and extralegal, that constituted genocide. In Oakland, similar actors at the local level carried out similar acts, especially within the flexible bounds of nineteenth-century governance and justice.

The story of California rests on white entitlement, a virus from colonialist Europe that, with each expansionist wave westward, mixed genes with capitalist entitlement. Every age has its conquerors and its mercenaries. Just as the three squatters who founded Oakland made their initial underhanded move under a pretext that the American takeover of 1848 erased all previous land titles, so geologists—my people—were the paid servants of expansionism in exploiting public lands, erasing their native overseers' claims, for private profit and national glory. Geologists armed with academic credentials, traditionally persons male and white, participated in a centuries-long wave of exploration that began in the 1830s with the first state geological surveys and swept west with the flag and telegraph and railroad, then overseas with the American empire. They are my scientific ancestors. It was a glorious age of scientific progress, borne on the horses of crushing imperial conquest.

Oakland was founded and built by men of that imperium, self-assured men, ruthless by upbringing, men who sought an advanced, idealized life for themselves worthy of the particular kinds of natural wealth and beauty they perceived. Among geologists in the generation now gone, I used to see a sort of lingering cowboy privilege, a pride that I think was inherited from those days in the vanguard, roaming and plundering the western frontier. We were on the winners' side of imperialism.

Yet our science is also sensually rich and intellectually sublime. I think that by the last chapter this will be plain. The geologist looks for principles in the swarm of particularities that make up landscapes and regions. The point of finding the scientific laws of rocks and landscapes is to apply them, using those laws to gain insight into every place on Earth, each in its own particularity. The aim of geology is to help us awaken tomorrow and know our home ground afresh. The fact that geologists can have jobs of mundane routine and careers of applied expertise does not erase their dream.

Readers who aren't geologists may not notice that I use geological terms that look like everyday words. *Clay*, *silt*, *sand* and *gravel* are size classes of sediment particles, but in everyday terms clay is creamy, silt looks smooth but chews gritty (yes, we taste rocks), sand is grainy (from barely visible to millet size) and gravel is larger than pea size. *Mud* is another of these terms; geologists use it to mean a mixture of clay and silt.

Readers who are geologists may notice that I use some geological terms in this book without the rigor they might prefer. For instance, I refer to the segments of the geologic time scale as "periods," although working geologists are particular about using the correct time rank in the nested series that consists of ages, epochs, periods, eras and eons. To them I say: believe me, as someone who's made a living enforcing our terminology, it was hard to relax.

I speak in this book as a member of the geological community, where I have spent my working life since college in a supporting role. When I speak of the attitudes and attributes of "my tribe," I reflect only my own opinions based on long experience and do not speak for anyone else. Neither do I wish to pretend that my community is truly tribal.

Before I start, a few orienting notes. The East Bay is a belt of territory, coastal flats in front of a range of high hills, that is generally aligned north–south with a distinct leftward lean of about 32 degrees. People here ignore that lean when they talk about directions—they go north to Richmond and south to Fremont. But Oakland lies on a wider lump of East Bay land that sticks out into San Francisco Bay, such that downtown is decidedly west of the southern end of the city. Southern Oakland has been called East Oakland since the early days. The traditional division between East Oakland and the rest of Oakland is at Lake Merritt, an arm of the Bay that intrudes deep into the coastal plain.

Much of Oakland is covered by a system of numbered streets, and new residents quickly learn that the Avenues, 1st through 109th, are in East Oakland running perpendicular to the coast, while the Streets, 2nd through 66th, lie west of Lake Merritt and run parallel to the shore. (East 8th through East 34th Streets extend the scheme partway into East Oakland.)

Oakland shares California's Mediterranean climate: a seasonal cycle, unique in the United States, of rainless summers and cool, wet winters. Our landscape turns gold in summer as the grasses die back, then green with the late fall rains. Most native trees, but not all, are evergreen species that never shed all their leaves. Snow in Oakland is rare enough to make the evening news; so is heat above body temperature.

My experience of Oakland, my city for over thirty years, is one of growing intimacy with its unusual geological complexity. I have walked every block of its streets, inspected all of its stairways and trails, and done a fair amount of off-trail bushwhacking. Oakland is a mosaic of long-gone lands—lost worlds—some of which have traveled great distances, over great stretches of time, to spend time with us. Its parts have been gathered and sculpted, by the aimless forces that operate the Earth, and stitched into a landscape rich in personality. Geologic Oakland is the core of my home and the navel of the world.

Every geologist has what might be called a natal landscape: the kind of country they lived in as a child, the landscape they imprinted on. The Bay Area's hills and peaks are the first mountains I ever saw. As with my father before me, my natal landscape is the Bay Area; but also like him I have deep family roots in the Northeast and spent important parts of my life there. Landscape was my childhood fascination, and it still is. I was raised on both the East and West Coasts, but not until my geology degree sank in did I see and understand their profound differences. The East Coast, in plate-tectonic terms, is a passive continental margin: for over one hundred million years, since the Atlantic Ocean opened up, it has stayed quiet long enough for erosion to do its work, keeping the coastal plains flat and the mountains fairly low. The West Coast is an active margin, where tectonic forces have cut and rearranged the Earth's crust in dramatic fashion and where earthquakes remind us it's still on the move. Thus this book begins with the Hayward Fault and ends with the Oakland Hills, which owe their existence to it. Every California city has a view of mountains, but our hills are special, as the Ohlones still living among us have always known. Come see.

[2023]

INTRODUCTION
(abridged)
from *Alice*
Ivy Anderson and **Devon Angus**

On January 25, 1917, more than two hundred prostitutes gathered inside a San Francisco church and staged what might have been the first sex workers' rights protest in modern history. Since the gold rush of 1849, prostitutes in San Francisco had plied their trade openly, but by 1917, the wave of Progressive-era reforms that swept the nation had reached the shores of the Paris of the West, and San Francisco's red-light district came under the scrutiny of moral reformers. While these self-appointed guardians of decency saw the closure of the brothels as a means to not only purify society of sin but also protect the sex workers themselves, many of the prostitutes saw it as a mass eviction. With few options left to them, hundreds of the women stormed the church of one of the city's most virulent anti-vice reformers, the Reverend Paul Smith, and demanded that he answer their cry: "You want . . . the city cleaned up . . . but where do you want the women to go?"

It would be generations before the concept of a sex workers' rights movement existed in any official form (COYOTE, which stands for Call Off Your Old Tired Ethics, was founded in California in 1973 and is considered the first sex workers' rights organization), but in 1917, two madams named Reggie Gamble and Maude Spencer organized a political demonstration and demanded their voices be heard. Spencer and Gamble enlisted the help of their friend Fremont Older, the editor of the *San Francisco Bulletin*, who in 1913 had earned their trust by publishing "A Voice from the Underworld," the serialized memoir of a prostitute going by the name "Alice Smith." The publication sparked public reaction, and the paper also published 291 letters sent to the *Bulletin* by sex workers and others. We must of course question the historical authenticity of the narrative and accompanying letters—the *Bulletin* was notoriously sensationalistic, and nationwide media was rife with dubious "true" accounts of prostitution and white slavery—and we must even go so far as to ask whether or not "Alice Smith" was a real person. And yet regardless, Alice Smith certainly existed for the women who followed "A Voice from the Underworld" in 1913 and marched with Gamble and Spencer four years later. The madams in fact approached Fremont Older to help them organize local prostitutes for their march because it was his publication of Alice Smith's narrative that provided a public platform from which echoed the stories of these women who had long been silenced.

The marginalization of sex workers' voices is a critical issue that still shapes debates about sex work today. On August 11, 2015, Amnesty International adopted a policy calling for the worldwide decriminalization of consensual sex work. "As a global human rights organization . . . it is right and fitting that we should look at one of the most disadvantaged groups of people in the world, often forced to live outside the law and denied their most basic human rights: sex workers," wrote the organization's policy advisor several days later. Certain prominent anti-trafficking organizations argued against the policy, claiming that decriminalization would allow vicious pimps, johns, and brothel owners to exploit innocent victims of the sex trade without fear of legal recourse. The debate ran in international newspapers for weeks, and a letter—penned by the Coalition Against Trafficking Women—opposing AI's policy drew attention after it was signed by a number of Hollywood celebrities, including actors Kate Winslet, Meryl Streep, and Lena Dunham. Dozens of editorials filled the pages of the *New York Times*, the *Guardian*, and the *Washington Post*, highlighting the illustrious signatures backing the opposition. On the other side, journalist and sex worker Molly Smith (a pseudonym) openly criticized these news sources for failing to consult actual sex workers on the topic, in effect putting the opinions of multimillionaire actors at the center of the argument. "If this criminalization is so beneficial for us," wrote Smith, a sex worker in Europe, "it's hard to imagine why the organizations campaigning for it are unable to find and quote even one sex worker in the world in support of it. . . . We are hopeful that the quieter voices of sex workers remain audible next to those of Hollywood stars."

What Molly Smith and many other contemporary sex workers are demanding is the same request that Alice Smith and the letter writers to the *Bulletin* insisted upon in 1913: to be heard. As politicians, clergymen, and clubwomen across the state of California debated an anti-vice law that would finally close California's brothels, the prostitutes whose lives would inevitably be changed by this law went largely ignored. In publishing Alice Smith's memoir and the accompanying letters, *Bulletin* editor Fremont Older was undoubtedly capitalizing on the national obsession with prostitution in order to sell papers and increase circulation, but, taking into consideration Older's political and philosophical transformation during the years leading up to the publication of "A Voice from the Underworld," one can argue that he was also taking a stance: one that said everyone deserved a chance to be heard, no matter how "criminal" or how outside of proper society one was.

Nevertheless, we must always take the accuracy of "A Voice from the Underworld" with a grain of salt, as we must with all memoirs and all popular media. But whether it is read as a story of one woman's life or as a revealing portrait of the role and attitudes of the media in Progressive-era San Francisco, this narrative has great value as a direct link between the shantytown brothels of gold rush San Francisco and the potent sex workers' rights movement today.

Despite questions surrounding Alice's true identity, her narrative has an air of authenticity that certainly rang true with the hundreds of other prostitutes and working-class women who read her story. Although Alice herself doesn't appear to advocate for any specific political measures, her narrative is inherently political, as it reveals pointed instances of gender discrimination and economic injustice that shaped the course of her life, and the lives of others like her. That said, the tale does not come across as having a specific agenda, and Alice refrains from summing up her personal views on prostitution until the very end of her narrative. Instead, she focuses on detailing her life as she moves through many jobs and locales across the country.

Beginning as a Midwestern farm girl, Alice moves west to California and spends time variously as a laundry worker in Oakland, a waitress in a small mining town, a "free lance" sex worker, a brothel girl, and a madam. For a time, Alice moves in and out of the world of prostitution, holding down other low-paying jobs to supplement her earnings. Alice's story deals with a number of shockingly revealing topics, including abortion, police abuse, and brothel life, and it does so in a way that is both informative and humanizing. The characters in Alice's story are not caricatures; the women she works alongside are not portrayed as victims to be pitied or beasts to be reviled. Throughout the narrative, we witness Alice's own accounting of the many circumstances in her life that led her to prostitution; contrary to what other members of society had claimed on both sides of the debate over the Red Light Abatement Act, she is neither a woman enslaved nor an entirely free agent.

News from Native California

Vol. 1, No. 1 March/April 1987 $3.00

A Yurok Story

Harry Roberts

NEWS • FROM NATIVE CALIFORNIA

Vol. 1 No. 4 September/November 1987 $3.00

Acorns: *Historical Uses, Modern Preparation, Recipes*

Regional Museums: *An Indian Perspective*

Point Arena Roundhouse

- Calendar
- Archaeology
- Art
- Education
- And more

News from NATIVE CALIFORNIA

INDIANS IN OVERALLS—PIT RIVER COUNTRY IN THE 1920S AND TODAY • THE RETURN OF THE HUNDRED-AND-ELEVENS TO NORTHWEST CALIFORNIA • REBURIAL VERSES • CHAW'SE BIG TIME • THE NEW FEDERAL ACKNOWLEDGEMENT BILL • INDIAN MUSEUMS • ART • BOOKS • EDUCATION • LANGUAGE • DR. COYOTE SPEAKS

News from NATIVE CALIFORNIA

AN INSIDE VIEW OF THE CALIFORNIA INDIAN WORLD

Selected covers of *News from Native California* magazine, 1987–present

Selected covers of *News from Native California* magazine, 1987–present

NEWS
from NATIVE CALIFORNIA
VOL 33 / ISSUE 4
Summer 2020
ACJACHEMEN
qayáawi
'omáay
$5.95

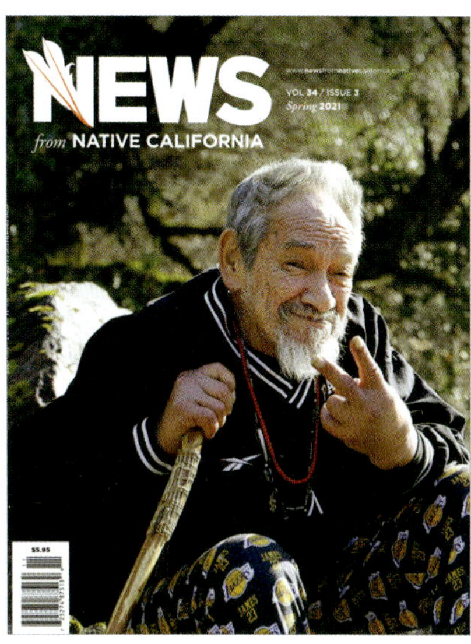
NEWS
from NATIVE CALIFORNIA
www.newsfromnativecalifornia.com
VOL 34 / ISSUE 3
Spring 2021
$5.95

NEWS
from NATIVE CALIFORNIA
www.newsfromnativecalifornia.com
VOL 36 / ISSUE 3
Spring 2023
$5.95

NEWS
from NATIVE CALIFORNIA
www.newsfromnativecalifornia.com
VOL 37 / ISSUE 1
Fall 2023
$5.95

Photos from *Chími Nu'am* by Sara Calvosa Olson, 2023

Illustrations by Lyn Risling, from *A Is for Acorn* by Analisa Tripp, 2015

B
basket

Illustrations by Carly Lake, from *Waa'aka'* by Cindi M. Alvitre, 2020

Last was Waa'aka', sleek and beautiful.
Her white feathers glowed like pearls in sand,
and she became Wiyot's favorite.

Things You Can Do with Your Chart for Calculating Quantum of Indian Blood

Do you have extra BIA Blood Quantum charts left over from those heady days of proving up? Don't just waste them; use every part! Here are some ideas to get you started:

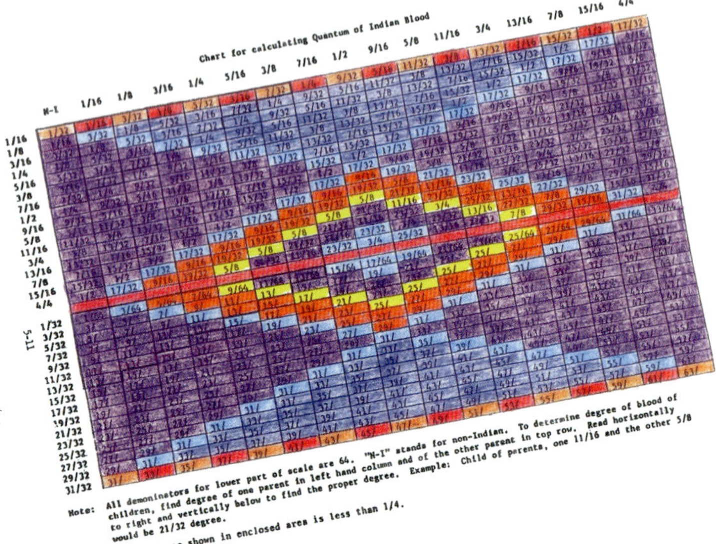

Fig. 1. "Wannabe Creations." Make up a beautiful, totally fake "Indian" design that means absolutely nothing to any North or South American tribe. Sell it for a lot of money. Tell everyone you're from the Wha-Naw-Bee Tribe.

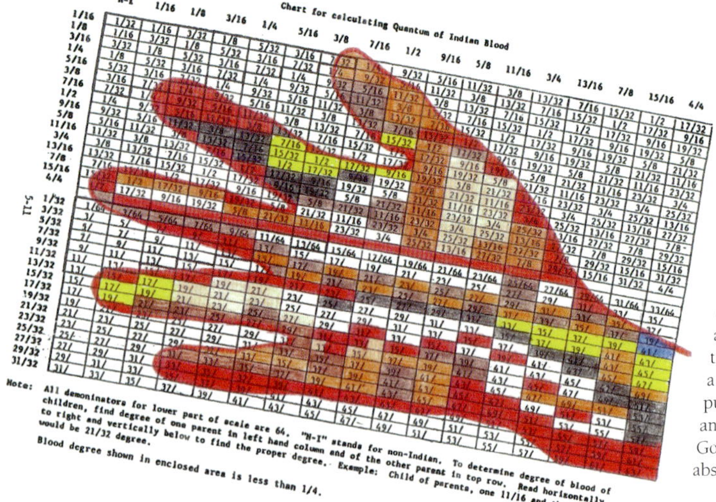

Fig. 2. "Hand of God." What if God was one of us? What would His blood quantum be? Should He be enrolled in a federally recognized tribe? Can it have a casino? Go ahead, put your hand down and trace it; you're God's proxy in His absence.

Images from *Bad Indians* by Deborah A. Miranda, 2013

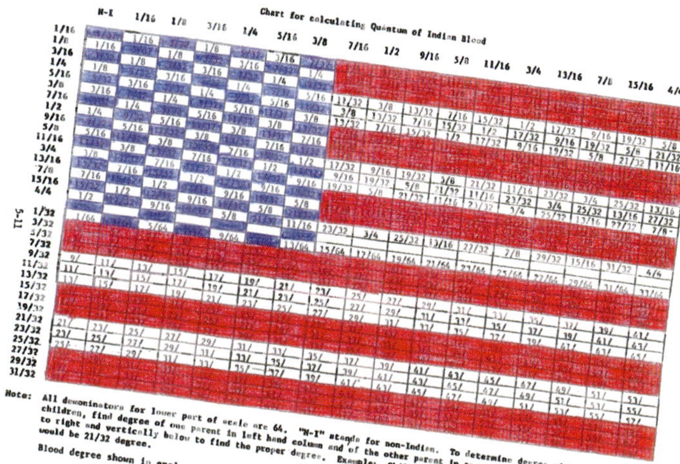

Fig. 3. "Patriotism Percentages." Why is blood quantum so important to the US government? It must be a measure of Indian patriotism. Create a flag that expresses your patriotism. Whatever you do, be respectful of another's nation's symbols.

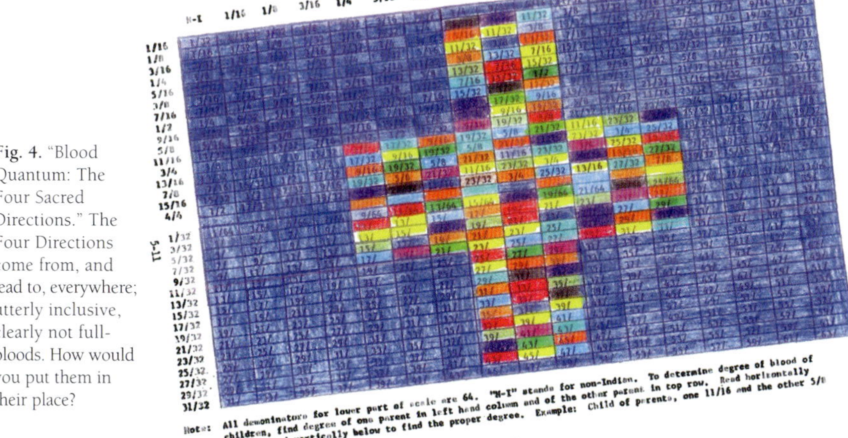

Fig. 4. "Blood Quantum: The Four Sacred Directions." The Four Directions come from, and lead to, everywhere; utterly inclusive, clearly not full-bloods. How would you put them in their place?

"Cousin Fred, Truckee, 1982" (left) and "Hunge Ka Pu, Chaw'se, 1995" (right) from *She Sang Me a Good Luck Song* by Dugan Aguilar, edited by Theresa Harlan, 2015

Photo from *The Mission* by Dick Evans, 2017

Photo from *San Francisco's Chinatown* by Dick Evans, 2020

Logo designed by Archie Ferguson for Heyday's 50th anniversary, 2024

Over the course of the publication of "A Voice from the Underworld," the *Bulletin* received more than four thousand letters in response, many of which came from other prostitutes inspired to tell their own stories. In some ways, it is the publication of these letters that makes "A Voice from the Underworld" a truly remarkable document. For two months, readers of the *Bulletin* were exposed to narratives detailing the lives, hopes, fears, needs, and desires of a class of women whose voices had previously been largely ignored by reformers and anti-vice activists whose overall aim was to close the brothels and shuffle the prostitutes into settlement homes and employment agencies. These letters are as diverse as they are impassioned. Some express feelings of entrapment and hopelessness, while some beg for assistance; others lambast the reformers for their prejudice and demand the dignity to live without interference. Some call for the development of a workers' state; others proclaim masculine sexuality to be the root of all evil. Some were raped or molested before entering prostitution, some were coerced by pimps, and many others entered "the life" of their own volition. Some of the letters are not from prostitutes but working-class women who felt they may, too, be on the road to sex work. Other letters were written by johns and the husbands of prostitutes, by social scientists, philosophers, novelists, and clergymen, and by politicians both local and far-flung. The varied voices of those published in the pages of the *Bulletin* can be read as a sort of time capsule, a representation of the many arguments placed on the table in California in 1913 in response to one question: What is to be done about the prostitution problem?

Just months after the sex worker march and closure of the Barbary Coast, the United States entered World War I. In response, social purity became wrapped up with national security, as reformers feared venereal disease spread by prostitutes would weaken the country's military. A new national social-purity law demanded the arrest of any prostitute found within five miles of an army base, and since essentially the whole of San Francisco fell within five miles of the Presidio, a rash of arrests followed. Today, the pictures of these women, and some men, can be seen lining numerous pages in "Sex Crimes and Muzzlers," a police mug book from 1918 now held in the archives of the San Francisco Main Library's History Center.

As historian Neil Larry Shumsky has noted, the Progressive era failed to eradicate prostitution; it merely scattered it. While the more dangerous industry of streetwalking became much more common, brothels continued to operate illegally in San Francisco and elsewhere. In one of the most dramatic chapters of Alice's narrative, she describes her oppressive fear of streetwalking, and the dangers associated with it, after hearing of the experiences of a friend who had worked the streets in Chicago. Since the 1917 closure of the Barbary Coast and the quasi-legal brothel system, San Francisco's sex workers have had to navigate the criminal underworld through a combination of their own self-organized networks; finding work on the streets and in underground brothels, bars, strip clubs, nightclubs, bathhouses, and massage parlors; and, more and more with the development of the Internet, online. Anti-vice campaigns in San Francisco have likewise continued to flourish and fade periodically based on instances of local and national backlashes against sex work.

While the sixties brought "free love" to the tip of the nation's tongue, a series of police backlashes at San Francisco's Compton Cafeteria and New York's Stonewall Inn simultaneously ignited the nation's gay rights and sex worker rights movements. This broadening of the national dialogue about sex coincides with what is considered to be the beginnings of the contemporary sex worker rights movement. While the 1960s caused a tidal wave of discussion, revolution, and reform about the critical issue of sex worker rights that is, if anything, increasing in momentum today, the forgotten history of the 1917 Prostitute March on the Reverend Paul Smith's Central Methodist Church and the publication of the story of Alice Smith by a sympathetic San Francisco newspaper are necessary links to the history of this continuing movement. In 1913, readers of the *San Francisco Bulletin* were discussing feminism, economic justice, labor rights, prison reform, and the inherent dignity of sex workers as human beings. Alice's story and the accompanying letters serve as a mark of how far we as a society have come—and how far we have left to go.

[2016]

SPEAKEASY TACOS

from *LAtitudes*

Michael Jaime-Becerra

Your family makes it all by hand. The meat. Beans and rice, nopales, and potato salad. A large platter of freshly cut fruit. Garnishes of finely minced white onions and cilantro and two kinds of salsa, red and green. One spiced enough to thrill the palate. One for those that prefer to be set aflame, because it is better to make your clients sweat and suffer than to overhear veiled insults about the salsa being tasty, but not hot.

Including your mother, Maria, there are four of you. You may be Miriam, the oldest child, now in your twenties. Your high-school years would have been spent either making tacos or keeping an eye on your brothers, but now you have a chair in an upscale hair salon and you plan on owning your own shop one day. Or you are Samuel, just old enough to buy beer, but already showing the talent and sensibility of a chef on the way to greatness. You were hired at Pollo Loco to wipe down tables and your years of making tacos vaulted you to unofficial Grill Master in a week. Now the goal is to be a nurse. To have solid, stable, official work. Or you are Eli, the youngest. The one who gets to go to college, to study United States history and try out accounting because it seems like it would be interesting and useful.

For three hours of catered taco service at a Saturday party, the preparation begins the Wednesday before. While you're cutting hair or tending to convalescents or studying, your mother is beating other taqueros to the best produce when local markets post their weekly specials. With the meat, she insists that the beef for her carne asada be shredded by the wholesale butchers' knives because it is damaged when they do it with the machine. Purchased in El Monte, it's the best any of you have ever found, the contents of the ten-pound bags tender and raw, blood pooling at the corners. Her pork adobada and her chicken come from a second wholesaler in Azusa. He's from Jalisco as well. Not the same pueblo as your family, but close enough that his seasoning is correct and trustworthy, the chicken tinged the yellow of saffron, the chunks of pork a deep orange that will become the color of charred brick as you tend to it in the pan. When beef tongue is requested, your mother will poach it in a broth of onion and garlic. In the morning, one of you will peel the rough outer layer, then dice the rich inner meat into tiny, succulent cubes to later be simmered in their own fat.

The prep work continues on Friday. In South El Monte, your mother picks lemons from her cousin's tree, and that night, instead of going out, you watch *Qué bonito amor* together, peeling and chopping into the early hours of Saturday. After a few hours' rest, you start again. Your hands become pruned because they're constantly wet—from bloody meat, from rinsing radishes, and dozens of white onions releasing musky milk. You wash and rewash the same knife and cutting board. You work the knife until it seems the top of the blade is slicing your index finger. A quick double-check to make sure you're holding the blade with the sharp side down.

Sweating constantly and eating as you go. No stopping for breakfast or lunch because time is passing and you're expected to serve a hundred hungry people in a few hours. Sampling along the way, carne asada scooped from the pan, salsa spooned out of the blender jar, pineapple plucked from the cutting board. Eat something now, your mother reminds you. There won't be time to eat later.

The stove is on the entire time, the same four gas burners as any household stove, but on this one, only two still work. Three of the four knobs are gone, a remaining white plastic stem melted like a used birthday candle. The large pans atop it are blackened and a little misshapen from countless hours of simmering meat. The pots' plastic handles are cracked or missing.

Stirring, keeping things in motion because whatever isn't moving is absorbing heat immediately and might soon burn. In the minute it takes to transfer rice from the pot to the chafing dish, the chafing dish will get hot enough to scorch your hand, pain then pulsing under cool water. A rookie mistake. For the next two weeks, your fingerprints will have the smooth, warped texture of Silly Putty.

Maria has made airplane parts in one El Monte factory and has assembled trophies in another. To clean offices in downtown Los Angeles high-rises, she had to learn how to drive, doing so in a car so questionable that the steering wheel popped off during the test drive. Thereafter, she'd stick to the first lane of the 10 freeway until she reached the Alameda exit. Before that, she sold popsicles at the Edward's Drive-In swap meet in Arcadia, her first job in the US, one that made her cry at night from the shame of being recognized by others from home. Remembering her as a proud, willful young woman, they asked, "¿Que haces aquí? ¿Por qué haces esto?"

What are you doing here?

Why are you doing this?

Thirty-some years later and she is still willful, still proud, though these aspects of her personality are now applied to the things that matter most: her three children and her taco business.

The business became "The Business" nearly a decade ago in the emergency room at Queen of the Valley Hospital, on the evening when her husband died. Prior to this, Maria and her husband would sometimes make tacos on the weekends in the backyards of relatives and family friends. It had been extra money, supplementary to his work as a gardener and her time in the factories. Miriam was seventeen then. Samuel was thirteen. Eli, twelve. In the plain white room, where the doctor said he had done everything he could, that the heart attack was just too much, the moment was a whirlwind of shock, grief, and panic about what to do next.

There was also the understanding that God had to take him. Miriam remembers a sense of peace accompanying this thought. Responsibility settling in. Certainty that they would eventually be fine.

Tacos then become the means to survive. How the mortgage gets paid. How the utilities stay on. Literally putting food on their table. Without any licenses, permits, or written contracts. No Yelp reviews and no requests to friend them on Facebook. Just business cards with two phone numbers, one for Spanish-speaking clients and one for those that only know English. Those who have this card have probably been at a party Maria's family catered, because this is the main way they're distributed. But word of mouth is fluid, and with Maria's food, the word is good. Her tacos are the sort that are remembered. *She* is remembered.

When she is not working the business, she is searching out cardboard and scrap metal, and on trash nights, she goes through a regular route of recycling bins. She keeps busy not just for the extra income, but because when she stops moving, her body is wracked with mysterious pain. Her hands now shake so uncontrollably that she has trouble serving tacos. Some regular clients have promised her a cure from Mexico, medicine purportedly blessed by the Pope, and when she falls asleep, her children witness her exhaustion and wonder about Parkinson's. Despite all this, Maria will still say that the taco business is greatest job she's ever had. It allows her to meet people from all walks of life, to be at a different party every week. But the very best part about the business is that it has kept her children with her. It has ensured that they remain together.

For one event, it's relentless heat all the way to Lancaster. In their father's truck, named "Guapa" by its original owners, now dented and scratched, flaking blue paint, something always needing to be fixed. Now the temperature gauge is creeping up. The event is at a retirement home, and when they arrive, radiator steam gushes from the hood.

The business grows to the point that they are often booked for two parties on the same day, with half the calls coming from clients in increasingly higher tax brackets. While Guapa isn't out of place on the eastern side of Los Angeles, she might not seem presentable to an NBC producer or a trust-fund kid or a family that spent thirty-thousand dollars to celebrate their daughter turning sixteen.

Miriam stretches her credit to its limit on a new truck, a V-8 engine to haul all the equipment and an extra cab to fit the family. Still at the Toyota dealership, the negotiations over, the loan papers signed in the sales manager's office. Since she's given him some business, why not return the favor? Two weeks later, she's back, the grill set up beside the service bays. Tacos for fifty: car techs, salesmen, the girls who answer the phones.

The business is torn between two different philosophies:

Maria accommodates her clients as fully as possible. If she's told that there are still people coming at the end of her three contracted hours, she'll wait for the latecomers at no extra charge. Fifteen minutes. Thirty minutes. An hour. The extra time doesn't matter because it lets her become part of the party. She'll gather everyone around the cake to sing "Las mañanitas" or "Happy Birthday." If there's dancing to be done, she'll get it started. Pour her a shot of Patrón and she'll cheer loudest during the toast. Her spirit is infectious, and it is genuine, for these are not just clients to her. Maria considers those who book her for recurring annual or semiannual parties as family. These clients often call her "Tía Maria" and their children are encouraged to say hello and hug her as if she were a blood relative. Sometimes these hugs seem awkward, the child's embrace tentative and reluctant. Sometimes the hugs are real because Maria is kindly remembered from the last time as "la señora de los tacos."

Besides the extra time, these are the people who also get a tray of potato salad and an overloaded fruit platter they didn't specify in their order. They might also get an added portion of lengua or fifteen pounds of carne asada instead of ten, the extra meat packed in one of the family's clear Tupperware containers that Samuel and Eli are reminded and reminded and reminded not to forget.

Maria sees these extras both as gifts to her regular clients for their loyalty and as investments in the business's future. She believes a potential new client will recall being poolside or before an inflatable jumper, in their hand an empty Styrofoam plate smeared with the last swirls of orange grease and salsa, their mouth pleasantly smoldering. Their appetite called for more and their body didn't have room for another bite. This person won't know that their satisfaction is the same satisfaction Maria and her children get from having seen their food enjoyed.

Maria's children know that each of those extras cuts into the profit margin. At $4.99 per pound, the two beef tongues for an extra chafing dish of lengua cost nearly fifty dollars, and that's without the additional garlic, onions, and seasonings to prepare them, the cooking time, and the time needed for peeling and cubing them the following morning. It all might be used for something else. Like a new stove or a professional-grade onion cutter. At the end of the night, Maria's boys can wait another ten or twenty minutes if the party hosts were generally respectful and paid what they owe. But, unlike their mother, Samuel and Eli believe that when the three hours are up, the three hours are up. Part of this is the fact that it is Saturday night. They both have girlfriends waiting for them and their phones buzz with text messages.

But their thinking is also rooted in confidence. Samuel and Eli have been doing this work, weekend after weekend, since they were in junior high. Eli knows that if you're calling him, you've probably had their tacos and you know they are very, very good. If you try to talk down the price he quotes you, he will feel mildly insulted because he knows eight dollars per person is more or less what other people charge. He'll work with you, removing extras until he hits a number you like. But if you live outside a ten-mile radius, he'll also charge you a fifty-dollar transportation fee to cover the cost of extra gas.

You are up in Silver Lake, up a narrow street, both sides lined with cars. Just enough room for the truck to approach the two-story glass-wall experiment attached to the hillside. Up concrete steps, a geometric hike past ripening grapefruit and kumquats, to the patio, the lighter of the two grill pans, a seventy-pound slab of stainless steel, hoisted by your brother. The grill stand is next, a two-person task guided by someone on the other end, you backing up and being careful not to scratch the silver Jaguar parked at the base of the steps, lifting, angling your way. Next is a second, smaller and circular grill for today's requested vegetarian preparation of grilled mushrooms, multicolored bell peppers, and onions.

Up with the propane tanks and a cooler the size of a coffin for anything perishable.

Most times the event is a birthday party, and today is no different. Today a father turns eighty, the milestone used to reunite three generations. T-shirts for the occasion sported by family from all over California. Nashville also represented. Munich, too. Talk of how cousins are related. Grandmothers the children never got to meet. The mandatory trip to Disneyland.

A quick connection to the propane tank under the grill stand, followed by three flicks from a long-stemmed lighter, and then the grill begins radiating unceasing heat at four-hundred degrees. There are four different kinds of tacos this afternoon. Rice and beans in the chafing trays beside the grill pan, a separate table with the potato salad, nopales, and fruit. The two kinds of salsa and a tray of freshly roasted jalapeños. The line moves quickly, forty-some curious and hungry people. Orders for one of each taco, absolutely to beans and rice because this is better than anything they've had in Tennessee, because there's absolutely no Mexican food in Germany. The men ask if the jalapeños are hot, then goad one another to try them. You suggest that two be taken in case they're not lucky with the first one.

Your family has worked parties at this home for nearly a decade. These clients, a husband and wife, know your family. They ask how your mother's doing. They knew your father. When they found out that he'd died, they took up a tip collection that amounted to over five hundred dollars. As the years went by, their friends began to hire you. Their friends' friends too. Each of them in parts of LA you'd never been to before. And so this husband and wife have become two of the business's most important clients, meaning that with them you adhere to your mother's philosophy of giving out extras for free. After a full shift at the hair salon the day before, your sister worked until three, peeling, blanching, and chopping the nopales, nopales that go untouched—partly because the tacos rule the evening and partly because this clientele doesn't really have the appetite or appreciation for a salad of minced cactus paddles.

The grill is cleared to make way for a slide show, and you remove the other equipment and supplies with the same sort of hurry you had when carrying them up. There is plenty of remaining food—food for days, as the host notes with resignation. People did come back for seconds, a few for thirds, and still the meat is piled high in the chafing dishes. Emptied, packaged up, and set next to the other side dishes with the inescapable sense that much of it will eventually be in trash. Even as you prepared it, you knew this would happen. When you were younger, the squandered expense, the wasted labor and time bothered you. Maybe it still does. Your mother's way of doing things makes you want to leave the business to focus on your hairdressing clients. Or move out of the house. Or dream of teaching high school students about the Louisiana Purchase. When there was nothing else, tacos allowed your family to live on. Now they hold you back. Each job comes with the deepening sense that either you or the business must change. And until something gives, you must tell yourself that wasted side dishes don't matter because your tacos were loved by those that ate them. You must tell yourself that's what matters most.

A few words on tortillas: The ones that Maria uses are slightly smaller than a compact disc, ordered by the box from a tortilleria in Baldwin Park and picked up the morning of the event. There are at least three other tortillerias minutes from her home, but they've never been considered because as far as Maria's concerned, the

Baldwin Park tortillas are perfect. A supple texture that gives slightly to the touch. That doesn't harden easily when heated. The subtle, sweet taste of the corn coming through each bite.

One Christmas Eve is spent doing the usual prep work, all four of them. Christmas morning in an industrial park. A bakery assembly line. Tacos intended as a thank-you for employees packing trays of fancy Danishes and madeleines. Afterwards, a fifty-dollar tip to be split four ways. That night it's decided they'll no longer work holidays.

Next it's nightfall at a horse property at the easternmost edge of the county. A full banda going. White Stetsons and white ostrich-skin belts and white boots that curl upward at the toe. Synchronized trumpets and trombones. A tuba. Dancing makes dancers hungry, and soon the chafing dishes are empty. The host sends someone out and he returns with another twenty-five pounds of carne asada. The tacos keep coming and the banda keeps playing, horses trained to prance in time with the music. Tamborazo a toda madre. Tipped $150 at the end of the night.

After three hours over the grill, your face is always sunburned, no matter if you've been outside or indoors. You've sweated enough to have felt embarrassed as you served food to your clients and to also feel thoroughly wrung out. Dehydrated. Now that the gear has cooled off and has been loaded onto the truck, everything about you also seems coated with the unique oily sheen that comes from adobada and asada smoke.

The ride home is quiet. Relief that cash is in your pocket and that looming bills will be paid, that this job is over. Curving along dark freeway lanes, all roads leading back to El Monte, the occasional rattles of shifting equipment in the truck bed reminding you that there is still more to be done once you get home.

You swing the cooler through the front door and collapse onto the couch. The answering machine blinks, the house quiet because your mother is still out at the other event booked for today. Everything in the back of your truck must be washed and cleaned, but if this evening is the first of a weekend with back-to-back events, the washing and cleaning must happen tonight instead of tomorrow. This maintenance will be the last thing you want to do. If you wait until tomorrow, your mother will be up before you, with degreaser and a pumice stone, scouring blackened oil off the spots where the grill pan gets hottest. You can already hear her complaining that you always use too much oil when you cook. The chaffing dishes and the utensils are waiting for you too, as are the pans and pots from the morning's prep work. And because they'll be the first things you'll need tomorrow morning, you begin by washing them. You can hear your mother saying, "Cada quien tiene que traer su tortilla a la casa." And you can sense the answering machine's light pulsing behind you. The empty weekend spaces on the calendar will taunt you until you play the message.

It will be a woman looking for tacos. She will be someone you don't already know and she will start in English, her voice unsure of itself because there is purposely no identifying greeting on the answering machine. She will switch to Spanish, and it will be clear from how poorly she speaks it, her pronunciation wooden and stilted, that this was the language of her parents or her grandparents, that it is no longer her own. She will sound out her phone number in the protracted manner of someone recollecting numerals for an exam.

She may be from someplace that you've never heard of before except for traffic updates and weather reports. She will say that she is a friend of Vijay. Or that she knows Adriana. Or that she was at the party for someone named Douglas. She will be expecting fifty people, but from the way she will describe the event, you can tell that it will more likely be twenty. Or a hundred. She will hope that you can work with her budget and you can already sense that she's the kind that probably won't tip.

In a few years, there may not be a business to receive this call. The business depends on your mother's health. And it depends on what you decide to do with your life. These ideas press intense guilt upon you, and yet the business no longer existing may also be its best possible outcome. If that day comes, it will be because you've each achieved something with your individual lives, something greater than what tacos can currently offer it. And you will have used skills passed down from your mother and honed in front of the grill: resourcefulness, tenacity, and the ability to be fearless in front of strangers.

But on this evening you will write down the woman's phone number and her name. You will do this with the same pen that you use to book appointments for your hairdressing clients, or that you used to fill out the paperwork for a position as a certified nursing assistant, or that you have in history class when you're taking notes on the Great Depression.

It will be too late to call the woman back tonight, but tomorrow morning, early, she will definitely hear from you.

[2015]

LETTER TO A YOUNG REFUGEE

from *Perfume Dreams*

Andrew Lam

On the news last night I saw you amidst a sea of desperate Albanian refugees and afterward I couldn't get the image out of my mind. You with your wide eyes and shy smile, your hand gripping your mother's as if it were a lifesaver, you are repeating my story of a few decades ago.

Listen, even if I know so little about your country's tumultuous history, even if I don't know your name, I think I know what you are going through. When I was eleven, about your age, I too fled from my homeland with my mother and sister and two grandmothers when the communist tanks came rolling into Saigon, Vietnam. We ended up in a refugee camp while our father was left behind.

Back then I couldn't make any sense out of what had happened to me or my family. History, after all, is always baffling to the young. One day I am reading my favorite comic book in my mother's garden, my two dogs sleeping lazily at my feet, and the next day I am running for my life with a small backpack in which I only managed to save my stamp collection. Everything else was burnt—photographs, mementos, books, toys, letters, identifications.

For the first few days in the refugee camp I walked about as if in a kind of trance. I kept thinking I would return home. I kept thinking this was just camping and soon my father would rescue us, would take us home to what I knew and loved. I had no words, no references to what I was experiencing. But now I know: I was dispossessed, an exile.

My young friend, there are so many things I want to tell you, so many experiences I want to share with you, but most of all I want to warn you that the road ahead is a very difficult and treacherous one and you must be brave, strong, and cunning. There are crucial things you should learn and learn quickly and then there are things you must mull over for the rest of your life.

The immediate thing is to learn to rise as early as possible. The food line is always long, and no matter how early you are, there will always be a line. You must have a hat or a scarf to protect your head from the cold and then from the sun.

When you get to the end of the line, try to act as helpless and as sad as possible. Tell the person in charge of food that your frail grandmother is bedridden and could not wait in line, that you are feeding her. Cry if you can. Try not to feel ashamed. That you never begged before in your life means nothing. Swallow your pride. Another plate will save you or your mother or sister many hours of waiting for the next meal. It will give them time to stand in line for medicine or clothes, if there are any.

Listen carefully, a new reality is upon you and you must rise to it as best you can. It entails a drastic change in your nature, in your thinking. It requires new flexibility and courage. Be aggressive even when you are naturally shy. Be brave even though until recently you still hugged your teddy bear in your own bed going to sleep.

Be fierce. Do not let others take advantage of you. Do not show that you are weak. In the worst circumstances, the weak get left out or beaten and robbed. Arm yourself if you can—a knife, a stone—and guard your family and what possessions you have left like a mad dog its bone. People can sense that you are willing to fight for what you have and most will back away.

Be alert. Listen to gossips and news. Find out what is coming down the line: food, donated clothes, blankets, tents, medicines.

Always get more than you need if you can manage it because what you have extra can be traded with others for something you don't have or can be given away to the elderly and feeble who are not as quick as you. An extra blanket is so helpful on a cold spring night, as you, I'm sure, have already found out.

Be hopeful. Maybe your father has made it somewhere else, to another camp possibly. The same can be said of your aunts and cousins, friends and neighbors. Never give up hope. Soon enough the camp will organize and there'll be a newsletter with information regarding lost relatives looking for each other or there'll be a bulletin board with names and agencies that will track displaced loved ones. Go every day to check to see whether your father has sent word. Console your inconsolable mother and sister. Hug them as often as you can.

My young friend, I close my eyes now and cast my mind back to that time spent in the refugee camp and all I hear are the sounds of weeping. I imagine it is not that different from what you are hearing now each morning, each afternoon, each night. Throughout the green tent city that flapped incessantly in the wind was the music of sorrow and grief. A woman who saw her husband shot in front of her wailed until she was hoarse and breathless. A man who left his feeble father behind cried quietly into his blanket. A woman whose teenage son was lost in the escape stared out into the dark as if she had lost her mind. For a while, the sound of weeping was my refugee camp lullaby.

Life in limbo is difficult and humiliating, but you must remember that being robbed of what you loved does not speak to your weakness or frailty. It only speaks of the inhumanity and fear and hatred of those who caused you to flee and endure in this new dispossessed reality.

I implore you, do not give in to their hatred. I know it is very hard, if not impossible, for someone who has just been forced out of his homeland, but you must try. Those who killed and robbed and caused so much pain and suffering to you, your family, and your people are, in fact, trying to make you into their own image, even if they don't realize it yet. They want you to hate just like them. They want you to be consumed with the fire of their hatred.

But don't hate. It will take great strength not to hate. And it will take even greater resilience to not teach hatred to those who come after you. Hatred consumes oppressed and oppressors alike and its terrible expressions—revenge is chief among them—always result in blood and tears and injustice and unspeakable suffering, an endless cycle of grief.

Learn to love what you have instead, learn to love those who suffered along with you, for their suffering and yours are now part of your inheritance.

Above all, don't forget. Commit everything—each blade of grass, each teary-eyed child, each unmarked grave—to memory. Then when you survive and are older, tell your story. Tell it on your bruised knees if you must, tell it at the risk of madness, scream it from the top of your lungs.

For though the story of how you suffered, how you lost your home, your loved ones, and how you triumphed is not new, it must always be told. And it must, by all means, be heard. It is the only light we ever have against the overwhelming darkness.

[2005]

INTRODUCTION

from *The Questions That Matter Most*

Jane Smiley

When I moved to California in 1996, I was following a horse. The horse's name was Terson (I called him Mr. T). I bought him from a stable in Wisconsin in 1993, and kept him in a barn outside Ames, Iowa, where I taught at Iowa State. But I was tired of nearly freezing to death when I rode him in the winter, and, by the way, my husband, Steve, who had grown up in Iowa, had spent some time in Santa Barbara and wanted to move back. Eventually, Steve and Mr. T. agreed on Carmel Valley, California. I could have said I was the native Californian, because I was born in LA, and my parents lived near Hollywood Park until I was about a year old, then moved back to the Midwest. Steve was born in Iowa, Mr. T in Germany. But no matter—like all migrants to California, we looked around and fell in love instantly with the new landscape and the everchanging but (almost) always pleasant weather.

At the time, I was known for *A Thousand Acres* and *Moo*, one of them openly set in Iowa and the other one sort of set in Iowa, at a land grant university. The first thing I did (inspired by Mr. T) was decide that of course I could breed racehorses, and I did, though none of them were successful. But Mr. T and the horses I bred gave birth to *Horse Heaven*, and in order to understand racing and breeding, I took a wonderful tour of California—Del Mar, Santa Anita, Hollywood Park, Golden Gate Fields, Temecula, Coalinga, and Davis, with many stops in between (San Francisco, Los Angeles, Santa Barbara, San Diego). The first thing I learned about California was how beautiful it is; the second thing I learned was that the climate and the scenery change every time you turn a corner or go over a mountain. I experienced this just the other day when I was walking in Monterey, and I left the Del Monte Shopping Center for Don Dahvee Park. I saw a path that I had never taken before, and it took me straight into the woods along a creek, natural, chaotic, and messy, not half a mile from the designer handbags at Macy's.

Before I came to California, the only California writer I knew much about was John Steinbeck, from Salinas, who, judging by his works, was interested not only in the social world and the history of his native land but also in the landscape. In my favorite of his novels, *East of Eden*, he begins by describing the diversity of the Salinas Valley—the lupines and the poppies, the trees and the Spanish moss, the changing nature of the soil, and the danger and beauty of the Salinas River. All of his works take on economic and political themes too (obviously in *The Grapes of Wrath* and *Of Mice and Men*), but one of the things you can't help doing if you are a writer based in California is attempting to convey what it feels like to be here, moment by moment.

My family had one small connection to California—one of my grandfather's many older sisters ended up in Vallejo, married to an astronomer who was a true crackpot, and who was also from central Missouri. His name was Thomas Jefferson Jackson See, and he earned his stripes as a crackpot by ruthlessly opposing Einstein's theory of relativity until the day he died, convinced that the universe was made of ether. He worked for the US Navy, and was sent to Mare Island to use astronomy to tell the exact time of day and to let the captains of the ships know so that they could embark on their missions in the proper way. And so I went to Vallejo and Mare Island to look around, gathering the information I needed to write *Private Life* (published in 2010). I also discovered a blot on US, and California, history that I hadn't known about: the internment of the Japanese during World War II. (If you grew up in St. Louis, or elsewhere in Missouri, slavery and abolition and segregation were frequent topics of conversation.) What I learned about my great-aunt taught me more about the complicated history of California and more about the complicated history of my family.

When I began teaching creative writing at UC Riverside in 2015, I was pleased that my students were much more diverse than they had been in Iowa, and they all had stories to tell that were enlightening and dramatic. A term was ten weeks long, so every student had to produce a draft a week—three drafts each for the first three stories—and then to choose the story that most interested them and write a fourth draft of that one. Discussions of each draft lasted about twelve to fifteen minutes, and the students discussing each draft could not use words of judgment or praise—if they didn't like something, they had to ask a question, such as "Why does Mary disappear after the first three pages?" The result was that the students got more intrigued by the stories they were writing, and as they fixed things, the stories grew more complex and unique. Often, what the students who were reading the stories did not understand had to do with the connection between where the story was set and how this affected the main character and his or her friends and family. This meant that over time my students became more aware of the ecosystems and communities that they grew up in, and also more eager to depict them. Reading these stories worked for me, too, since there are so many enclaves in California that most of them are under the radar. Two examples of stories that my students were working on were one written by a female grad student about an insane asylum from the early twentieth century that was run by her ancestors, which explores the cruelty of the system, in part from the point of view of one of the women who works at the asylum; the other was by a male undergrad student, about a family escaping from Mexico after the father is killed by gang members—some members of the family have transportation, but some of them have to walk the whole way.

The books I assigned were meant to be an exploration for my students, but turned out to be an exploration for me, too. I was quite familiar with Sue Grafton and had been enjoying her mysteries since the late 1980s—in some sense she replaced my youthful obsession with Agatha Christie, and both my students and I enjoyed the way Grafton created suspense, but also how she portrayed the idiosyncratic locations in and around Santa Barbara. I was also familiar with *The Woman Warrior*, and I wanted my students to learn from the complexity of how the narrative mixes personal experience with traditional stories. We did not exactly read it as nonfiction, because the elements seemed imaginative to us and therefore worth learning from, for both fiction writers and nonfiction writers. In some sense, these books served my students as historical novels, about events and places that existed before they were born and that have now changed—I had felt the same pleasure in books I had read in school, such as *David Copperfield* and *Giants in the Earth*.

One book that my students and I found astonishingly compelling and informative was *Kindred*, by Octavia Butler, a novel that immerses modern readers in the experience of being enslaved in the mid-nineteenth century, and how that contrasts with the life the protagonist is leading in the present day. We understood that Butler was using science fiction to explore important issues that many of my students were familiar with but hadn't been asked to imagine in such detail before. *Little Scarlet*, by Walter Mosley, offered similar insights and feelings. Some of my students were from the LA area, and Mosley's dramatic depiction of the Watts riots and the racial issues surrounding them, plus the way he incorporated them into a thriller, was very alluring.

The more recent novels that we discussed showed them what they could aim for. I had spent a lot of time on an Ojibwa reservation in northern Wisconsin, but what Tommy Orange showed me and my students about the experiences of Native Americans in Oakland was completely new. The way that *There There* jumps around between the points of view of different characters (using first person, second person, and third person) also sparked discussions of the benefits that each point of view offers the reader and the author. I think that Orange, as the youngest of the authors, also provided my students a pathway to a fresh literary voice. I did not make them read *The Greenlanders*, but they had a similar experience when I assigned *The Good Men*, by Charmaine Craig, which was about religious conflicts in France in the fourteenth century, was a little shorter, and was written in a more accessible style than my novel. Many of my students were fascinated by events they had experienced or heard about, and *The Good Men* offered a way to talk about how to imagine those events in detail and put them on the page, even if, when you start, you have very little idea of how to understand them.

The book I assigned that I think my students and I appreciated the most was *The Sellout*, by Paul Beatty. I taught it in my comic novel class, and it was the perfect example of using a comic and satiric voice to lure the reader into seeing the absurdity of the world that the narrator is living in. It was a major prizewinner, but easy for my students, and for me, to relate to. It fit perfectly into the desire that I had for my students to feel the presence of the writers around them, busily working and depicting the places in California that my students knew and wanted to write about themselves.

What is my justification for collecting these essays? For me, it is that every novelist's life has taken place during times of turmoil, and many novelists choose to explore that turmoil (for example, Émile Zola). In this way, being a novelist becomes a form of education. Let's say that first comes fear, then comes rage, then comes curiosity, then comes a more complex curiosity as our imaginations encompass our characters and their feelings. One of the most controversial essays included here is a comparison of *Uncle Tom's Cabin* and *Huckleberry Finn*, titled "Say It Ain't So, Huck." I had read *Huckleberry Finn* in school and knew it was considered a great American novel, but I had never read *Uncle Tom's Cabin* until I was forty-five and stuck in bed with a broken leg. *Uncle Tom's Cabin* is often derided, but when I read it, I thought it was much more complex and informative than *Huck Finn*, partly because Uncle Tom was not "an Uncle Tom"—he was a thoughtful and spiritual character—but mostly because the critics had overlooked Cassy, a determined and enterprising woman slave who manages to escape across the Ohio River with her child. I was incensed that a female author and her brave female character had to be denigrated while a male author who doesn't quite work out his plot gets to be number one. Before the age of the internet, my essay earned as much opprobrium as any essay ever printed in the *Atlantic*. What it did for me was make me consider the history of racism in the US in a way I'd never done before. I had been naive—I figured that if schools and public transit and our neighborhood were integrated, as they were when I was a child in St. Louis, racism must be behind us. Writing about those issues taught me how much further we had to go.

And then there was female exploitation and power, another aspect of *Uncle Tom's Cabin*. When I was a child, my mother worked at a newspaper, and then I went to a coed private school in

St. Louis, and then I went to Vassar and the Iowa Writer's Workshop. There was never a moment when I suspected that being a girl and then a woman was somehow standing in my way. I wrote about what interested me; it got published. I was dedicated to doing what I wanted, and it never occurred to me to look at our junk house when I was in elementary school and compare it to the luxurious house a mile away that some relatives lived in. I didn't understand class or capitalism until I took up with a basketball-playing socialist in college. We lived in a small Marxist commune, had many discussions about exploitation and class, but never talked about feminism or art. Or race—there were no African Americans in our commune. By the time I started my writing career, I knew that even though the nuclear war I had feared as a child had never actually taken place, there were plenty of issues all around me to think about, learn about, and portray. As I wrote more novels and got interested in more subjects, I became more eager to explore those issues.

There was recently a short essay in the *Guardian* about how historical novels shouldn't exist. It was written by a man who had just published a historical novel, and I think he meant it as something of a spoof, but if I had been arguing the issue with him, I would have said that all novels are historical novels, because those that outlive their authors teach future readers what life was like from the authors' point of view at the time when the authors were writing them. A good example is Sir Walter Scott, one of the first novelists to explore eras several hundred years in the past (*Ivanhoe*, *Quentin Durward*). At the beginning of the nineteenth century, Scott did not have the archeological evidence we have, or other aspects of research that historians now employ, but he had the stories, passed down over generations, and he reimagined them and set them down in a new form—the novel, the historical novel. His work was hugely popular. The books are still readable and dramatic. My favorite of his are the novels he wrote about the religious conflicts of the seventeenth century, especially *The Tale of Old Mortality*. Is it accurate? As I was reading it, I was both enthralled and motivated to look up the history of those times and compare what historians had to say with what Scott wrote. And that is one thing historical novels do—they pull you in and make you wonder, not only about what really happened but also about how and why the author portrayed the events as he did. Because of this, I think that I often forgive and even thank authors of novels for truthfully representing the era they lived in. Yes, Anthony Trollope shows signs of antisemitism, and I don't like that, but it shows me who he is—he can't help but reveal it. It is also true of Trollope that he was more interested in, and more insightful about, the lives of his female characters than any nineteenth-century male writer that I can think of. Was that because his wife read his work, day by day, and gave him advice? I suspect it is. Novels and novelists are complex, and that is why I prefer writing about complex issues in novels rather than in nonfiction.

The novel is, and always has been, a self-made form. We read them as children, go on reading them, and then decide to try writing one, to see how our own experiences look on the page. Not all of my students will have enough luck (or maybe dedication) to write about their experiences and stories, and not all of them will find a publisher or an audience, but I hope that the ones who are really dedicated do so, because their depictions of one of the largest, most beautiful, most populous, most diverse, and most contradictory states in the US are revealing and fascinating.

Most of the essays in this book have been assignments—I am handed a topic and asked to reveal my thoughts. I hope that I have used them in the same way that I have used my novels—to learn more about something that I thought I understood, and to understand that topic, or issue, with more clarity and nuance.

[2023]

REPRESENTATION

from *What You Don't Know Will Make a Whole New World*

Dorothy Lazard

Culturally, Sarah couldn't have picked a better area for us to live. I had always been a fiend for movies, so I was happy to find a few old theaters within walking distance of our apartment. During the early 1970s, movie theaters were being torn down for new commercial buildings, but there was still the Lux on Broadway and the Roxie on 17th Street, screening the latest from Hollywood. Sometimes Sarah and I would venture north to the MacArthur–Broadway Mall or to the Piedmont Theatre to catch a movie, but the downtown theaters were our favorites.

The Black Arts Movement, launched in the late 1960s, was at its zenith in the mid-1970s. For young people like me, coming of age during this time was more visually and ideologically stimulating than any other period in our lives. It was the first, best time to be a Black kid in this country. The Afrocentric art that seemed suddenly everywhere taught us to value our own natural, Black selves, our hair and our heritage. This mental rewiring was a challenge after so many years of being fed white standards, white images. This movement was a gift more powerful and long-lasting than any gun battle, civil rights demonstration, or political manifesto. It was foundational, demonstrating in so many creative ways that if we couldn't love ourselves, appreciate our own value, how in the world could we convince anyone else to value us?

My teen years were radically different from my early years. We had cast off the word "Negro" and begun to call ourselves "Black." That's Black with a capital B, thank you very much. It caused a rift in a lot of families across the country, with the older generation clinging to the "Negro" moniker and the slow and steady agenda of integration. Meanwhile, we young folks were declaring, as James Brown had a few years earlier, "I'm black and I'm proud." We began to realize that we had to name ourselves to claim our value. We had to change the minds of those who sought to undervalue us as a community, to bar us from what was rightfully ours. The arts movement that now centered the Black body and Black culture was predicated on reinvention. It stimulated my desire to write and to add to this amazing explosion of expression.

Sarah was a museumgoer, and I would tag along with her sometimes to check out what was on display. Art popped up everywhere in Oakland—in galleries, in people's houses, in recreation centers. The Rainbow Sign in South Berkeley was a mecca for aspiring and established Black artists—poets, essayists, dancers, singers—and the community was always welcome to partake of the art exhibits, the readings, the talks about the power of art.

What helped open up the barn doors was the new era of filmmaking. In the early 1970s, on the heels of Gordon Parks's success in directing *Shaft*, Hollywood got a sniff of the money to be made from the Black community, and suddenly there were loads of Black-themed films: gangster movies, thrillers, police procedurals, horror flicks, romances. Not all of them were as well-made as *Shaft* or the Motown-backed *Lady Sings the Blues*, but we flocked to them anyway, just as we had flocked to television sets to see Black performers years before. We were just so happy to see *anybody* resembling us on screen, we didn't much care about the plot of the film. A Black private detective working a case, a Black vampire chewing up L.A., brothers karate-chopping their way through Hong Kong, a Black family struggling for respect, an urban kid chasing seemingly impossible dreams. We were there for it. We were learning how to view ourselves, magnified and beautiful. Despite all the C-grade scripts, mediocre acting, and pedestrian directing, we were learning how to critique these cinematic selves.

My film obsession was fueled by a trip to the Oakland Museum in February 1973. In observance of Black History Month, the museum's Cultural Affairs Guild hosted a film festival to celebrate the history of Black presence in American cinema. A few hundred people crowded into the James Moore Theater over a number of days to see the wide-ranging series, which showed everything from early Paul Robeson films (*The Emperor Jones*) to earnest, socially conscious midcentury films like *Bright Road*, with Dorothy Dandridge and Harry Belafonte. After the screenings, Albert Johnson, a UC Berkeley professor and film historian (who knew there was such a thing!), showed clips from early films—*Rufus Jones for President*, featuring a four-year-old Sammy Davis Jr., and *St. Louis Blues*, with blues singer Bessie Smith—and he explained their historical significance to the audience.

The film screenings became a popular annual event at the museum, with Professor Johnson moderating the lively Q&A that followed. The talks mainly centered on Black portrayals in Hollywood—not just the ones we got but the ones we wanted. Hollywood for decades had been banking on our denigration, and the typical movie fare, if Blacks were included at all, often demeaned, abused, or sacrificed us in some way. Like most Black kids, I learned early in my film consumption that Black folks rarely made it to the end credits. We not only wanted representation, we wanted to see ourselves in all our humanity and complexity. We also wanted to see ourselves win, being resourceful and heroic. Young people condemned the old Stepin Fetchit and Black mammy movies from the 1930s and 1940s, but, to be honest, a lot of recent movie fare offered just new versions of those early "shuckin' and jivin'" portrayals that had unnerved us earlier. Instead of being set on Southern plantations or in Manhattan boudoirs, these new portrayals were in urban settings, usually drug-saturated ghettos.

Simply seeing Black faces on the silver screen was not enough anymore. We wanted to see recognizable characters.

The audience peppered Professor Johnson with questions at every event: How much power do Black folks really have in Hollywood? How many Black screenwriters are working in Hollywood? Why aren't films made by Black filmmakers getting distributed widely? How does film distribution work? How does film financing work?

Professor Johnson introduced us to early Black filmmaker Oscar Micheaux, who made independent movies on a shoestring budget in the 1920s and '30s that elevated our people, portraying them in all their psychological, class, and moral diversity. Micheaux hired Black actors, some of whom would make the leap to mainstream Hollywood films, like Paul Robeson, who, having grown disgusted with the limited opportunities in America, went to England to act in movies of substance.

During the 1970s, a period that would become known as the Blaxploitation era in film history, the debate about what type of film Black folks *should* appear in got complicated by bringing class concerns into the mix. Many in the community felt there were positive depictions (teachers, ministers, hardworking parents) that Black audiences support, while other characterizations (drug dealers, prostitutes, junkies, criminals) should be condemned. The museum audience became especially charged after the screening of Melvin Van Peebles's controversial *Sweet Sweetback's Baadasssss Song*.

At the same time we were being introduced to these controversies, the independent film *The Mack*, starring Max Julien and Richard Pryor, hit theaters. Shot on the streets of West Oakland, it tells the story of an ex-con who becomes a successful pimp and the underworld life he inhabits. Despite all the hue and cry about "proper" representation, this film was very popular with Black audiences, and in the decades after its release it would continue to be highly influential in popular culture and fashion.

The film series at the museum had me buzzing, making me rethink all the movies I had absorbed and what they were not so subtly telling me about myself and my place in society. From my earliest days, I had ingested a steady diet of white victors and Black subordinates—slaves, maids, butlers, and feeble-minded, shuffling old men. Professor Johnson exhibited clips from films like *The Pirate* and *Ziegfeld Follies*, which featured Black actors, dancers, and singers in segments that were edited out when the movies were shown in segregated Southern theaters. We were dispensable, Hollywood always seemed to be telling us. Learning things like this, I reassessed all those films in which no Black people appeared, not even as servants. Each question led to more questions. How did Black actors justify working in an industry where they were so disregarded? How did any of them make a steady living with such limited opportunities? White audiences never had to search far for positive, or even interesting, portrayals. White actors had access to every type of role. I realized that all those times I'd heard Bette Davis blithely say in her films, "I'm free, white, and twenty-one," that there was cultural currency in that off-the-cuff remark, which I read as code for "I can do what I want." It was true. And I wondered when I'd see a Black woman on screen sail through life so confidently.

Some of the organizers of the museum's film festival would go on to create the nonprofit organization Black Filmmakers Hall of Fame, Inc., which would sponsor, over the next twenty-six years, film screenings, annual film symposia, and screenwriting competitions. The organization also held at Oakland's newly refurbished Paramount Theatre a swanky annual awards ceremony, complete with star-studded red carpet reception, to celebrate Black actors, directors, producers, and other creatives working in the film industry. It felt good to see so many stars in little ol' Oakland receiving acclaim for not just excelling (like Sidney Poitier and Diahann Carroll) but enduring (like Beah Richards, Woody Strode, and Clarence Muse). The ceremony was named in honor of the trailblazing Oscar Micheaux.

[2023]

THERE OUGHT TO BE A BOOK, A BEAUTIFUL BOOK

from *The Heyday of Malcolm Margolin*

Malcolm Margolin, interviewed by **Kim Bancroft**

Why such a focus on creating beautiful books? You may as well ask why I breathe.

Part of it is shame. I'd be ashamed to do something that *wasn't* beautiful. Somebody puts years of work into a book; they've got all their aspirations, all their ego in it. They're putting it out into the world. They've given me the best piece of their work, and we're going to do a lousy-looking book? I'd be ashamed to face them. So it's partly pride in what we do. But I'd just cringe with embarrassment if something didn't turn out very well.

And then it's so puzzling: Why doesn't *everybody* make beautiful books? Why do a book if it's not beautiful? Why do something ugly? Ugliness has always puzzled me. I've never quite understood it.

Beauty is also puzzling. There's something about beauty—it's not prettiness. Beauty is something else. There's a ferocity to it, a power to it. There's a wonderful Rilke quote from the first of his *Duino Elegies* where he's wondering what beauty is. He says:

> Who, if I cried out, would hear me among the angels'
> hierarchies? And even if one of them pressed me
> suddenly against his heart: I would be consumed
> in that overwhelming existence. For beauty is nothing
> but the beginning of terror, which we still are just able
> to endure,
> and we are so awed because it serenely disdains

to annihilate us. Every angel is terrifying.

I collect quotes about beauty. I think about beauty all the time. If a day passes where I haven't thought about beauty, just for what it is, in the abstract, it's probably an odd day.

I like going to this French restaurant in Berkeley called La Note that has a courtyard in the back. I just sit in the back of La Note and enjoy it. It's so simple. A few trees, a few tables, a brick wall, some plants, but it's so lovely out there. It's so easy to create beauty. Why isn't it everywhere? Why do people tolerate the ugliness of place or personality?

My wonderful friend Dashrath Patel was active in the politics of Gujarat. He used to talk about the need for a Ministry of Beauty. Tourism already had someone to speak for it, commerce had somebody to speak for it, and the environment had somebody to speak for it. But who would speak for beauty?

One of the scariest things that ever happened to me was when Tom Killion brought me the book he had done with Gary Snyder on the High Sierra of California, a big, beautiful limited edition of one hundred copies, and he wanted us to do a trade book. It had hand-set type, special papers, and original prints. It exemplified the highest standards in book craft—a luxury liner of a book, deeply satisfying and utterly thrilling. I was simultaneously inspired and distressed. In doing a trade edition, I was going to take something beautiful and make it uglier! That kept me up nights.

The focus on beauty happens to some extent at our meetings. In other businesses they talk about the bottom line, profit, costs. We do, too, but it doesn't have the same sway as in other places. The main question here is how to make this thing beautiful. Beauty has a voice in our meetings. People are rewarded, praised, for doing beautiful work. When somebody comes in with something beautiful, I'm just so delighted by it. When a book comes in under budget, that's great, and I'm full of compliments. When a designer comes in and has done a beautiful cover, I'm gushing all over the place.

For example, we had a meeting recently about what to do with a book of photographs Cris Benton made, flying a kite over the South Bay salt flats. We talked about keeping it within budget, but that was so minor. The real conversation was what it should look like. We spend a whole lot of time on these books, thinking about what their soul is, what motivates the author, what's in there. We visualize people reading the book; they enter into that book, and when they come out of it, they're going to be a different person. How are they going to be changed? What are we going to do within that book to facilitate that change?

So it's all a matter of beauty. Why else would people work here? For the laughter, I suppose, and there's a lot of that. But the laughter would go away if these things were ugly. The whole thing would collapse. It's just a *sine qua non*.

What I do is hire people and give them the best of my feedback, the best of my thoughts, make certain that they've got enough time to do something wonderful. Frankly, I do a certain amount of protecting people's capacity to create beauty. I run interference when necessary. A couple of people have said something interesting about my taking blame. I hadn't been aware of what that meant for others, but it's true. When something goes wrong, I'll take the blame for it so they can do beautiful work.

There's that wonderful story about Moses Mendelssohn. He was the grandfather of Felix Mendelssohn, the composer and pianist. Moses Mendelssohn was famous as both a Talmudic scholar and an enlightenment philosopher. He straddled worlds. He was also deformed, a hunchback. When he was a young man, a marriage was arranged for him with a woman from a distant place. On the day of the marriage, the bride came and saw him for the first time. She said she couldn't go through with it. The relatives of the bride tried to talk to her, to tell her that beauty is skin deep, that he was the most capacious soul that the world had ever seen, kind and brilliant, and that she'd be happy with these internal qualities. But she just couldn't picture herself with a person like this.

Finally, the relatives came to Moses and told him, "Listen, here's what's happened. We're sorry. We're going to have to call the wedding off. We'll settle about the dowry."

He said, "Hey, I understand why she wouldn't want to marry me. But I ask for just a ten-minute conversation with her."

They agreed. She came in very reluctantly for this conversation. What he said was this: "There is an understanding that before we're born, we're in heaven with God. In heaven, we discuss Talmud and Torah with the angels. We're in total bliss. We can even see what our lives are going to be. However, at birth, that prior knowledge is erased so we can begin our lives afresh.

"For some reason, that knowledge was not erased for me, so I remember when I was with God and the angels. When I asked to see who I would be in the next life, I was shown a perfectly formed, handsome young man who pleased me greatly. 'And whom will I marry?' I asked. They brought before me a hunchbacked woman, gnarled and deformed. I said, 'No, she must be beautiful. Let *me* have the hunchback.' "

So there's something valuable about creating a place where other people can do beautiful work. I'm just amazed at the people that have written these books, that have designed these books, that have kept this thing going.

What I love about publishing is creating books. I've never been very good at long-term planning, mission statements, those kinds of summations. I've been good at stories. Behind each is some kind of value, courage, excellence, and generosity. It's a life of tapas rather than main courses.

People ask me why we keep publishing books about Indians and others at the social margins. The metaphor I often use is that they asked Willie Sutton why he robbed banks, and he said, "That's where the money is." I'm a publisher. I need stories that are passionate, something to believe in. So I find where the stories are. And they're great stories. But I keep returning to the question "Why aren't twenty-five Heydays mining these stories?" The stuff that slips through my fingers is daunting.

It's not always easy, but I tend to just live with things. There have been money problems for forty years, and there will always be money problems. Then there's catching up on emails, a flood of them. It's relentless. But here's one that begins, "Beloved Malcolm." So I can't complain! I'm completely disorganized. I have no idea how to put emails in files and folders. Stuff will stick in my mind that I'll respond to, and other stuff I'll forget and won't do. Sometimes I'll just shoot it over to an assistant. Sometimes I'll answer it briefly. Sometimes I'll say the truth: "Hey, listen, in a better world than this, I'd give it all the care and attention that it deserves, but I'm over my head, and I just can't do what you would like me to do and what I would like to do."

It can be overwhelming. I wish I could be more of what people want me to be. People have these genuine needs. One of the things I determined, though, was not to be a slave to the inbox. There's a part of me that's in a daydreamy world, so sometimes I just don't give a damn. At the same time, I just wish I could do more. So I do feel bad.

How do I cope with it? I get up at five in the morning. I work late, and I work weekends. But a whole lot of it is not all that laborious. Much of each day, I'm reading inspiring words, talking to people about their deepest thoughts and most intimate feelings. I go to several parties and receptions a week. I'm out in the world, active and engaged. If this is work, I can't help but wonder what play must be like.

[2014]

THE SAND DUNES OF OLD SAN FRANCISCO

from *Lost Worlds of the San Francisco Bay Area*

Sylvia Linsteadt

The dunes had always been home to hardy yellow lupines, and the pewter-blue butterflies called Xerces, whose only home in the world was the western, ocean-facing half of San Francisco. Great winds shaped the dunes like tides, moving sand in gusts so that the landscape was never the same from one day to the next. The dunes were an extension of the pounding and gale-filled seaboard, the edge of the world where land sifted into wave, only here and there touched with the speckled blue flash of a butterfly, the bronze and panting dash of a coyote, the scuttling green iridescence of a tiger beetle. When a strong wind came, it ran unimpeded—save for the low-growing lupines and deerweeds and little stunted willows along seeps and small creeks. The sand was vast in every direction like some seaside Sahara—from present-day Golden Gate Park all the way south to Lake Merced, and inland to Mount Sutro. On a dark night the winds might take your very name away for a moment in favor of cold stars and ocean and howling weather, bracing and clean as the beginning of time.

Until the early 1900s, San Francisco's expanse of dunes was called the Outside Lands, or, more simply, the Great Sand Waste, a place that most city residents considered desolate, barren, and forbidding—a kind of no-man's-land. Some of the dunes were over one hundred feet high, and caught the winds that blew unhindered northwest from the San Francisco Peninsula. The sand was defiant, and did not take easily to development: always transforming, always blowing, always getting into shoes and socks and even the heaviest coats, never offering a reliable foothold for more than a few moments. Even on a still day, fine sand undulating up and down in giant dunes was difficult to navigate on foot, but such a landscape was harder still to traverse by horse and carriage. Esteban Richardson, who grew up in the 1840s, the grandson of a presidio comandante, remembered how "the wind carried with it an almost incredible burden of both fine and coarse sand that got into clothes, eyes, nose, mouth—anything that was open in short—besides penetrating the innermost recesses of a household." This was not the place for a settlement, let alone a city, but San Francisco's population explosion and staggering growth from the start of the gold rush through the early 1900s sealed the fate of the sand dunes, which fell slowly but inevitably to builders, first marshaling steam shovels and later electric bulldozers.

As early as 1849, attempts were already being made to flatten some of the dunes—nothing could be done about the wind—but this was difficult work and it rarely took hold. In the years before the turn of the century, many of the sand dunes stayed mostly as wild as they had been for millennia, transformed only here and there by dairy ranches, a chicken farm, four cemeteries—a wasteland was a good place to bury a growing city's dead—and Samuel Brannan's Cliff House resort in 1863. Wealthy visitors to the resort demanded the city build a road over the sand dunes to make the place easier to get to, and while the road attracted more settlers to the area, houses were built slowly, a few at a time, with wooden planks laid over the sand for access. Displacement of sand by wind only grew worse as development increased because more and more of the lupines, wind-stunted little oaks, and coyote brush that had kept the sand in place were cleared or cut down for firewood. But the conjuring of Golden Gate Park right in the middle of all that sand in the 1870s and '80s stood as proof that the shifting, blustery "wasteland" could be conquered and transformed into gardens, stands of cypress and eucalyptus, and lawns so completely convincing that the sand below was soon forgotten.

In 1895, when the Market Street Railway Company started selling old horse-drawn streetcars in favor of new electric ones, people began to move in larger numbers to the "Outside Lands." The streetcars were complete house structures already, portable and finely finished—and they sold for ten dollars apiece without the seats. The great dunescapes of the city's western frontier were largely empty—a perfect place to put your new house-on-wheels! By 1900, one hundred streetcar-houses were nestled among the sand dunes facing Ocean Beach, a motley and bohemian enclave, like some gathering of nesting seabirds. In the beginning, many of the horse-car houses were actually restaurants, beach cottages, and clubhouses on then-mayor Adolph Sutro's land, among the women's Falcon Cycling Club, and a musical gathering place called La Bohème. After the 1906 earthquake, Carville-by-the-Sea, as the community was called, became a settlement for refugees, and by the 1950s, many of the streetcars had been absorbed into more traditional apartment structures.

By that time, the feats of modern engineering and sheer hubris that had transformed sand dunes into Golden Gate Park had likewise turned much of the once-"wasteland" into streets and apartment buildings that became proper city districts—the Sunset and the Richmond.

To the ravenous city, the sand dune "wasteland" was seen from the beginning as a nuisance and an impediment to progress—blowing where it shouldn't, shifting into the street when your back was turned, a chore to get a horse and carriage to traverse, un-pinnable, un-griddable, and worse still, notably infertile and difficult to grow any "useful" plants upon without large amounts of expensive water and manure. But the sand dunes were in truth far from barren—it just took an expert sort of eye to notice their own shy language of fecundity. From its earliest days, San Francisco attracted not only gold-seekers but also naturalists drawn to the abundance of plant and animal life around the bay, an abundance that is almost unimaginable today. The city's sand dunes inspired the devotion of a number of entomologists and amateur naturalists alike, including George Dunn, who in 1892 made a minute study of San Francisco's coastal strand ecosystem. A waste, people called the dunes, but not Dunn. Burrowing in sand, nesting in lupine branches, feeding on deerweed, fifty species of beetle and mollusk, twenty-nine species of spider, and seven kinds of mite, and numerous butterflies and moths were documented by Dunn. In all, he recorded some 221 insect species that called the sand dunes home, attuned as he was to their jeweled and infinitesimal worlds from his many hours crouched and peering into the grains.

One particularly beautiful little gem of a creature, the Xerces blue butterfly, carried the fate of the dunes on its silver and lapis wings. By the 1870s, naturalists and entomologists were growing vocal about the loss of butterfly abundance and diversity across the dunescape; the Xerces blue, endemic to the coastal dune ecosystem of the San Francisco Peninsula alone, its range constrained by the reach of fog, stirred special concern. Hans Hermann Behr, a German naturalist, butterfly expert, and early member of the California Academy of Sciences, predicted that the Xerces blue would become extinct within his lifetime. Behr had already observed the decline of countless butterfly species and their habitats across the city, and he did in fact watch the Xerces completely disappear from the San Francisco dunes by 1875. He wrote to a colleague in Chicago that "the locality where it used to be found is converted into building lots, and between German chickens and Irish hogs no insect can exist besides louse and flea," but in later years naturalists managed to relocate a small population to a lonely patch of dunes above Lobos Creek, where yellow bush lupine, the Xerces' primary food, still grew.

Despite these tender efforts, by 1941, the Xerces blue was last observed at the Laurel Hill Cemetery where a few odd lupines and deerweeds grew among the graves. It was the first butterfly to vanish completely from North America. The sands of San Francisco were gone too, except for a small patch at Ocean Beach. There, they were held in—and kept out of the roads—by a fortified retaining wall made in part by old gravestones from the very same Laurel Hill Cemetery, which was dug up to make way for housing and offices in the mid-forties. Bodies were relocated to a mass grave at no cost, but families had to purchase headstones back from the cemetery within ninety days if they wanted to keep them. Most were abandoned, used instead for breakwaters at the Marina and Aquatic Park, gutters in Buena Vista Park, and the retaining wall at Ocean Beach. The names of San Francisco's dead were scattered throughout the city, epithets and surnames and dates of birth and death fragmented and mortared into its corners, underbellies, and seams.

In years of exceptional wind and tide, the sands at Ocean Beach shift with all of their old wildness, baring pieces of the wall at the top edge of the beach. Every few decades, beautiful granite gravestones and bits of tomb marker from the nineteenth century are found exposed along the strand, bearing the ghostly names of people who once lived here when the city was young, when the sand dunes still danced under the howling hands of wind, mysterious and unknowable people who are long since gone. Sometimes the letters are faded, sometimes they are clear. "Delia Presby, Wife of E.B. Oliver, died April 9. 1890, aged 26 yrs. 10 mos. 27 days. REST," read one gravestone, stark in the wet sand in the summer of 2012. After a few months, it was pushed and covered again by strong tides and heaving sand, lost once more to time—like the great sweeping dunescape, like the tiny powdered wings of the Xerces blue, alighting on a fragrant bush lupine for the last time.

Some gardeners claim that without irrigation or fertilizer, Golden Gate Park would return to dunes in a matter of ten years. Always underneath the city there are the ghosts of sand dunes; there are chrysalises that never hatched; there are seeds that will wait forever if they must, hoping to bloom again.

[2017]

SELECTED LIST OF PUBLICATIONS

The following list covers much of Heyday's publishing history, but it does not include every edition of every book Heyday has been involved with. When Heyday has released multiple editions of a book, or when a book was released by another publisher before Heyday, we have noted the year and details of Heyday's first edition. As a general rule, we have not included books that Heyday distributed but did not directly publish or place its imprimatur on. We have listed editors and illustrators, but for reasons of space we have not included most front-matter credits.

1974

The East Bay Out: An Unauthorized Guide to Hiking, Camping, Swimming, and Fishing in the East Bay Regional Parks. Malcolm Margolin; Illustrations by Nancy Curry.

1975

The Earth Manual: How to Work on Wild Land without Taming It. Malcolm Margolin.

1978

The Ohlone Way: Indian Life in the San Francisco–Monterey Bay Area. Malcolm Margolin.

1981

Stickeen. John Muir.

The Way We Lived: California Indian Reminiscences, Stories and Songs. Edited with Commentary by Malcolm Margolin.

1982

Gender. Ivan Illich.

1983

Portraits of California Indians.

Yamino-Kwiti: A Story of Indian Life in the Los Angeles Area. Donna Preble.

1984

Roads to Ride: A Bicyclist's Topographic Guide to Alameda, Contra Costa and Marin Counties. Grant Petersen with Mary Andersen.

1985

55 1/2 Running Trails of the San Francisco Bay Area. Tony Burke.

The Musicians and the Servants: A Novel of India. Carolyn North.

Roads to Ride South: A Bicyclist's Topographic Guide to San Mateo, Santa Clara, and Santa Cruz Counties. Grant Petersen and John Kluge.

Straight with the Medicine: Narratives of Washoe Followers of the Tipi Way. As told to Warren L. d'Azevedo.

1986

Cyclists' Route Atlas: The Delta, Farm, & Wine Country. Randall Gray Braun.

Cyclists' Route Atlas: Yolo, Solano, Napa, & Lake Counties. Randall Gray Braun.

Humphrey the Wayward Whale. Ernest Callenbach and Christine Leefeldt; Illustrations by Carl Dennis Buell.

1987

Bitter Melon: Inside America's Last Rural Chinese Town. Jeff Gillenkirk and James Motlow.

Cyclists' Route Atlas: The Gold Country & High Sierra/North. Randall Gray Braun.

H_2O and the Waters of Forgetfulness. Ivan Illich.

Strawberries in November: A Guide to Year-Round Gardening in the East Bay. Judith Goldsmith.

Toward a History of Needs: Includes Energy & Equity. Ivan Illich.

1987–present

News from Native California. Magazine edited by Vera Mae Frederickson, Malcolm Margolin, and David W. Peri (1987–1989); Malcolm Margolin and David W. Peri (1989); Jeannine Gendar,

Malcolm Margolin, and David W. Peri (1990–2000); Margaret Dubin (2000–2012); Lillian Fleer and Sylvia Linsteadt (2012); Lindsie Bear (2012–2015); and Terria Smith (2015–present).

1988

Cyclists' Route Atlas: The Gold Country & High Sierra/South. Randall Gray Braun.

The Harvest Gypsies: On the Road to the Grapes of Wrath. John Steinbeck; Introduction by Charles Wollenberg.

The Life of an Oak: An Intimate Portrait. Glenn Keator; Artwork by Susan Bazell.

1989

Berkeley Inside/Out: A Guide to Restaurants, Entertainment, People and Politics. Don Pitcher; History by Malcolm Margolin.

Celebration of Awareness: A Call for Institutional Revolution. Ivan Illich.

Life in a California Mission: Monterey in 1786. Jean François de la Pérouse. Copublished with Santa Clara University.

Tools for Conviviality. Ivan Illich.

1990

The Flavors of Home: A Guide to Wild Edible Plants of the San Francisco Bay Area. Margit Roos-Collins.

Into the Sunlight: Life after the Iron Curtain. Roger Rapoport.

Jack London and His Daughters. Joan London.

1991

The Bay Area at War: How We Reacted to the Persian Gulf Crisis. Edited by Eric Newton and Roger Rapoport.

It Will Live Forever: Traditional Yosemite Indian Acorn Preparation. Beverly R. Ortiz as told by Julia F. Parker; Photographs by Raye Santos.

Let's Park in San Francisco. Kenneth Fried.

The Maidu Indian Myths and Stories of Hanc'ibyjim. Edited and Translated by William Shipley.

To the American Indian: Reminiscences of a Yurok Woman. Lucy Thompson, Che-na-wah Weitch-ah-wah.

1992

Alcatraz! Alcatraz! The Indian Occupation of 1969–1971. Adam Fortunate Eagle.

Never Buy Anything New: A Guide to 400 Secondhand, Thrift and Consignment Stores in the San Francisco Bay Area. Charlene Akers.

1993

Indian Summer: Traditional Life among the Choinumne Indians of California's San Joaquin Valley. Thomas Jefferson Mayfield. Copublished with the California Historical Society.

1994

Ararapikva: Traditional Karuk Indian Literature from Northwestern California. Julian Lang.

Flutes of Fire: Essays on California Indian Languages. Leanne Hinton.

Life on the Edge: A Guide to California's Endangered Natural Resources—Wildlife. Biosystems Books.

Mourning Dove—ʔoʔrowiʔ: A Yurok/English Tale.

Open to the Public: A Guide to the Museums of Northern California. Copublished with the California Historical Society.

1995

General Vallejo and the Advent of the Americans. Alan Rosenus. Copublished with Urion Press.

Grass Games and Moon Races: California Indian Games and Toys. Jeannine Gendar.

Native Ways: California Indian Stories and Memories. Edited by Malcolm Margolin and Yolanda Montijo.

Photographing the Second Gold Rush: Dorothea Lange and the Bay Area at War, 1941–1945. Dorothea Lange; Introduction by Charles Wollenberg.

1996

The Fine Art of California Indian Basketry. Brian Bibby. Copublished with the Crocker Art Museum.

First & Foremost: A Guide to Northern California's Independent Bookstores.

Charlene Akers.

Highway 99: A Literary Journey Through California's Great Central Valley. Edited by Stan Yogi. Copublished with the California Council for the Humanities.

Kashaya Pomo Plants. Jennie Goodrich, Claudia Lawson, and Vana Parrish Lawson.

Remember Your Relations: The Elsie Allen Baskets, Family, & Friends. Suzanne Abel-Vidor, Dot Brovarney, and Susan Billy.

1997

Adopted by Indians: A True Story. Thomas Jefferson Mayfield; Illustrated by Hilair Chism and Rick Jones.

Berkeley! A Literary Tribute. Edited by Danielle La France.

Bret Harte's Gold Rush: "Outcasts of Poker Flat," "The Luck of Roaring Camp," "Tennessee's Partner," and Other Favorites. Bret Harte.

In My Own Words: Stories, Songs, and Memories of Grace McKibbin, Wintu. Alice Shepherd.

Life Amongst the Modocs: Unwritten History. Joaquin Miller. Copublished with Arion Press.

No Rooms of Their Own: Women Writers of Early California, 1849–1869. Edited by Ida Rae Egli. Copublished with Santa Clara University.

Where on Earth: A Guide to Specialty Nurseries and Other Resources for California Gardeners. Barbara Stevens and Nancy Conner.

1998

The Ferry Building: Witness to a Century of Change. Nancy Olmsted. Copublished with the Port of San Francisco.

The Heart Is Fire: The World of the Cahuilla Indians of Southern California. Deborah Dozier.

Into a Wild Sanctuary: A Life in Music and Natural Sound. Bernie Krause.

Jazz on the Barbary Coast. Tom Stoddard. Copublished with the California Historical Society and the San Francisco Traditional Jazz Foundation.

The Morning the Sun Went Down. Darryl Babe Wilson.

The Shirley Letters: From the California Mines, 1851–1852. Louise Amelia

Knapp Smith Clappe; Edited by Marlene Smith-Baranzini.

Stories Grandma Never Told: Portuguese Women in California. Sue Fagalde Lick.

Wine Country: A Literary Companion. Edited by Benjamin Russack.

Women of the Gold Rush: "The New Penelope" and Other Stories. Frances Fuller Victor; Edited by Ida Rae Egli.

1999

Acorn Soup. L. Frank.

California Shorts. Edited by Steven Gilbar.

A Community of Words: A Directory of Literary Readings and Workshops in California. Compiled by Poets & Writers, Inc.

The Dumbbell Nebula. Steve Kowit.

The Geography of Home: California's Poetry of Place. Selected and Edited by Christopher Buckley and Gary Young.

In Danger. Suzanne Lummis.

Jack London's Golden State: Selected California Writings. Edited by Gerald Haslam.

One Hand on the Wheel. Dan Bellm.

Picturing California's Other Landscape: The Great Central Valley. Edited by Heath Schenker. Copublished with the Haggin Museum.

A World Transformed: Firsthand Accounts of California Before the Gold Rush. Edited by Joshua Paddison.

Writing Home: Award-Winning Literature from the New West. Edited by Brian Bouldrey.

2000

Acting for Nature: What Young People Around the World Are Doing to Protect the Environment. Sneed B. Collard III and Action for Nature; Illustrated by Carl Dennis Buell.

Doubleness. Richard Silberg.

Eldorado: Adventures in the Path of Empire. Bayard Taylor. Copublished with Santa Clara University.

LA Shorts. Edited by Steven Gilbar.

Listening to Winter. Molly Fisk.

Middle Ear. Forrest Hamer.

Only What We Could Carry: The Japanese American Internment Experience. Edited by Lawson Fusao Inada.

Topaz Moon: Chiura Obata's Art of the Internment. Chiura Obata; Edited with Text by Kimi Kodani Hill.

Unfinished Message: Selected Works of Toshio Mori. Toshio Mori. Copublished with Santa Clara University.

Unfolding Beauty: Celebrating California's Landscapes. Edited by Terry Beers. Copublished with Santa Clara University.

Water and the Shaping of California. Sue McClurg. Copublished with the Water Education Foundation.

Wishbone. Priscilla Lee.

2001

Courthouses of California: An Illustrated History. Edited by Ray McDevitt. Copublished with the California Historical Society.

Death Valley in '49. William Lewis Manly; Edited by LeRoy and Jean Johnson. Copublished with Santa Clara University.

Fool's Paradise: A Carey McWilliams Reader. Carey McWilliams. Copublished with Santa Clara University.

Giants in the Earth: The California Redwoods. Edited by Peter Johnstone.

Henry Sugimoto: Painting an American Experience. Kristine Kim.

How Much Earth: The Fresno Poets. Edited by Christopher Buckley, David Oliveira, and M. L. Williams.

In Full View: Three Ways of Seeing California Plants. Glenn Keator and Linda Yamane; Illustrations by Ann Lewis. Copublished with Headlands Center for the Arts.

Lands of Promise and Despair: Chronicles of Early California, 1535–1846. Edited by Rose Marie Beebe and Robert M. Senkewicz. Copublished with Santa Clara University.

Living in Color: The Art of Hideo Date. Karin Higa.

November Grass. Judy Van der Veer. Copublished with Santa Clara University.

Shades of California: The Hidden Beauty of Ordinary Life.

Edited by Kimi Kodani Hill.

The Trees of Golden Gate Park and San Francisco. Elizabeth McClintock; Edited and Arranged by Richard G. Turner, Jr. Copublished with the Pacific Horticultural Foundation.

Una Storia Segreta: The Secret History of Italian American Evacuation and Internment during World War II. Lawrence DiStasi.

2001–2004

Bay Nature. Magazine founded by Malcolm Margolin and David Loeb. Independent institution 2004–present.

2002

California: A Study of American Character. Josiah Royce. Copublished with Santa Clara University.

Coyote Fights the Sun: A Shasta Indian Tale. Mary J. Carpelan.

The Dirt Is Red Here: Art and Poetry from Native California. Edited by Margaret Dubin.

The High Sierra of California. Gary Snyder and Tom Killion. Copublished with the Yosemite Association.

How to Keep Your Language Alive: A Commonsense Approach to One-on-One Language Learning. Leanne Hinton with Matt Vera and Nancy Steele.

The Journey of the Flame. Walter Nordhoff. Copublished with Santa Clara University.

Make a Difference: Your Guide to Volunteering and Community Service. Arthur I. Blaustein.

One Day on Beetle Rock. Sally Carrighar. Copublished with Santa Clara University.

Quizzical Eye: The Photography of Rondal Partridge. Elizabeth Partridge and Sally Stein. Copublished with the California Historical Society.

Under the Fifth Sun: Latino Literature from California. Edited by Rick Heide. Copublished with Santa Clara University.

2003

920 O'Farrell Street: A Jewish Girlhood in Old San Francisco. Harriet Lane Levy.

At Work: The Art of California Labor. Edited by Mark Dean Johnson.

Bear in Mind: The California Grizzly. Susan Snyder.
Copublished with The Bancroft Library.

California Poetry: From the Gold Rush to the Present. Edited by Dana Gioia, Chryss Yost, and Jack Hicks.

Dark God of Eros: A William Everson Reader. William Everson, Edited by Albert Gelpi.

Hidden Treasures of San Francisco Bay. Photographs by Dennis E. Anderson. Copublished with Blue Water Pictures.

Indian Tales. Jaime de Angulo. Copublished with Santa Clara University.

Mark Twain's San Francisco. Edited by Bernard Taper. Copublished with Santa Clara University.

The Raccoon Next Door: Getting Along with Urban Wildlife. Gary Bogue; Illustrations by Chuck Todd.

River of Words: Images and Poetry in Praise of Water. Edited by Pamela Michael.

Storm. George R. Stewart. Copublished with Santa Clara University.

Structures of Utility. David Stark Wilson.

Two-Hearted Oak: The Photography of Roman Loranc. Roman Loranc.

2004

Addison Street: The Berkeley Poetry Walk. Edited by Robert Hass and Jessica Fisher.

Deeper Than Gold: A Guide to Indian Life in the Sierra Foothills. Brian Bibby; Photography by Dugan Aguilar.

Drawn West: Selections from the Robert B. Honeyman Jr. Collection of Early Californian and Western Art and Americana. Jack von Euw and Genoa Shepley. Copublished with The Bancroft Library.

Dream Songs and Ceremony: Reflections on Traditional California

Indian Dance. Frank LaPena.

Each a Mighty Voice: A Century of Speeches from The Commonwealth Club of California. Steven Boyd Saum.

Ecotopia. Ernest Callenbach. Copublished with Banyan Tree Books.

Ecotopia Emerging. Ernest Callenbach. Copublished with Banyan Tree Books.

The Golden Game: The Story of California Baseball. Kevin Nelson. Copublished with the California Historical Society.

Gunfight at Mussel Slough: Evolution of a Western Myth. Edited by Terry Beers. Copublished with Santa Clara University.

Jewish Life in the American West. Ava F. Kahn. Copublished with the Autry Museum of Western Heritage.

Journey to Topaz. Yoshiko Uchida; Illustrated by Donald Carrick.

The Land of Orange Groves and Jails: Upton Sinclair's California. Edited by Lauren Coodley. Copublished with Santa Clara University.

Letters to the Valley: A Harvest of Memories. David Mas Masumoto; Illustrated by Doug Hansen.

Merton of the Movies. Harry Leon Wilson. Copublished with Santa Clara University.

Peaceful Painter: Memoirs of an Issei Woman Artist. Hisako Hibi.

Precious Cargo: California Indian Cradle Baskets and Childbirth Traditions. Brian Bibby. Copublished with the Marin Museum of the American Indian.

Sierra Birds: A Hiker's Guide. John Muir Laws. Copublished with the California Academy of Sciences.

Skin Tax: Poems. Tim Z. Hernandez.

Unsettling the West: Eliza Farnham and Georgiana Bruce Kirby in Frontier California. JoAnn Levy. Copublished with Santa Clara University.

Walking the Flatlands: The Rural Landscape of the Lower Sacramento Valley. Mike Madison.

2005

AutoBioDiversity: True Stories from ZYZZYVA. Edited by Howard Junker.

The Autobiography of Lincoln Steffens. Lincoln Steffens.
Bloodvine: A Novel. Aris Janigian.
California Uncovered: Stories for the 21st Century. Edited by Chitra Banerjee Divakaruni, Jim Quay, and William E. Justice.
Chain Letter. Lucille Lang Day.
Dear People: Remembering Jonestown. Edited by Denice Stephenson.
El Corazón de la Muerte: Altars and Offerings for Days of the Dead. Oakland Museum of California.
Essential Saroyan: A Selection of William Saroyan's Best Writings. Edited by William E. Justice. Copublished with Santa Clara University.
Farmworker's Daughter: Growing Up Mexican in America. Rose Castillo Guilbault.
The Front Lines of Social Change: Veterans of the Abraham Lincoln Brigade. Richard Bermack.
Haslam's Valley. Gerald Haslam.
Lion Singer. Sylvia Ross.
Magpies and Mayflies: An Introduction to Plants and Animals of the Central Valley and Sierra Foothills. Derek Madden, Ken Charters, and Cathy Snyder.
No Other Life. Gary Young.
Peace Is a Four-Letter Word. Janet Nichols Lynch.
Perfume Dreams: Reflections on the Vietnamese Diaspora. Andrew Lam.
Samurai of Gold Hill. Yoshiko Uchida; Illustrated by Ati Forberg.
The Smokehouse Boys: Poems. Shaunna Oteka McCovey.
Tales of the Fish Patrol. Jack London. Copublished with Santa Clara University.
Workin' Man Blues: Country Music in California. Gerald Haslam, with Alexandra Haslam Russell and Richard Chon.

2006

The Anza Trail and the Settling of California. Vladimir Guerrero.
Birds of Napa County. Hermann Heinzel.
Blithe Tomato. Mike Madison; Drawings by Patrick McFarlin.
Bracing for Disaster: Earthquake-Resistant Architecture and Engineering

in San Francisco, 1838–1933. Stephen Tobriner.
Copublished with The Bancroft Library.

Dark Metropolis: Irving Norman's Social Surrealism.
Crocker Art Museum and Irving Norman Trust.

Discovering Nature's Alphabet. Krystina Castella and Brian Boyl.

Dream Town. Michelle Markel; Illustrations by Rick Reese.

Essential Mary Austin: A Selection of Mary Austin's Best Writings.
Edited by Kevin Hearle.
Copublished with Santa Clara University.

Essential Muir: A Selection of John Muir's Best Writings.
Edited by Fred D. White.
Copublished with Santa Clara University.

Inlandia: A Literary Journey through California's Inland Empire.
Edited by Gayle Wattawa.
Copublished with Santa Clara University.

Ira Nowinski's San Francisco: Poets, Politics, and Divas. Ira Nowinski
Copublished with The Bancroft Library..

The Oracles: My Filipino Grandparents in America. Pati Navalta Poblete.

Past Tents: The Way We Camped. Susan Snyder.
Copublished with The Bancroft Library.

Pleasure: Poems. Gary Young.

The Port Chicago Mutiny: The Story of the Largest Mass Mutiny Trial in U.S. Naval History. Robert L. Allen.
Copublished with the Equal Justice Society.

Testimonios: Early California through the Eyes of Women, 1815–1848.
Translated with Commentary by Rose Marie Beebe and Robert M. Senkewicz. Copublished with The Bancroft Library.

Theodore Wores in the Southwest. Edited by Stephen Becker.
Copublished with the California Historical Society.

Treasures of the Conservatory of Flowers. Nina Sazevich;
Photographs by Kevin J. Frest.

What Anna Loves. Written by Andra Simmons;
Illustrated by Gina Capaldi.

Woman of Ill Fame: A Novel. Erika Mailman.

2007

The Architecture of Ratcliff. Woodruff Minor; Photography by Kiran Singh.

Califauna: A Literary Field Guide. Edited by Terry Beers and Emily Elrod. Copublished with Santa Clara University.

Changing Course: Windcall and the Art of Renewal. Susan Wells.

Chief Marin: Leader, Rebel, and Legend. Betty Goerke.

Chumash Ethnobotany: Plant Knowledge Among the Chumash People of Southern California. Jan Timbrook, with Botanical Watercolors by Chris Chapman. Copublished with the Santa Barbara Museum of Natural History.

Dawson's Avian Kingdom: Selected Writings by William Leon Dawson. William Leon Dawson; Edited by Anna Neher. Copublished with Santa Clara University.

Essential Bierce: A Selection of the Writings of Ambrose Bierce. Edited by John R. Dunlap. Copublished with Santa Clara University.

Fast Cars and Frybread: Reports from the Rez. Gordon Johnson.

First Families: A Photographic History of California Indians. L. Frank and Kim Hogeland.

Flora of the Santa Ana River and Environs: With References to World Botany. Oscar F. Clarke, Danielle Svehla, Greg Ballmer, and Arlee Montalvo.

Forgotten Bread: First-Generation Armenian American Writers. Edited by David Kherdian.

Gables and Fables: A Portrait of San Francisco's Pacific Heights. Anne Bloomfield and Arthur Bloomfield; Illustrated by Kit Haskell.

Geological Ramblings in Yosemite. N. King Huber. Copublished with the Yosemite Association.

Heirlooms: Letters from a Peach Farmer. David Mas Masumoto; Illustrated by Doug Hansen.

Impressions of the East: Treasures from the C. V. Starr East Asian Library, University of California, Berkeley. Deborah Rudolph.

The Laws Field Guide to the Sierra Nevada. John Muir Laws. Copublished with the California Academy of Sciences.

No Time to Nap. Mike Madison; Illustrated by Mary Peterson.

Our People, Our Lands, Our Images: International Indigenous Photographers. Edited by Hulleah J. Tsinhnahjinnie and Veronica Passalacqua.

Our Valley, Our Choice: Building a Livable Future for the San Joaquin Valley. Great Valley Center.

A Sweetness Rising: New and Selected Poems. Roberta Spear; Edited by Philip Levine.

There's an Opossum in My Backyard. Gary Bogue; Illustrated by Chuck Todd.

Ticket to Exile: A Memoir. Adam David Miller.

Under the Dragon: California's New Culture. Lonny Shavelson and Fred Setterberg.

2008

Above All: Mount Whitney and California's Highest Peaks. Photographs by David Stark Wilson; Text by Steve Roper. Copublished with the Yosemite Association.

All the Saints of the City of the Angels: Seeking the Soul of L.A. on Its Streets. J. Michael Walker.

Allensworth, the Freedom Colony: A California African American Township. Alice C. Royal with Mickey Ellinger and Scott Braley.

Archy Lee: A California Fugitive Slave Case. Rudolph M. Lapp.

Edges of Bounty: Adventures in the Edible Valley. William Emery; Photographs by Scott Squire.

Grassroots Philanthropy: Field Notes of a Maverick Grantmaker. Bill Somerville with Fred Setterberg.

He Flies through the Air with the Greatest of Ease: A William Saroyan Reader. Edited by William E. Justice.

Jazz Idiom: Blueprints, Stills and Frames. The Jazz Photography of Charles L. Robinson; Poetic Takes and Riffs by Al Young.

Legends of the Yosemite Miwok. Compiled by Frank LaPena; Craig D. Bates, and Steven P. Medley, Illustrated by Harry Fonseca. Copublished with the Yosemite Association.

Life on the River: The Archaeology of an Ancient Native American Culture. William R. Hildebrandt and Michael J. Darcangelo.

Luminous Mountains: The Sierra Nevada of California. Photographs and Text by Tim Palmer. Copublished with the Yosemite Association.

Nature's Beloved Son: Rediscovering John Muir's Botanical Legacy. Bonnie J. Gisel with Images by Stephen J. Joseph.

Norman Clyde. Robert C. Pavlik. Copublished with the Yosemite Association.

Seaweed, Salmon, and Manzanita Cider: A California Indian Feast. Margaret Dubin and Sara-Larus Tolley.

A Seed of Modernism: The Art Students League of Los Angeles, 1906–1953. Will South, Marian Yoshiki-Kovinick, and Julia Armstrong-Totten. Copublished with the Pasadena Museum of California Art.

Spring Salmon, Hurry to Me! The Seasons of Native California. Edited by Margaret Dubin and Kim Hogeland. Copublished with Santa Clara University.

Sudden and Solitary: Mount Shasta and Its Artistic Legacy, 1841–2008. William C. Miesse with Robyn G. Peterson. Copublished with Turtle Bay Exploration Park.

Tree Barking: A Memoir. Nesta Rovina.

Two Bear Cubs: A Miwok Legend from California's Yosemite Valley. Retold by Robert D. San Souci; Illustrated by Daniel San Souci. Copublished with the Yosemite Association.

Walking Tractor: And Other Country Tales. Bruce Patterson.

Wallace Stegner's West. Edited by Page Stegner. Copublished with Santa Clara University.

Where Light Takes Its Color from the Sea: A California Notebook. James D. Houston.

2009

A Community Organizer's Tale: People and Power in San Francisco. Mike Miller.

Dream Street. Douglas McCulloh.

First Light: Five Photographers Explore Yosemite's Wilderness.

Charles Cramer, Karl Kroeber, Scot Miller, Mike Osborne, and Keith S. Walklet. Copublished with the Yosemite Association.

Flowering Shrubs of Yosemite and the Sierra Nevada. Shirley Spencer. Copublished with the Yosemite Association.

Granite, Water, and Light: The Waterfalls of Yosemite Valley. Photographs and Text by Mike Osborne. Copublished with the Yosemite Association.

Medicine Trails: A Life in Many Worlds. Mavis McCovey and John F. Salter.

Mother Goose in California. Conceived and Illustrated by Doug Hansen.

Mountains and Molehills. Frank Marryat. Copublished with Santa Clara University.

No Place for a Puritan: The Literature of California's Deserts. Edited by Ruth Nolan. Copublished with Santa Clara University and the Inlandia Institute.

Nothing Left in My Hands: The Issei of a Rural California Town, 1900–1942. Kazuko Nakane.

O, My Ancestor: Recognition and Renewal for the Gabrielino-Tongva People of the Los Angeles Area. Claudia Jurmain and William McCawley.
Copublished with the Rancho Los Alamitos Foundation.

A Rare Botanical Legacy: The Contributions of Ruby and Arthur Van Deventer. Edited by Rick Bennett and Susan Calla.

Riverbig: A Novel. Aris Janigian.

Tamalpais Walking: Poetry, History, and Prints. Tom Killion and Gary Snyder.

Wheels of Change: From Zero to 600 M.P.H., the Amazing Story of California and the Automobile. Kevin Nelson.
Copublished with the California Historical Society.

Wherever There's a Fight: How Runaway Slaves, Suffragists, Immigrants, Strikers, and Poets Shaped Civil Liberties in California. Elaine Elinson and Stan Yogi.

2010

Baby Yosemite. Katherine Brumage.
Copublished with the Yosemite Foundation.

Blood Strangers: A Memoir. Katherine Briccetti.

Blue Jay Girl. Sylvia Ross.

A California Bestiary. Rebecca Solnit and Mona Caron.
Copublished with the Oakland Zoo.

Discovering Early California Afro-Latino Presence. Damany M. Fisher.

East Eats West: Writing in Two Hemispheres. Andrew Lam.

Frozen Music: A Literary Exploration of California Architecture.
Edited by David Chu.
Copublished with Santa Clara University.

The Illuminated Landscape: A Sierra Nevada Anthology.
Edited by Gary Noy and Rick Heide. Copublished with Santa Clara University and Sierra College Press.

The Laws Pocket Guide Set: San Francisco Bay Area. John Muir Laws.

Remaking California: Reclaiming the Public Good.
Edited by R. Jeffrey Lustig.

Rivers of California: Nature's Lifelines in the Golden State.
Photographs and Text by Tim Palmer.

A State of Change: Forgotten Landscapes of California.
Text and Art by Laura Cunningham.

Tahoe beneath the Surface: The Hidden Stories of America's Largest Mountain Lake. Copublished with Sierra College Press.

Take Me to the River: Fishing, Swimming, and Dreaming on the San Joaquin. Edited by Joell Hallowell and Coke Hallowell.
Copublished with the San Joaquin River Parkway and Conservation Trust.

There's a Hummingbird in my Backyard. Gary Bogue;
Illustrated by Chuck Todd.

Turned Round in My Boots: A Memoir. Bruce Patterson.

Word on the Street. Photographs by Richard Nagler.

A Yankee in Mexican California, 1834–1836. Richard Henry Dana Jr.
Copublished with Santa Clara University.

2011

Beyond Words: 200 Years of Illustrated Diaries. Susan Snyder. Copublished with The Bancroft Library.

Black California: A Literary Anthology. Edited by Aparajita Nanda.

A Californian's Guide to the Trees among Us. Matt Ritter.

Cityscapes: San Francisco and Its Buildings. John King.

Entangled: A Chronicle of Late Love. Don Asher and Lois Goodwill.

Everyday Dogs: A Perpetual Calendar for Birthdays and Other Notable Dates. Mary Scott and Susan Snyder. Copublished with The Bancroft Library.

Fup. Jim Dodge.

Grave Matters: Excavating California's Buried Past. Tony Platt.

How Do I Begin? A Hmong American Literary Anthology. The Hmong American Writers' Circle.

Jesse's Ghost: A Novel. Frank Bergon.

Lunch Bucket Paradise: A True-Life Novel. Fred Setterberg.

Making Home from War: Stories of Japanese American Exile and Resettlement. Edited by Brian Komei Dempster.

New California Writing 2011. Edited by Gayle Wattawa.

Paris Portraits: Stories of Picasso, Matisse, Gertrude Stein, and Their Circle. Harriet Lane Levy.

A Queen's Journey: An Unfinished Novel about Hawaii's Last Monarch. James D. Houston.

Ranchos Los Alamitos: Ever Changing, Always the Same. Claudia Jurmain, David Lavender, and Larry L. Meyer. Copublished with the Rancho Los Alamitos Foundation.

Releasing the Days. Stephen Meadows.

Rise of the Ranges of Light: Landscapes and Change in the Mountains of California. David Gilligan.

2012

All of Us or None: Social Justice Posters of the San Francisco Bay Area. Lincoln Cushing.

Califlora: A Literary Field Guide. Edited by Terry Beers. Copublished with Santa Clara University.

California Glaciers. Photographs and Text by Tim Palmer.
Children of Manzanar. Edited by Heather C. Lindquist.
Essential Art: Native Basketry from the California Indian Heritage Center. Brian Bibby.
Giving with Confidence: A Guide to Savvy Philanthropy. Colburn Wilbur with Fred Setterberg.
Kodoku. William Emery; Illustrations by Hanae Rivera.
The Laws Guide to Drawing Birds. John Muir Laws.
Many Worlds: Native Life along the Anza Trail. Katherine Brumage; Illustrations by Mona Caron.
Married at Fourteen: A True Story. Lucille Lang Day.
Masha'allah and Other Stories. Mariah K. Young.
My Yosemite: A Guide for Young Adventurers. Mike Graf; Illustrations by Annette Filice. Copublished with Yosemite Conservancy.
Nature Notebook. Tammy Stellanova. Copublished with Yosemite Conservancy.
New California Writing 2012. Edited by Gayle Wattawa.
Pairing of Polarities: The Life and Art of Sonya Rapoport. Edited by Terri Cohn.
The Photographer's Guide to Yosemite: Revised and Updated. Michael Frye. Copublished with Yosemite Conservancy.
Room to Breathe: The Wild Heart of the San Francisco Peninsula. Edited by Kristi Britt. Copublished with the Midpeninsula Regional Open Space District.
Rose Hill: An Intermarriage before Its Time. Carlos E. Cortés. Copublished with the Inlandia Institute.
So Far from Home: Russians in Early California. Edited by Glenn J. Farris. Copublished with Santa Clara University.
Soul Calling: A Photographic Journey through the Hmong Diaspora. Joel Pickford.
Valley of Shadows and Dreams. Ken Light and Melanie Light.
The Wildness Within: Remembering David Brower. Kenneth Brower.

2013

Aesop in California. Doug Hansen.

Bad Indians: A Tribal Memoir. Deborah A. Miranda.

Bringing Our Languages Home: Language Revitalization for Families. Edited by Leanne Hinton.

Brother and the Dancer: A Novel. Keenan Norris.

The Court That Tamed the West: From the Gold Rush to the Tech Boom. Richard Cahan, Pia Hinckle, and Jessica Royer Ocken.

Father Junipero's Confessor: A Novel. Nick Taylor.

Here Tomorrow: Preserving Architecture, Culture, and California's Golden Dream. J. K. Dineen.

Hetch Hetchy: Undoing a Great American Mistake. Kenneth Brower.

Lela Rhodes, Pit River Woman. As told to Molly Curtis.

Manzanar to Mount Whitney: The Life and Times of a Lost Hiker. Hank Umemoto.

A Naturalist's Guide to the Santa Barbara Region. Joan Easton Lentz. Copublished with the Santa Barbara Museum of Natural History.

New California Writing 2013. Edited by Gayle Wattawa and Kirk Glaser. Copublished with Santa Clara University.

Sacrament: Homage to a River. Photographs by Geoff Fricker; Text by Rebecca Lawton.

Saltscapes: The Kite Aerial Photography of Cris Benton. Cris Benton.

San Francisco: Arts for the City: Civic Art and Urban Change, 1932–2012. Susan Wels.

Scrape the Willow until It Sings: The Words and Work of Basket Maker Julia Parker. Deborah Valoma.

Spiders in Your Neighborhood: A Field Guide to Your Local Spider Friends. Patrick Stadille.

Vital Signs. Poetry by Juan Delgado; Photography by Thomas McGovern. Copublished with the Inlandia Institute.

2014

California Bees and Blooms: A Guide for Gardeners and Naturalists. Gordon W. Frankie, Robbin W. Thorp, Rollin E. Coville, and Barbara Ertter.

Copublished with the California Native Plant Society.

Enough for All: Foods of My Dry Creek Pomo and Bodega Miwuk People. Kathleen Rose Smith.

Fightin' Words: 25 Years of Provocative Poetry and Prose from "The Blue Collar" PEN. Edited by Judith Cody, Kim McMillon, and Claire Ortalda. Copublished with PEN Oakland.

The Heyday of Malcolm Margolin: The Damn Good Times of a Fiercely Independent Publisher. Kim Bancroft.

The Laws Pocket Guide to the Birds of the Sacramento Valley. John Muir Laws.

Literary Industries: Chasing a Vanishing West. Hubert Howe Bancroft; An Abridged Edition by Kim Bancroft.

Looking at Art, the Art of Looking. Photographs by Richard Nagler.

On Track: A Field Guide to San Francisco's Historic Streetcars and Cable Cars. Rick Laubscher. Copublished with Market Street Railway.

San Francisco's Jewel City: The Panama-Pacific International Exposition of 1915. Laura A. Ackley. Copublished with the California Historical Society.

Secrets of the Oak Woodlands: Plants and Animals among California's Oaks. Kate Marianchild; Illustrations by Ann Meyer Maglinte. Copublished with California Wildlife Foundation/ California Oaks.

A Short History of San Francisco (Expanded and Updated). Tom Cole.

Sierra Stories: Tales of Dreamers, Schemers, Bigots, and Rogues. Gary Noy. Copublished with Sierra College Press.

Trail Posts: A Literary Exploration of California's State Parks. Edited by Malcolm Margolin and Mariko Conner. Copublished with California State Parks Foundation.

Under Spring: Voices+Art+Los Angeles. Jeremy Rosenberg. Copublished with the California Historical Society.

Wonderments of the East Bay. Sylvia Linsteadt and Malcolm Margolin.

2015

A Is for Acorn. Analisa Tripp; Illustrations by Lyn Risling.

The Bay Area Forager: Your Guide to Edible Wild Plants of the San Francisco Bay Area. Mia Andler and Kevin Feinstein.
The Bay Area Through Time. Laura Cunningham.
California's Fall Color: A Photographer's Guide to Autumn in the Sierra. G Dan Mitchell.
California's Wild Edge: The Coast in Poetry, Prints, and History. Tom Killion with Gary Snyder.
Cityscapes 2: Reading the Architecture of San Francisco. John King.
Fylling's Illustrated Guide to Pacific Coast Tide Pools. Marni Fylling.
Game Changers: Twelve Elections That Transformed California. Steve Swatt with Susie Swatt, Jeff Raimundo, and Rebecca LaVally. Copublished with the California Historical Society.
High Spirits: The Legacy Bars of San Francisco. J. K. Dineen.
John Muir's Book of Animals. John Muir, Illustrations by Lisel Jane Ashlock.
LAtitudes: An Angeleno's Atlas. Edited by Patricia Wakida.
The Laws Pocket Guide: Yard and Garden Birds. John Muir Laws, Copublished with Audubon California.
She Sang Me a Good Luck Song: The California Indian Photographs of Dugan Aguilar. Dugan Aguilar, Edited by Theresa Harlan.
Sierra Starlight: The Astrophotography of Tony Rowell. Tony Rowell.
The Wolf Who Ate the Sky. Text by Mary Daniel Hobson and Anna Isabel Rauh; Illustrations by Charles Hobson.

2016

Alice: Memoirs of a Barbary Coast Prostitute. Ivy Anderson and Devon Angus. Copublished with the California Historical Society.
BART: The Dramatic History of the Bay Area Rapid Transit System. Michael C. Healy.
California, the Magic Island. Doug Hansen.
California's Wild Coast Note Card Box. Tom Killion.
Changing Season: A Father, A Daughter, A Family Farm. David Mas Masumoto with Nikiko Masumoto.
De-Bug: Voices from the Underside of Silicon Valley. Edited by Raj Jayadev and Jean Melesaine.

Dear Miss Karana. Eric Elliott.
Empire. Photographs and Essays by Lewis deSoto. Copublished with the Inlandia Institute.
The High Sierra Note Card Box. Tom Killion.
The Horribly Hungry Gingerbread Boy: A San Francisco Story. Elisa Kleven.
It's Nice to Be a Pika. Text by Molly Woodward; Photographs by Tom and Pat Leeson.
It's Nice to Be an Otter. Text by Molly Woodward; Photographs by Tom and Pat Leeson.
King Sequoia: The Tree That Inspired a Nation, Created Our National Park System, and Changed the Way We Think about Nature. William C. Tweed. Copublished with Sierra College Press.
The Laws Guide to Nature Drawing and Journaling. John Muir Laws.
The Laws Sketchbook for Nature Journaling. John Muir Laws.
The Mountains of California. John Muir.
My First Summer in the Sierra. John Muir.
Quirky Berkeley. Tom Dalzell; Illustrations by Traci Hui; Photographs by John Storey.
Running Wild. Elaine Miller Bond.
Sam Maloof: 36 Views of a Master Woodworker. Fred Setterberg. Copublished with the Sam and Alfreda Maloof Foundation for Arts & Crafts.
The San Francisco Bay Note Card Box. Tom Killion.
The Sea Forager's Guide to the Northern California Coast. Kirk Lombard; Illustrations by Leighton Kelly.
Vintage: California Wine Labels of the 1930s. Edited by Christopher Miya and Ashley Ingram. Copublished with the California Historical Society.
Well Aged: California Whiskey and Spirits Labels of the 1930s. Edited by Christopher Miya and Ashley Ingram. Copublished with the California Historical Society.
Wild Suburbia: Learning to Garden with Native Plants. Barbara Eisenstein.

The Winter Note Card Box. Tom Killion.

2017

ABC Oakland. Michael Wertz.

The California Field Atlas. Obi Kaufmann.

A Californian's Guide to the Birds among Us. Charles Hood.

City of Vines: A History of Wine in Los Angeles. Thomas Pinney. Copublished with the California Historical Society.

Discovering Nature's Alphabet (board book). Krystina Castella and Brian Boyl.

Discovering Nature's Hidden Alphabet. Krystina Castella and Brian Boyl.

Fred Korematsu Speaks Up. Laura Atkins and Stan Yogi; Illustrations by Yutaka Houlette.

Gold Rush Stories: 49 Tales of Seekers, Scoundrels, Loss, and Luck. Gary Noy. Copublished with Sierra College Press.

The Haas Sisters of Franklin Street: A San Francisco Memoir of Family and Love. Frances Bransten Rothmann. Copublished with San Francisco Heritage.

How a Mountain Was Made: Stories. Greg Sarris.

Living Wild. Elaine Miller Bond.

Lost Worlds of the San Francisco Bay Area. Sylvia Linsteadt.

The Mission. Photographs by Dick Evans.

Our Dishonest President. The *Los Angeles Times* Editorial Board; Introduction by Davan Maharaj and Nicholas Goldberg.

Trees in Paradise: The Botanical Conquest of California. Jared Farmer.

2018

The Bakersfield Sound: How a Generation of Displaced Okies Revolutionized American Music. Robert E. Price.

Bird Songs Don't Lie: Writings from the Rez. Gordon Lee Johnson.

Birds of Berkeley. Oliver James.

California Comeback: The Genius of Jerry Brown. Narda Zacchino.

The California Field Atlas Note Card Set: Mammals. Obi Kaufmann.

The California Field Atlas Note Card Set: Raptors. Obi Kaufmann.

California Fights Back: The Golden State in the Age of Trump. Peter Schrag.
Coyote at the Big Time: A California Indian 123. Lyn Risling.
Is That a Skunk? Gary Bogue; Illustrated by Chuck Todd.
It's Nice to Be a Mountain Lion. Text by Molly Woodward; Photographs by Tom and Pat Leeson.
The Last Stand: The War Between Wall Street and Main Street over California's Ancient Redwoods. David Harris.
Our National Disgrace: Homelessness in the City of Angels. The *Los Angeles Times* Editorial Board; Introduction by Nicholas Goldberg.
Quirky Berkeley, Volume 3. Tom Dalzell; Illustrations by Traci Hui; Photographs by John Storey.
Ransoming Pagan Babies: The Selected Writings of Warren Hinckle. Warren Hinckle.
Unlikely Ally: How the Military Fights Climate Change and Protects the Environment. Marilyn Berlin Snell.

2019

The Battle for People's Park, Berkeley 1969. Tom Dalzell.
Biddy Mason Speaks Up. Arisa White and Laura Atkins; Illustrations by Laura Freeman.
The Birds of Oliver James Note Card Set: Volume 1. Oliver James.
The Birds of Oliver James Note Card Set: Volume 2. Oliver James.
A Californian's Guide to the Mammals among Us. Charles Hood.
The Curious World of Seaweed. Josie Iselin.
The Curious World of Seaweed Note Card Box. Josie Iselin.
Foucault in California: A True Story—Wherein the Great French Philosopher Drops Acid in the Valley of Death. Simeon Wade.
It's Nice to Be a Kit Fox. Text by Molly Woodward; Photographs by Donald Quintana.
Just Another N——: My Life in the Black Panther Party. Field Marshal Don Cox.
Maestrapeace: San Francisco's Monumental Feminist Mural. Juana Alicia, Miranda Bergman, Edythe Boone, Susan Kelk

Cervantes, Meera Desai, Yvonne Littleton, and Irene Perez. Copublished with San Francisco Heritage.

Mark Twain's Civil War: The Private History of a Campaign That Failed. Mark Twain; Edited by Benjamin Griffin. Copublished with The Bancroft Library.

Muir Woods and Mt. Tam Note Card Box. Tom Killion.

Northern California Coast Note Card Box. Tom Killion.

The Once and Future Forest: California's Iconic Redwoods. Save the Redwoods League. Copublished with Save the Redwoods League.

Sierra Wildflowers: A Hiker's Guide. Written and Illustrated by John Muir Laws.

The State of Water: Understanding California's Most Precious Resource. Obi Kaufmann.

Wild Colors of the West. Elaine Miller Bond.

2020

Bohemians West: Free Love, Family, and Radicals in Twentieth-Century America. Sherry L. Smith.

The Botanical World of Lesley Goren: California Native Flowers No. 1. Lesley Goren.

The Botanical World of Lesley Goren: California Native Flowers No. 2. Lesley Goren.

The David Lance Goines Note Card Collection: Chez Panisse. David Lance Goines.

The David Lance Goines Note Card Collection: Movies. David Lance Goines.

The Forests of California: A California Field Atlas. Obi Kaufmann.

Fylling's Illustrated Guide to Nature in Your Neighborhood. Marni Fylling.

Harlem of the West: The San Francisco Fillmore Jazz Era. Elizabeth Pepin Silva and Lewis Watts.

Heirloom Fruits of America: Selections from the USDA Pomological Watercolor Collection. Introduction by Daniel J. Kevles.

Hellacious California! Tales of Rascality, Revelry, Dissipation, and Depravity, and the Birth of the Golden State. Gary Noy. Copublished with Sierra College Press.

How to Teach Nature Journaling: Curiosity, Wonder, Attention. John Muir Laws and Emilie Lygren.

My Country 'Tis of Thee: Reporting, Sallies, and Other Confessions. David Harris.

Native California Flash Cards: For Culture and Language Learning. Lyn Risling.

The Naturalist's Illustrated Guide to the Sierra Foothills and Central Valley. Derek Madden, with Erinn Madden and Ken Charters.

Patriotic Dissent: America in the Age of Endless War. Daniel A. Sjursen.

Redress: The Inside Story of the Successful Campaign for Japanese American Reparations. John Tateishi.

San Francisco's Chinatown. Photographs by Dick Evans; Kathy Chin Leong.

Waa'aka': The Bird Who Fell in Love with the Sun. Cindi M. Alvitre; Illustrations by Carly Lake.

2021

Birds of Lake Merritt. Alex Harris.

The Complete Ecotopia. Ernest Callenbach.

Czesław Miłosz: A California Life. Cynthia L. Haven.

Deep Hanging Out: Wanderings and Wonderment in Native California. Malcolm Margolin.

Dream State: California in the Movies. Mick LaSalle.

Freedom to Discriminate: How Realtors Conspired to Segregate Housing and Divide America. Gene Slater.

Full Ecology: Repairing Our Relationship with the Natural World. Mary M. Clare and Gary Ferguson.

Hansen's Field Guide to the Birds of the Sierra Nevada. Keith Hansen, Edward C. Beedy, and Adam Donkin. Copublished with Sierra College Press.

An Indian among los Indígenas: A Native Travel Memoir. Ursula Pike.

The Magic Years: Scenes from a Rock-and-Roll Life. Jonathan Taplin.

Making Revolution: My Life in the Black Panther Party.
Field Marshal Don Cox.
A Salad Only the Devil Would Eat: The Joys of Ugly Nature.
Charles Hood.
Why to These Rocks: 50 Years of Poems from the Community of Writers.
Edited by Lisa Alvarez. Copublished with the Community of Writers.

2022

Becoming Story: A Journey among Seasons, Places, Trees, and Ancestors. Greg Sarris.
The Coasts of California: A California Field Atlas. Obi Kaufmann.
The Cold Canyon Fire Journals: Green Shoots and Silver Linings in the Ashes. Robin Lee Carlson.
The Curanderx Toolkit: Reclaiming Ancestral Latinx Plant Medicine and Rituals for Healing. Atava Garcia Swiecicki.
Feels Like Home: A Song for the Sonoran Borderlands. Linda Ronstadt and Lawrence Downes; Photographs by Bill Steen.
The Private Lives of Public Birds: Learning to Listen to the Birds Where We Live. Jack Gedney.
San Bruno Mountain: A Guide to the Flora and Fauna. Doug Allshouse and David L. Nelson.
The Sierra Winter Note Card Box. Tom Killion.
This Bell Still Rings: My Life of Defiance and Song. Barbara Dane.
The Trees of California Note Card Box. Tom Killion.
Wild Sonoma: Exploring Nature in Wine Country. Charles Hood with Lynn Horowitz and Jeanne Wirka; Illustrations by John Muir Laws.
Writing Themselves into History: Emily and Matilda Bancroft in Journals and Letters. Kim Bancroft. Copublished with The Bancroft Library.

2023

Berkeley Walks: Revised and Updated Edition. Robert E. Johnson and Janet L. Byron.

Birds of Point Reyes. Keith Hansen.

Boom Times for the End of the World. Scott Timberg.

California Against the Sea: Visions for Our Vanishing Coastline. Rosanna Xia.

Chími Nu'am: Native California Foodways for the Contemporary Kitchen. Sara Calvosa Olson.

Deep Oakland: How Geology Shaped a City. Andrew Alden.

The Deserts of California: A California Field Atlas. Obi Kaufmann.

Know We Are Here: Voices of Native California Resistance. Edited by Terria Smith.

Nocturnalia: Nature in the Western Night. Charles Hood and José Gabriel Martínez-Fonseca.

The Questions That Matter Most: Reading, Writing, and the Exercise of Freedom. Jane Smiley.

The Scandal of Cal: Land Grabs, White Supremacy, and Miseducation at UC Berkeley. Tony Platt.

The Sierra Forager: Your Guide to Edible Wild Plants of the Tahoe, Yosemite, and Mammoth Regions. Mia Andler.

Stranded: Finding Nature in Uncertain Times. Maddalena Bearzi.

What You Don't Know Will Make a Whole New World: A Memoir. Dorothy Lazard.

2024

Bay Area Wildlife: An Irreverent Guide. Jeff Miller; Illustrated by Obi Kaufmann.

Bird of Four Hundred Voices: A Mexican American Memoir of Music and Belonging. Eugene Rodriguez.

The Birds in the Oaks: Secret Voices of the Western Woods. Jack Gedney.

California Snakes and How to Find Them. Emily Taylor.

The California Sky Watcher: Understanding Weather Patterns and What Comes Next. William A. Selby.

The Forgetters: Stories. Greg Sarris.
Heyday at Fifty: Selected Writings from Five Decades of Independent California Publishing. Edited by Emmerich Anklam; Introduction by Steve Wasserman and Gayle Wattawa.
The Laws Field Guide to Sierra Birds. John Muir Laws.
Louder Than the Lies: Asian American Identity, Solidarity, and Self-Love. Ellie Yang Camp.
The Poet and the Silk Girl: A Memoir of Love, Imprisonment, and Protest. Satsuki Ina.
Portrait in Red: A Paris Obsession. L. John Harris.
The State of Fire: Why California Burns. Obi Kaufmann.
Tell Me Something, Tell Me Anything, Even If It's a Lie: A Memoir in Essays. Steve Wasserman.
Unnatural Habitat: The Native and Exotic Wildlife of Los Angeles. Craig Stanford.
What Kind of Bird Can't Fly: A Memoir of Resilience and Resurrection. Dorsey Nunn with Lee Romney.

ABOUT THE CONTRIBUTORS

Andrew Alden is a geologist and geoscience writer who has worked for the US Geological Survey and reported for KQED and *Bay Nature*. He is the author of *Deep Oakland*, published by Heyday in 2023. His website is oaklandgeology.com.

Cindi M. Alvitre is the author of *Waa'aka'* (2020). She is a descendant of the original inhabitants of Los Angeles and Orange Counties. She currently teaches American Indian Studies at California State University, Long Beach.

Ivy Anderson is a San Francisco–based writer who focuses on issues of ecology and radical history. Her reportage on water management issues was published in *Water Efficiency Magazine* and her poetry in *Poecology*. She is coeditor of *Alice*, published by Heyday in 2016.

Devon Angus is an artist, activist, and historian based in San Francisco. He composed and performed a conceptual folk operetta based on San Francisco history, *The Ghosts of Barbary*, throughout the Bay Area, Switzerland, and Italy. He is coeditor, with Ivy Anderson, of *Alice*.

Emmerich Anklam is managing editor at Heyday. Born and raised in Santa Rosa, California, he lives in Berkeley and has been a member of the Heyday staff since 2015.

Laura Atkins is an author, teacher, and children's book editor with over twenty years of editorial experience. She worked at Children's Book Press, Orchard Books, and Lee and Low Books. She is coauthor of *Fred Korematsu Speaks Up* (with Stan Yogi, 2017) and *Biddy Mason Speaks Up* (with Arisa White, 2019), both published by Heyday. She is also author of the picture book *Sled Dog Dachshund*. She is based in Berkeley, California. Find out more at lauraatkins.com.

Kim Bancroft is the author of *The Heyday of Malcolm Margolin* (2014) and *Writing Themselves into History* (2022), both published by Heyday. Her edited edition of Hubert Howe Bancroft's autobiography, *Literary Industries* (2014), was also published by Heyday. She lives in Northern California. Learn more at kimbancroft.com.

Sara Calvosa Olson (Karuk) is a food writer and editor living in the Bay Area with her husband and two teenage sons. She is the author of *Chími Nu'am*, published by Heyday in 2023, and her writing has appeared in *News from Native California* and *Edible Shasta-Butte*. Visit her website at akihsara.com, and follow her on Instagram at @thefrybreadriot.

Lawrence Downes is a writer and editor in New York. For more than thirty years, he worked in newspapers, including the *Chicago Sun-Times*, *Newsday*, and the *New York Times*, where he was an editor and member of the editorial board. He is coauthor, with Linda Ronstadt, of *Feels Like Home*, published by Heyday in 2022.

Elaine Elinson was the communications director of the ACLU of Northern California and editor of the *ACLU News* for more than two decades. She is coauthor, with Stan Yogi, of *Wherever There's a Fight*, published by Heyday in 2009. Her articles have been published in the *San Francisco Chronicle*, the *Nation*, *Poets and Writers*, and numerous other periodicals. Her website is elaineelinson.com.

Dick Evans is a photographer whose books include *San Francisco and the Bay Area: The Haight-Ashbury Edition* (InTransit Images and The Booksmith, 2011), *The Mission* (Heyday, 2017), and *San Francisco's Chinatown* (Heyday, 2020).

L. Frank (Ajachmem/Tongva) is an artist and decolonizationist who has exhibited in numerous shows. A cultural activist, L. Frank is one of the founding board members of the Advocates for Indigenous California Language Survival. L. Frank's books include *Acorn Soup* (1999) and *First Families* (coauthored with Kim Hogeland, 2007), both published by Heyday.

Laura Freeman, a Coretta Scott King Illustrator Honoree, is the illustrator of *Biddy Mason Speaks Up* (2019).

Jack Gedney was born in California and studied literature and natural history at UC Berkeley. He is the author of *The Private Lives of Public Birds* (2022) and *The Birds in the Oaks* (2024), both published by Heyday. He is also the author of a compact field guide to the trees of the San Francisco Bay Area and co-owner of a wild bird feeding and nature shop in Novato, California.

Keith Hansen is the author and illustrator of *Birds of Point Reyes* (2023), as well as illustrator and coauthor of *Hansen's Field Guide to the Birds of the Sierra Nevada* (2021).

Leanne Hinton is professor emerita at the University of California, Berkeley, and a founding member of the board of the Advocates for Indigenous California Language Survival. She has authored many articles and several books on language revitalization, including *Flutes of Fire* (1994, new edition 2022) and *How to Keep Your Language Alive* (with Matt Vera and Nancy Steele, 2002), both published by Heyday.

Kim Hogeland has an MA in history from UC Davis and has been a regular contributor to *News from Native California*. She is coauthor, with L. Frank, of *First Families* (2007).

Charles Hood, a poet and naturalist, is the author of numerous books, including four published with Heyday: *A Californian's Guide to the Birds among Us* (2017), *A Californian's Guide to the Mammals among Us* (2019), *A Salad Only the Devil Would Eat* (2021), and *Nocturnalia* (with José Gabriel Martínez-Fonseca, 2023). He lives in the Mojave Desert.

Yutaka Houlette is a web developer and the illustrator of *Fred Korematsu Speaks Up* (2017).

Michael Jaime-Becerra grew up in El Monte, California, a working-class suburb east of East Los Angeles. An associate professor of creative writing at UC Riverside, he is the author of the story collection *Every Night Is Ladies' Night* and the novel *This Time Tomorrow*. His essay "Speakeasy Tacos" was included in the collection *LAtitudes: An Angeleno's Atlas*, published by Heyday in 2015.

Gordon Lee Johnson (Cahuilla/Cupeño) lives and writes on the Pala Indian Reservation. A former newspaperman, he was last a columnist and feature writer for the *Press-Enterprise*, covering Southern California's Inland Empire. He is the author of three books: *Rez Dogs Eat Beans* (2001), *Fast Cars and Frybread* (Heyday, 2007), and *Bird Songs Don't Lie* (Heyday, 2018).

Obi Kaufmann is the author of *The California Field Atlas* (2017), *The State of Water* (2019), *The Forests of California* (2020), *The Coasts of California* (2022), *The Deserts of California* (2023), and *The State of Fire* (2024), all published by Heyday. When he is not backpacking, you can find the painter-poet at home in the East Bay, posting trail paintings at his handle @coyotethunder on Instagram. His website is coyoteandthunder.com.

Tom Killion is a woodcut and letterpress artist. He is the founder of The Quail Press and his extensively illustrated books include *The High Sierra of California* (2002), *Tamalpais Walking* (2009), and *California's Wild Edge* (2015, republished as *California's Wild Coast* in 2020), all created in collaboration with Gary Snyder and published by Heyday. His website is tomkillion.com.

Carly Lake is the illustrator of *Waa'aka'* (2020). She lives and makes art near the San Gabriel Mountains in Los Angeles. Her website is carlylake.com.

Andrew Lam is the author of the essay collections *Perfume Dreams* (2005) and *East Eats West* (2010), both published by Heyday, as well as the story collection *Birds of Paradise Lost*. He cofounded and was editor of New

America Media, an association of more than three thousand ethnic media outlets in the United States. Followed by a film crew back to his homeland, Vietnam, he was featured in the documentary *My Journey Home*, which aired nationwide on PBS.

John Muir Laws is a principal leader and innovator of the worldwide nature journaling movement. He is the founder and president of the Wild Wonder Foundation, as well as the founder and host of the Nature Journal Club. His books include *The Laws Field Guide to the Sierra Nevada* (2007), *The Laws Guide to Drawing Birds* (2012), *The Laws Guide to Nature Drawing and Journaling* (2016), *How to Teach Nature Journaling* (with Emilie Lygren, 2020), and *The Laws Field Guide to Sierra Birds* (2024), all published by Heyday. Visit his website at johnmuirlaws.com.

Dorothy Lazard was born in St. Louis and grew up in San Francisco and Oakland. A librarian for nearly forty years, she joined the staff of the Oakland Public Library in 2000. From 2009 until her retirement in 2021, she was the head librarian of OPL's Oakland History Center, where she encouraged people of all ages and backgrounds to explore local history. Her first book, *What You Don't Know Will Make a Whole New World*, was published by Heyday in 2023. She lives in Oakland. Her website is dorothylazard.com.

Sylvia Linsteadt is the author of two story collections, *The Venus Year* and *Our Lady of the Dark Country*; two novels for young readers, *The Wild Folk* and *The Wild Folk Rising*; and the folkloric novel *Tatterdemalion* with painter Rima Staines. Her works of nonfiction include *Wonderments of the East Bay* (2014) and *Lost Worlds of the San Francisco Bay Area* (2017), both published by Heyday. Her website is sylviavictorlinsteadt.com.

Malcolm Margolin is the publisher emeritus of Heyday, an independent nonprofit publisher and unique cultural institution, which he founded in 1974. His books include *The East Bay Out* (1974), *The Earth Manual* (1975), *The Ohlone Way* (1978), *The Way We Lived* (as editor, 1981), and *Deep Hanging Out* (2021). He helped found the Bay Nature Institute and the

Alliance for California Traditional Artists, and he is the founder and creative director of the California Institute for Community, Art, & Nature.

Kate Marianchild is the author of *Secrets of the Oak Woodlands*, published by Heyday in 2014. A graduate of UC Berkeley, she founded the seaweed business Rising Tide Sea Vegetables and has worked for several nonprofits. She lives in Mendocino County, and her website is katemarianchild.com.

David Mas Masumoto grows organic peaches and grapes on his family farm in Del Rey, California. He is the author of numerous books, including three published by Heyday: *Letters to the Valley* (2004), *Heirlooms* (2007), and *Changing Season* (with Nikiko Masumoto, 2016). An active proponent of organic farming, Masumoto has won numerous literary awards. He is also active in foundation work and in the cultural life of California and beyond. Visit his website at masumoto.com.

Deborah A. Miranda is an enrolled member of the Ohlone/Costanoan-Esselen Nation of the Greater Monterey Bay Area in California, with Santa Ynez Chumash Ancestry. She is the author of *Bad Indians*, published in 2013 by Heyday, as well as the author of four poetry collections and coeditor of *Sovereign Erotics: A Collection of Two-Spirit Literature*. A retired professor of English at Washington and Lee University, she lives in Eugene, Oregon. Learn more at deborahmiranda.com.

Gary Noy is the author of *Sierra Stories* (2014), *Gold Rush Stories* (2017), and *Hellacious California!* (2020), all published by Heyday. A Sierra Nevada native and current resident, Gary Noy taught history at Sierra College from 1987 until 2012. He founded the Sierra College Center for Sierra Nevada Studies and served as its director until his retirement.

Dorsey Nunn began advocating for the rights of California prisoners and their families while incarcerated. As codirector of Legal Services for Prisoners with Children (LSPC), in 2003 he cofounded All of Us or None

(AOUON), a grassroots movement of formerly incarcerated people working on their own behalf to secure their civil and human rights. AOUON is now the policy and advocacy arm of LSPC, which Nunn has led as executive director since 2011. He is the author of *What Kind of Bird Can't Fly*, published by Heyday in 2024.

Ursula Pike is a graduate of the MFA program at the Institute of American Indian Arts. She is the author of *An Indian among los Indígenas*, published by Heyday in 2021. An enrolled member of the Karuk Tribe, she was born in California and grew up in Daly City, California, and Portland, Oregon. She lives in Austin, Texas. Her website is ursulapike.com.

Tony Platt is the author of thirteen books and 150 essays and articles on race, inequality, and social justice in American history. His books include *Grave Matters* (2011) and *The Scandal of Cal* (2023), both published by Heyday. A Distinguished Affiliated Scholar at Berkeley's Center for the Study of Law and Society, Platt has taught at the University of Chicago, UC Berkeley, and CSU Sacramento. He lives in Berkeley and Big Lagoon, California.

Lyn Risling is an artist whose work reflects the revival and continuation of cultural traditions and the natural world of her tribal peoples, the Karuk, Yurok, and Hupa. She is the illustrator of *A Is for Acorn* (2015) and the author and illustrator of *Coyote at the Big Time* (2018), both published by Heyday.

Lee Romney spent twenty-three years as a reporter at the *Los Angeles Times*, where she developed expertise in criminal justice and mental health. She is currently collaborating with a former public defender on the podcast *November in My Soul*. Dorsey Nunn wrote *What Kind of Bird Can't Fly* (Heyday, 2024) with Romney.

Linda Ronstadt, the great-granddaughter of Friedrich and Margarita Ronstadt of Sonora, Mexico, is one of the world's most acclaimed singers. Her six-decade career encompassed rock, folk, country, light opera, Mexican songs, and American standards. Her book *Feels Like Home* was published by Heyday in 2022.

Greg Sarris is currently serving his sixteenth term as Chairman of the Federated Indians of Graton Rancheria and his first term as board chair for the Smithsonian's National Museum of the American Indian. His publications include *How a Mountain Was Made* (2017), *Becoming Story* (2022), and *The Forgetters* (2024)—all published by Heyday—as well as *Keeping Slug Woman Alive* (1993), *Grand Avenue* (1994), and *Watermelon Nights* (1998). He lives and works in Sonoma County, California. Visit his website at greg-sarris.com.

Jane Smiley is a novelist and essayist. Her novel *A Thousand Acres* won the Pulitzer Prize and the National Book Critics Circle Award in 1992, and her latest novel, *Lucky*, was published in 2024. Her essay collection *The Questions That Matter Most* was published by Heyday in 2023. She lives in Carmel Valley, California.

Kathleen Rose Smith (Bodega Miwuk/Dry Creek Pomo, and a member of the Federated Indians of Graton Rancheria) grew up in the Healdsburg area. An artist from early childhood, she graduated from the San Francisco Art Institute in 1977. Her jobs included park naturalist, art instructor, archaeology field technician, and foods columnist for *News from Native California*. She is the author of *Enough for All*, published by Heyday in 2014.

Gary Snyder is a poet, author, scholar, cultural critic, and professor emeritus at UC Davis. He has been a Guggenheim Fellow and is a member of the American Academy of Arts and Letters and the American Academy of Arts and Sciences. His *Turtle Island* won the Pulitzer Prize for poetry in 1975, and his book-length poem *Mountains and Rivers Without End* won the Bollingen Prize in poetry in 1997. He has collaborated with Tom Killion on three books published by Heyday: *The High Sierra of California* (2002), *Tamalpais Walking* (2010), and *California's Wild Coast* (2015, 2020).

Rebecca Solnit is the author of more than twenty books, including *A Field Guide to Getting Lost*, *Men Explain Things to Me*, *Recollections of My Nonexistence*, and *Orwell's Roses*. Her collaboration with artist Mona Caron, *A California Bestiary*, was published by Heyday in 2010. Her website is rebeccasolnit.net.

Susan Straight is the author of several novels, including *Mecca* and *Highwire Moon*, as well as the memoir *In the Country of Women*. She was born and continues to live in Riverside, California, where she serves as Distinguished Professor of Creative Writing at UC Riverside. Visit her website at susanstraight.com.

Analisa Tripp is the author of *A Is for Acorn*. She is a graduate of the Native American Studies Program at UC Berkeley. A member of the Karuk Tribe, she currently lives with her family in their ancestral territory located in beautiful northwestern California.

Patricia Wakida maintains her own linoleum block and letterpress studio under the Wasabi Press imprint. She is editor of the anthology *Only What We Could Carry* (2000) and the essay collection *LAtitudes* (2015), both published by Heyday. She lives in Oakland, and her website is wasabipress.com.

Steve Wasserman is publisher of Heyday. He has been editor of the *Los Angeles Times Book Review*, editorial director of New Republic Books, publisher and editorial director of Hill and Wang at Farrar, Straus & Giroux and of the Noonday Press, editorial director of Times Books at Random House, and editor at large for Yale University Press. His first book, published by Heyday in 2024, is *Tell Me Something, Tell Me Anything, Even If It's a Lie*. He lives in Berkeley, California.

Gayle Wattawa is general manager and editorial director at Heyday. A member of the Heyday staff since 2004, she is editor of *Inlandia: A Literary Journey through California's Inland Empire*, published by Heyday in 2006.

Arisa White is a Cave Canem–graduate poet and an associate professor in English and creative writing at Colby College. Her books include *Biddy Mason Speaks Up* (2019), coauthored with Laura Atkins and published by Heyday, as well as the poetry collection *You're the Most Beautiful Thing That Happened* and the poetic memoir *Who's Your Daddy*. Visit her website at arisawhite.com.

Rosanna Xia is an environmental reporter for the *Los Angeles Times*, where she specializes in stories about the coast and ocean. She was a Pulitzer Prize finalist in 2020 for explanatory reporting, and her work has been anthologized in the Best American Science and Nature Writing series. She is the author of *California Against the Sea*, published by Heyday in 2023.

Stan Yogi is coauthor of *Wherever There's a Fight* (with Elaine Elinson, 2009), coauthor of *Fred Korematsu Speaks Up* (with Laura Atkins, 2017), and editor of the literary anthology *Highway 99* (1996), all published by Heyday. He managed development programs for the ACLU of Northern California for fourteen years. His work has appeared in the *San Francisco Chronicle*, *MELUS*, and several anthologies.

ABOUT HEYDAY

HELP CO-WRITE HEYDAY'S NEXT CHAPTER

In 1974, Malcolm Margolin founded Heyday in the living room of his Berkeley, California, home. What began as a do-it-yourself labor of love ended up making history, launching a trailblazing new chapter of California's literary story.

From day one, Heyday has introduced the world to a diversity of voices that may have otherwise gone unheard. From Deborah Miranda's *Bad Indians* to Obi Kaufmann's beloved *California Field Atlas* series, from John Muir Laws's nature journaling guides to Dorothy Lazard's memoir *What You Don't Know Will Make a Whole New World*, everything we publish underscores the message that stories about California, by Californians, are not niche narratives. They have universal urgency, beauty, and import.

In contrast with a mainstream publishing industry that tends to ignore or compartmentalize California voices, perspectives, and histories, Heyday is a breath of fresh air. We've never been beholden to corporate stakeholders telling us what to publish. We listen to our readers, and to a vibrant grassroots community of creators, artists, writers, naturalists, and activists that we learn from and grow with every day.

That's why, fifty years after our founding, Heyday is still a labor of love. The fruits of that labor, highlighted in this special anniversary volume, span four pillars: Nature, History, Social Justice, and California Indian Cultural Renewal.

Each selection included in this anthology is, to quote our founder, "something only Heyday could publish." We're proud of that.

We hope you are too, because you deserve some of the credit. As a nonprofit publisher, we derive 65 percent of our budget from book sales, and the remaining 35 percent from donations.

To say we can't do this without you is an understatement. Your love of great literature and your support of our work is what enables us to take bold creative risks that bring one-of-a-kind books to life.

At our half-century mark as an independent publisher, we're not only celebrating the work you read in this anthology, but looking toward the future. More than ever, the world needs books that break new ground, dazzle the imagination, and challenge the status quo.

We're excited to meet this moment—and the next fifty years—with vision and inspiration. If you are too, please make a gift to Heyday. Your gift will become books, and those books just might help change the world, one reader at a time.

WAYS TO GIVE

By Mail: Make a check out to Heyday and mail to Heyday, PO Box 9145, Berkeley, CA 94709

Online: Make a donation online at heydaybooks.com/community/ Questions about donating? Send them to development@heydaybooks.com.

Heyday is a 501(c)(3) nonprofit organization. Our tax ID is 94-3268357.

STAFF

Steve Wasserman, Publisher
Gayle Wattawa, General Manager/Editorial Director
Emmerich Anklam, Managing Editor
Kalie Caetano, Marketing and Publicity Director
Chris Carosi, Sales Manager
Tavi Carpenter, Graton Roundhouse Intern
Archie Ferguson, Art Director
Marlon Rigel, Production Manager
JiaJing Liu, Development Manager
Marthine Satris, Senior Acquisitions Editor
Eve Sheehan, Office Manager
Terria Smith, Director of the Berkeley Roundhouse
Christine Trudeau, Roundhouse Fellow

Malcolm Margolin, Founder

BOARD OF DIRECTORS

ADVISORY COUNCIL

A NOTE ON TYPE

This book is set in Schneidler, a typeface created in 1936 and named after its designer, Ernst Schneidler. First published through the Bauer Type Foundry, then through Stempel, Schneidler has a cupped serif style and is informed by Renaissance-period Venetian type design.